LOVE
ITS FORMS, DIMENSIONS AND PARADOXES

Love

Its Forms, Dimensions and Paradoxes

İlham Dilman

palgrave

Published by
PALGRAVE
Houndmills, Basingstoke, Hampshire RG21 6XS and
175 Fifth Avenue, New York, N. Y. 10010
Companies and representatives throughout the world

PALGRAVE is the new global academic imprint of
St. Martin's Press LLC Scholarly and Reference Division and
Palgrave Publishers Ltd (formerly Macmillan Press Ltd).

Outside North America
ISBN 0–333–73544–7

Inside North America
ISBN 0–312–21643–2

This book is printed on paper suitable for recycling and
made from fully managed and sustained forest sources.

A catalogue record for this book is available
from the British Library.

Library of Congress Cataloging-in-Publication Data
Dilman, Ilham.
Love : its forms, dimensions, and paradoxes / Ilham Dilman.
p. cm
Includes bibliographical references and index.
ISBN 0–312–21643–2
1. Love. I. Title.
BD436.D54 1998
128'.46—dc21   98–23463
                                                               CIP

10   9   8   7   6   5   4   3   2
09 08 07 06 05 04 03 02 01

Printed and bound in Great Britain by
Antony Rowe Ltd, Chippenham, Wiltshire

Contents

Acknowledgements   viii

Preface   xi

1   Human Togetherness and the Reality of
Other People   1

   1.1   Human Separateness: Does it Separate?   1
   1.2   The Individual's Dual Reality: in Himself
and for Others   5
   1.3   Summing Up   11

2   Love and Hate: Are They Opposites?   13

   2.1   Mature and Immature Love   13
   2.2   Asymmetry between Love and Hate   16
   2.3   Richness of Love and Poverty of Hate   18
   2.4   Love and Hate: Goodness and Evil   21

3   Forms of Love: Emotional Maturity and
Reciprocity   24

   3.1   Love and Reciprocity: Troubadour Love   24
   3.2   Love and Maturity: 'Ecstatic Love'   26
   3.3   'La Folie de l'Amour'   31
   3.4   'The Terribleness of Love': Lady Macbeth   33
   3.5   Conclusion   37

4   Conflicting Aspects of Sexual Love Revisited:
Can They Be Reconciled?   41

   4.1   A Problem for Love   41
   4.2   Are Sex and Love One Thing or Two?   46
   4.3   Sexual Desire and the Caring Aspect of Love   49
   4.4   Exclusive Love and Regard for the Beloved:
Are They Compatible?   51
   4.5   Quest for Reciprocity and Unconditional
Giving: How Can They Be Reconciled?   53
   4.6   Sexual Passion and the Restraint of Love   56
   4.7   Conclusion   58

5   Proust: Sexual Love and its Longing for Union   .   60

5.1   Proust and Sartre on the Reality of what our
      Emotions Reveal   60
5.2   The Solipsism of Proustian Love   63
5.3   Proust and Freud on Transference Love   68
5.4   Conclusion   72

6   Freud on Love and Sexuality: a Critique   74

6.1   Sexual Love   74
6.2   Love and Creativity   86

7   D.H. Lawrence: Sexual Love, A Vital
     Relationship between Opposites   98

7.1   Introduction   98
7.2   Sexual Love and the Separateness of the
      Individual   98
7.3   Polarity of the Sexes: How is Communion
      Possible in Sexual Love?   105
7.4   Profane and Spiritual Love: Are they
      Compatible?   109
7.5   Summing Up: Sex, Love and Beyond   112

8   Erich Fromm on 'Love as an Art'   117

8.1   Introduction   117
8.2   Love and Human Existence   118
8.3   'Love as an Art and so a Practice'   125
8.4   Love and its Different Objects   128
8.5   Fromm's Criticisms and Revisions of Freud   135

9   C.S. Lewis in Four Loves: Our Natural Loves   138

9.1   Introduction   138
9.2   Beginning at the Beginning with our Natural
      Propensities   139
9.3   Affection   144
9.4   Friendship   148
9.5   Eros or Sexual Love   151

10 C.S. Lewis in Four Loves: Charity and the
    Christian Love of God   155

    10.1 Natural Loves and the Supernatural   155
    10.2 The Christian Love of God   159
    10.3 Charity or Compassion: Love of One's
          Neighbour   161
    10.4 The Transmutation of our Natural Loves   166
    10.5 Some Concluding Remarks   170

11 Kierkegaard on the Christian Injunction to
    Love One's Neighbour   172

    11.1 Preliminaries   172
    11.2 'You Shall Love your Neighbour as Yourself'   177
    11.3 Christian Love in Relation to Erotic
          Love and Friendship   189

12 Kierkegaard on the Works of Love   199

    12.1 Introduction   199
    12.2 Spiritual Love and its Character   200
    12.3 Love's Work in Forming the Heart   216
    12.4 Kierkegaard, Plato and Simone Weil on
          Loving the Beautiful   224
    12.5 Conclusion   229

Bibliography   234

Index   237

Acknowledgements

I am grateful to Eric Gill and the Wolseley Fine Arts Museum, London, for permission to reproduce the fine drawing on the jacket of this book. I would also like to acknowledge my thanks to Mrs Helen Baldwin for her impeccable secretarial work in getting this book ready for publication. I would like to acknowledge Heinemann as the first publisher of the book *The Prophet*, by Kahlil Gibran, from which the poem 'Of Love', quoted on page ix of this book, comes. Finally I would like to express my thanks to Mr Tim Farmiloe, Publishing Director, and Ms Charmian Hearne, Senior Commissioning Editor at Macmillan, for the confidence they have shown in me in accepting this book after having seen only the first few chapters of it; and also to Mr Julian Honer for all his help in getting the book ready for the press.

Of Love

(from *The Prophet*)

When love beckons to you, follow him,
Though his ways are hard and steep.
And when his wings enfold you yield to him,
Though the sword hidden among his pinions
may wound you.
And when he speaks to you believe in him,
Though his voice may shatter your dreams
as the north wind lays waste the garden.

For even as love crowns you so shall he
crucify you. Even as he is for your growth
so is he for your pruning.
Even as he ascends to your height and
caresses your tenderest branches that quiver
in the sun,
So shall he descend to your roots and
shake them in their clinging to the earth.

Like sheaves of corn he gathers you unto
himself.
He threshes you to make you naked.
He sifts you to free you from your husks.
He grinds you to whiteness.
He kneads you until you are pliant;
And then he assigns you to his sacred fire, that
you may become sacred bread for God's sacred feast.
All these things shall love do unto you that
you may know the secrets of your heart, and in that
knowledge become a fragment of Life's heart.

But if in your fear you would seek only love's
peace and love's pleasure,
Then it is better for you that you cover your
nakedness and pass out of love's threshing-floor,
Into the seasonless world where you shall laugh,
but not all of your laughter, and weep, but not
all of your tears.

Love gives naught but itself and takes naught
but from itself.

Love possesses not nor would it be possessed;
For love is sufficient unto love.

When you love you should not say, 'God is in
my heart' but rather, 'I am in the heart of God.'

And think not you can direct the course of love,
for love, if it finds you worthy, directs your course.

Love has no other desire but to fulfil itself.

But if you love and must needs have desires, let
these be your desires:

To melt and be like a running brook that sings
its melody to the night.

To know the pain of too much tenderness.

To be wounded by your own understanding of love;
And to bleed willingly and joyfully.

To wake at dawn with a winged heart and give
thanks for another day of loving;

To rest at the noon hour and meditate love's
ecstasy;

To return home at eventide with gratitude;

And then to sleep with a prayer for the beloved
in your heart and a song of praise upon your lips.

Kahlil Gibran

Preface

This book is concerned with questions about love: questions about its many forms, its many strands and aspects and the relation in which they stand to each other. It is concerned with questions about love's relation, in its different forms, to the self and also to sex, about the obstacles to love, its frustrations, corruptions, arrests and developments in the face of them. It also seeks the views of some writers who have suggested some distinctive solutions to the existential problems which love poses in the face of its obstacles.

What are these obstacles? Can they be overcome? Are the different aspects of love in conflict with one another? Is there any rivalry between different forms of love? If there is an inherent connection between love and generosity, between love and creativeness, as the book argues there is, then how can love *itself* be selfish, destructive, tyrannical? These are *conceptual* questions. How is love to be transformed so as to transcend and overcome its obstacles? Where they pull the lover in different directions how are the demands of different forms or aspects of love to be reconciled in the lover? These are *existential* questions, questions concerning the lover's mode of existence. But these two forms of question – questions relating to problems for our thinking which call for a clearer understanding and questions relating to problems of life encountered by the individual in his experience of love – run into each other. The enquiry which the book undertakes thus encompasses both these aspects – conceptual and existential.

In considering these questions the book also seeks the views of some writers who have had something to say about love and have suggested distinctive solutions to the existential problems which love poses in the face of its obstacles. There are in the main two perspectives from which the writers in question view love and offer solutions to its problems: a psychoanalytic perspective and a religious one. The book is interested in the *variety* of the views and solutions suggested by the writers it considers and also in the *affinities* between what comes to view in the contrasting perspectives considered.

All the writers considered stress that love is something from which people have something to learn and that in the course of what he learns the lover changes and so does the love of which he

comes to be capable. The changes in question are seen as developments and, when there is no learning, as arrests, and hence the
perspectives from which they are so seen are obviously not morally
neutral. The book finds some striking affinities in the ways in
which the different writers considered conceive this development:
the direction in which we have to ascend to a love mediated by a
recognition of goodness (Plato's Diotima), move towards a more
mature love (Balint and Fromm), purify our hearts (Plato's Socrates,
C.S. Lewis and Kierkegaard). There is also a wider measure of
agreement than we would think at first about what a person comes
to or finds in himself in moving towards purity of heart and greater
affective maturity: compassion and gratitude, trusting and trustworthiness, forgiveness and forgivenness, commitment to the loved
one and loyalty. Indeed it seems to me that 'affective maturity' on
the one hand and 'selflessness and purity of heart' on the other are
the two sides of the same coin.

This is one of the 'conclusions' towards which the book moves.
Another one is that while there are many different forms of love
and that, contrary to what Freud held, many of them are not sexual
in character, nevertheless sex has a natural affinity to love. I mean
that this is so despite the fact that sex can exist apart from love and
can be a vehicle for aggression, hatred and destructiveness. As for
love itself it can, for instance, be selfish. But while generosity is an
expression of love, selfishness is not. Another and central 'conclusion'
towards which the book moves is that love is the source of what
constitutes goodness in human life as conceived by most of the
writers considered. Indeed the affective development in which a
person moves towards a more mature love is an ascent towards
greater goodness. The characteristics of such love, such as generosity, mercifulness, humility, patience, forgiveness, trust and courage,
are at the same time the constituents of goodness.

The book argues, in this connection, that love is creative; it opens
a person up, makes him accessible to contact with 'the outer world':
capable of forgiving and open to learning. Whereas in lovelessness
a person is shut in himself, deprived of what sustains growth.
Indeed in hatred, vindictiveness, malice and envy a person is stuck;
he turns round and round the same spot, and repeats himself. Such
repetition is the opposite of creativeness which implies begetting
something new.

The book thinks of the human soul as bipolar. On the one hand it
has the propensity to protect itself when under threat. It closes itself

against danger. This propensity, especially where a person lacks conviction in his own reality in so far as he is unable to believe that he matters to others, can turn into self-seeking. In any case there is much in what he meets in the human world to encourage it to develop in that direction – so much so that we may be excused for speaking of self-seeking itself as a natural propensity of the human soul. On the other hand the human soul has a propensity which faces it in the opposite direction. This is a natural propensity to open up, take an interest in and give itself to what exists outside, is other than itself. This natural propensity of the human soul or human heart is love. But though the opposite of each other, in the variety of expressions they take in human life these two propensities can get entangled with each other. Thus love desires its return or reciprocation. This is of course a desire for contact and communion with the loved one and as such a natural component of love itself. But it often is also a desire for psychological sustenance, satisfaction and perhaps confirmation too and as such in the service of what constitutes the other pole of the human soul, namely self-seeking. It introduces a conflict for the individual in love. The book examines some of the forms which this conflict takes in human life and the way it is seen from different perspectives.

Can the desire for reciprocity be purified from the self which seeks its own fulfilment? Or does it have to be abandoned if love is to grow? But in the case of sexual love can it be abandoned without at the same time taking away the sexual character of the love? These are some questions which recur in the different chapters of the book: Can love be sexual and spiritual at one and the same time?

Love, as a natural inclination to open up to another, the loved one, is a risky business. It leaves the lover vulnerable before another. It calls on his capacity for trust, which itself belongs to love, and trusting another person means taking a risk. Giving one's heart exposes it to the risk of being broken. Therefore it takes a certain confidence in one's own capacity to hold together to be able to open up and give oneself to another in love. Given the frailties of human nature, both lover and loved one have their own share of pain, disappointment, the battering of their resistances, the taxing of their commitment and loyalty to endure. Love is a trial of the lover and grows as the lover is tried so long as he keeps his heart open and does not turn away from love. As the poet Kahlil Gibran puts it in the poem I quote at the beginning of this book: 'even as he

[love] is for your growth so is he for your pruning'. The growth comes with the pruning.

The pruning of the individual is the shedding of his defences and his learning to live and love without their protection. It is this that tests his capacity to hold together. If he can come through he finds himself and is able to give himself, give up himself, in love. What the defences protect and sustain is the ego, the self which seeks itself. As they are pruned he becomes more accessible to love. This is part at least of what Kierkegaard calls 'the work of love in forming the heart'. Again as Gibran puts it:

> He [love] threshes you to make you naked.
> He sifts you to free you from your husks.
> He grinds you to whiteness.

Both D.H. Lawrence and Erich Fromm, in their different ways, point out how much today we have lost our way in love. As Lawrence puts it, our love has become something 'mental', it comes from the mind rather than from the blood. Fromm puts this by saying that the soul of modern man and his love relations have been taken over by 'the marketing orientation'. They point out that we live in a world in which sex and love are something we copy rather than something that wells from within. In becoming part of that world we lose our soul. Without it we cannot be ourselves in sex and we have no self to give in love, no self with which to be naked – like an onion you can peel without ever reaching a solid core. As Lawrence puts it of modern men: 'No matter how they pull their shirts off they never arrive at their own nakedness. They have none. They can only be undressed. Naked they cannot be' (1977, p. 104). This is part of Lawrence's argument that 'love is a counterfeit feeling today' and that 'as with counterfeit emotions there is no real sex at all' today. It takes real giving for this to be otherwise and a real self to give. You cannot have it when, as Lawrence puts it, sex is merely 'a thing to be naughty with' and 'to be naughty with it' is the done thing today. The argument is that sexuality has become largely something in which men and nowadays sometimes women too copy the herd, emulate an ideal of liberation and machismo, and do so to find an inflation of the ego. The point of interest for the book to which this is leading is that there is such a thing as counterfeit sex and love and that to find real sex, real desire, real love what makes a person false and his sex and love counterfeit has to be threshed out of him. Only then can a person have the opportunity to learn from love and grow to maturity.

The next question concerns the desire for oneness which is at the heart of love – at any rate of sexual love: Is this desire an expression of immaturity? And can the lovers who are drawn to one another find the oneness they long for? This is a question that figures prominently throughout the book. Sartre (see Chapter 4) thinks that this oneness which we long for in love is a pipedream: 'The other is in principle out of my reach. When I try to reach him he runs away from me and when I turn away from him he pursues and tries to possess me' (1943, p. 479). Sartre's answer is that the lover must learn to live in conflict with the other and maintain his freedom or autonomy as an individual. Individual autonomy and communion with the other are irreconcilable; communion in harmony with the other is impossible. Indeed it involves a contradiction since autonomy is a necessary condition for it and yet at the same time excludes it. Sartre here fails to make a distinction we meet in Fromm, namely between 'symbiotic union' or 'fusion without integrity' and 'union with integrity' which Gabriel Marcel calls 'communion'. (For a discussion of Marcel's criticism of Sartre on this question see Dilman 1993, Chapter 7).

Simone Weil has said something similar to Sartre without accepting his answer:

> I want the person I love to love me. But if he is totally devoted to me he does not exist any longer and I cease to love him. If, on the other hand, he is not totally devoted to me, he does not love me enough.

And again:

> When a human being is attached to another by a bond of affection which contains any degree of necessity, it is impossible that he should wish autonomy to be preserved both in himself and in the other (1959, p. 156).

She attributes this to 'the mechanism of nature'; but she believes that in such a situation what is impossible can be made possible by 'the miraculous intervention of the supernatural'. This brings a change in the lovers' affective focus with a loss of its self-centred orientation. As a result they are able to 'fully consent to be two and

not one'. They learn to 'respect the distance which the fact of being
two distinct creatures places between them' (ibid., p. 157). As Kahlil
Gibran puts it:

> … let there be spaces in your togetherness
> And let the winds of heaven dance between you.

In the portraits of love he draws in *A la Recherche du Temps Perdu*,
Proust too emphasizes the loved one's inaccessibility to the lover
(see Chapter 5). In love, he emphasizes, we thirst to overcome the
barriers that separate the loved one from us – as lover. But he is
firmly convinced that the more we try to do so the more they separate us. His answer to this problem is that it is only when the passion in which we thirst to possess what we love has calmed down,
and in our affective memory we re-live that which escaped us in
our thirst, that we can savour it and appreciate its beauty. What we
long for in love can thus only be captured in art and its creativeness
after we have lived and suffered this longing. This he tries to do in
his big novel. Art is thus Proust's religion and he practices it in
what he gives of himself to writing his great work.

Lawrence too has something distinctive to say about love, sex
and human separateness (see Chapter 7). He thinks that for love to
flourish there must be something more in the lover's life than the
interest belonging to his love. This, I think, is portrayed well by
Tolstoy in his novel *Anna Karenina*. Vronsky gives up his career and
everything that goes with it for Anna, and she in turn is separated
from the son she loves and shunned by society. They are thus
thrown on to each other and have no oxygen to breathe. The novel
portrays how as a result their love is slowly suffocated. They need a
life outside their love from which to replenish themselves and
nourish the love they give each other.

Although Lawrence argues this only for the male lover, I think
that *both* parties to the love relationship, the man and the woman,
must allow each other such a life if the lovers are to find communion. Lawrence makes a distinction between such communion,
which he reserves for friendship, and what he calls 'a conjugation
of the blood', which he confines to the lovers' 'night-time selves'.
He thinks that to seek intimacy in love and marriage is a disaster
and that lovers should preserve the purity of their sexual polarity
and remain 'other' to each other. For this otherness is necessary for
the magnetic attraction which is at the core of sexual passion.

He finds the solution in what he calls the dual movement of sexual love – sensuality in which the lovers remain separate individuals and communion in which they yield their individuality. But these two movements are irreconcilable and the lovers have to find a balance between them – between sensuality and communion.

Freud (see Chapter 6) thought of sexuality as at once pleasure-seeking and also directed to an object. When it is directed to a person, we have here the makings of sexual love. He further believed that all love is essentially sexual in character. In other words, for instance, such things that are as far apart as friendship and the love of God are seen as forms of sexual love – in the way for instance that in geometry the square and the circle are seen as forms of the polygon. It is the 'libido', the energy of human sexuality, that infuses sexual love. It has two 'currents', namely sensuality and affection. Normally in sexual love these are fused together; the character which each has in separation from the other is transformed and together they constitute a whole. That is how in sexual love sex, and love are *at one* with one another. But when sexual love contains nothing but tenderness this is a consequence of the repression of the libido's sensual current. Freud considers such love as lame in that it cannot achieve its aim, namely physical union – e.g. Prince Myshkin's love for Nastasya Phillipovna and also for Aglaya in Dostoyevsky's *The Idiot*. The libido, however, can take different aims; it enters into our other loves and interests, moving us to pursue their aims. Freud calls this 'sublimation'.

This is the gist of Freud's conception of all love as essentially sexual in character. In other words Freud regards carnal love as primary and spiritual love as a sublimated form of it. In contrast, Simone Weil points out, Plato reverses this order; for him carnal love is a degraded form of chaste love (Weil, 1953, p.69). A consideration of the relation between these two forms or aspects of love constitutes another one of the main themes of this book.

I criticize Freud's quasi-mechanistic conception of the relation between love and sexuality and also his biological conception of sex – as does Fromm too. I argue that sex, which indisputably plays an important role in all animal life, assumes a new dimension in human life for which there is no logical space in animal life. I also reject Freud's view that all love is sexual in character – an idea which Lawrence rejects too. The chapter ends with a consideration of the connection between love and creativity. (This last section is taken from Chapter 3, Section 2 of my book *Freud and Human*

Nature, 1983). What I say in this section is directly linked to my conception of the human soul as bipolar with love as one of its two poles, the other one being self-preservation which can easily turn into self-seeking. I argue throughout the book that self-seeking is the enemy of spirituality (see Plato) and is usually a destructive force in human life (see Kierkegaard). In contrast, love contains the elements which, when blended together in mature love, are a creative force in life. Freud could perhaps be seen as straining towards but altogether missing something like this in his conception of sex as 'the instinct of life' – life but not self-preservation.

Here let me add an idea which I do not discuss as such in the book, namely that sex divorced from love may nevertheless, in some cases, be a misguided search for love. It is not inconceivable that the prowler who seeks the satisfaction of his sexual urge with prostitutes may be looking for love in the only place where he feels it to be available for him. Sex, pure and simple, as a form of itch, may thus be rarer than we recognize. Indeed sex is hardly ever an itch, and more often than not it is a vehicle not only for love, but also for other things: for the expression of anger, for destructivity rather than creativity – as in rape, for instance. It may be put in the service of a person's quest for power, it may become a vehicle of self-seeking. All the same it seems to me that sex has a natural affinity with love and that when it becomes a vehicle for these other things it becomes corrupt. This is of course a value judgement. In any case in its relation to love it is entirely feasible to see sex as in the service of love rather than the other way around, namely as love in the service of sex.

The chapter on Fromm (see Chapter 8) contrasts his 'existential' orientation with Freud's quasi-biological conception of sexuality. For Fromm love is sought for the solution it offers to the existential problem which human separateness poses for all human beings. It is one attempt at the solution of this problem among several others and the most satisfactory of them. But this is true only in the case of *mature* love. For with such love 'the paradox occurs that two beings become one and yet remain two' (1979, p. 24). Maturity, however, is something that takes inner work and mature love, therefore, is something the individual *learns*. The learning involves coming to self-knowledge – learning to accept disappointment, criticism, contradiction, frustration, learning loyalty, gratitude, generosity, patience, the tolerance of faults and imperfections in the loved one, learning to consider and care for others, and learning to give up phantasy-thinking and to respect reality. This is the process of growing up, and that means of growing out of a childish mentality, a dependent affectivity, and a self-centred orientation to others.

There is much which in the chapter on Erich Fromm I find right in what he says, but I have several criticisms too and the main one is directed to his view of love, mature love, as sought for the solution it offers to the existential problem of human separateness. For human separateness, I argue, is not a problem for one until one falls in love. In any case when one genuinely falls in love one's love is gratuitous, it is not a means to anything. The way I put it throughout the book is that human separateness is a problem *for love* because of love's desire for communion and oneness with the loved one. It is in coming to maturity and so to mature love that this problem is resolved – provided *both* parties to the relationship are mature. Otherwise the mature partner's maturity helps him to cope with the problems of the relationship, not to add to them, and to give support to the other in the way she copes with them.

The two religious writers I examine in the last four chapters of this book, writing from a Christian perspective, recognize this problem well and find its solution equally in the transformation of the lover's love as he grows out of a self-centred orientation and learns respect, gratitude, forgiveness and acceptance of reality – the antithesis of which are idealization and wishful thinking. Thus Kierkegaard (see Chapter 12) speaks of such a transformation as the 'revolution' of love. With love so transformed there comes, as he puts it, a 'life-giving confusion' which obliterates the distinction for the lovers between *mine* and *yours* while at the same time keeping the *I* and the *you* distinct. 'For without *you* and *I* there is no love.' That is, the love which the lovers have and give to one another must come from them as individuals, they must be *themselves* in their love. 'And [at the same time] with *mine* and *yours* there is no love' (1962, p. 248). But this is a paradox, for '*mine* and *yours* ... are in fact formed out of *you* and *I* and consequently seem necessary wherever *you* and *I* are.' He adds that 'this holds true everywhere, except in love, which is the fundamental revolution'. 'The deeper the revolution, the more the distinction between mine and yours disappears, and the more perfect is the love' (pp. 248–9).

There is really a close affinity between this claim and Fromm's saying that with mature love 'the paradox occurs that two beings become one and yet remain two'. Man's existential situation which constitutes a problem for love, namely what I have called our separateness as individuals, is represented in a parody by Plato's Aristophanes in the *Symposium*. Plato's view, as articulated by Diotima, is that the answer to the situation parodied is to be found in an ascent to an impersonal love. Such a love is mediated by a love of the Good, it is undiscriminating between particular individuals and so is detached from the needs and desires in us, the satisfaction of which we seek in them. In the *Phaedo* this detachment is represented as achievable by means of the purification of the soul from the self. There is a close affinity between this conception of love and that found in Christianity.

The ascent of which Diotima speaks in the *Symposium*, ascent from the particular to the form of the good, the detachment from what we turn to in the particular and the individual for the satisfaction of our needs, does not imply indifference to the particular and the individual. Not at all. For the love of the good towards which we move in such an ascent and detachment is something that finds expression in our concern for individuals. It is only there that it can find expression. This ascent thus is not a flight into the abstract and the general, a flight from the world in which it is the individual that counts, the individual with whom we make contact. This is indeed well appreciated by both of the two Christian writers I examine in Chapters 9 to 12 of this book. In Plato this thought is expressed in the *Republic* in terms of the allegory of the cave in the idea of the return to the cave by the individual who has been freed from it.

In the title of the book I refer to the 'forms' and 'dimensions' of love. By 'form' I mean such things as sexual love, friendship, affection, gratitude, compassion. These are at the same time 'strands' and 'expressions' of love. Thus sexual love may contain affection and even compassion. Love in its different forms has many manifestations in common. By its 'dimensions' I mean what constitutes the directions in which love, in one or other of its forms, can develop or fail to do so, coming to be arrested and the love in question taking a corrupt form. These are the dimensions in which we assess and characterize a person's love. They are at the same time dimensions of the lover's personality and character. Thus we speak of a mature love and a mature person, a selfless person and a pure love, a false person and a counterfeit love, a shallow person and a shallow love.

So I quote a line from a book entitled *Women and Sometimes Men*: 'What a man is his love is' (Florida Maxwell-Scott, 1957, p. 186). I emphasize that there need be nothing fixed or immutable in this.

A man can learn from his experience of love, from its difficulties and his failures, and in the process change – become capable of mature judgement and mature responses. In what he thus comes to his love changes. Equally as his love changes so he changes. But, in the opposite direction, if he is embittered by his experiences, for instance of failure, betrayal or rejection, he may become incapable of love – he may become hard-hearted, cynical, unforgiving, withdrawn. This is where he is defeated instead of learning from love.

These things, such as hard-heartedness and cynicism, are defences against love, against what a person exposes himself to in love. As the poet Gibran puts it:

> All these things shall love do unto you that
> you may know the secrets of your heart, and in that
> knowledge become a fragment of Life's heart.

> But if in your fear you would seek only love's
> peace and love's pleasure,
> Then it is better for you that you cover your
> nakedness and pass out of love's threshing-floor,
> Into the seasonless world where you shall laugh,
> but not all of your laughter, and weep, but not
> all of your tears.

To live without love is to miss out on life's offerings, to turn away from life's blessings and to dry up.

İLHAM DİLMAN

1

Human Togetherness and the Reality of Other People

1.1 Human Separateness: Does it Separate?

Is there a sense in which each human being is inevitably at the centre of his life in the way he understands things and in the way they matter to him? I want to argue that there is a sense in which this is true. But in what sense is it true? If I am in the centre of my life and you are of yours how can we establish a relation of reciprocity and find togetherness in it? I want to take forward my discussion of this question.

The inevitable centredness of human life in the self, I shall argue, is the reverse side of the separateness which characterizes human existence, that is the existence of human beings as individuals. I argued (Dilman, 1987, Chapter 7) that it is in accepting this separateness that we find our individuality and that it is only as such that we can establish a genuine reciprocity in our personal relationships.

This is the reciprocity of love, trust and give and take. It is a gift of love when the love exists on both sides. It cannot be sought; one is blessed with it in the purification of one's love from ego-centricity *if* one is lucky. The love in question can be personal as in the case of the love between parent and child, or man and woman, or impersonal as in the case of compassion for the afflicted. Compassion is reciprocated in gratitude and in the constructive use of what is received.

The antithesis of such reciprocation is the rejection of what one is given in love, exploitation and betrayal of trust. Its very possibility is internal to human separateness and so written into human existence. It is a part of its character: we are intentional agents and in an important sense our centre of gravity lies within our own

1

individual lives. But in what sense? Before taking up this question I want to consider, once more, the question whether human separateness excludes reciprocity, whether in our separateness we are irremediably alone. My answer, briefly, was that while another person cannot take *my* decisions, face *my* difficulties, feel *my* distress, love or die in *my* place and vice versa (ibid., p. 97), he can enter into my situation and help me arrive at a decision that will be mine; he can share my distress in his concern, himself feeling distress at my distress. But he cannot take it away from me, however much he may wish to do so. All he can do is to bear it in silence, without burdening me with his pain. In this sharing we are *together*: we hold hands, so to speak, while we each continue to stand on our own feet. This is what I meant to illustrate in my choice of Matisse's 'The Dance' for the cover of my book, *Love and Human Separateness*.

A mother can hold her baby and press him to her breast, but she cannot make his distress hers, she cannot take it away from him. Similarly, where a man's wife has been taken hostage and is going to be killed, the man may offer himself to take her place in exchange for her life. But he cannot die her death. In this supreme sacrifice, if she accepts it for the sake of their young child who needs to be looked after by a mother, they are *together*. This is the togetherness that belongs to reciprocity.

Again, if I am your friend I shall support you in your love and take an interest in its object. Thus in our friendship we are *together*, but our interests even when they have the same object are distinct. This is what it is to share the same interest. Where I try to take it over through a form of identification at the expense of my independent existence my interest in what you are interested in will not be genuine. For it is not gratuitous, it is subordinated to my aim to step into your shoes. This destroys our togetherness and separates us in a way in which we need not be separated.

Put it like this: we are inevitably separate, but our separateness need not separate us. We can be together in our separateness in the only way in which it is possible for two human beings to be together. The impossibility of stepping into your shoes, in the sense I have indicated, does not make the togetherness I can find while remaining myself a limited kind of togetherness – a second-best as it were.

But what kind of impossibility are we speaking of here? In my early book *Matter and Mind* (1975), Pt II, I argued that in the claim that two people cannot have the very same after-image, feel the self-same pain, truth and falsity are intermingled and I tried to disentangle these. I quote the concluding paragraph of Chapter 6:

> when we insist that however similar two people's sensations they can never be identical 'since my pain is mine and your pain is yours' we misunderstand the use of the personal pronouns here. Still this is not to say that we should simply retract these words. For in them there is also the recognition of something important, namely that we cannot have another person's sensation *in the sense that* we may have his belongings, nor even *in the sense that* we may have his qualities, virtues and vices. For the identity of pain cannot be divorced from the person who gives expression to or conceals it (p. 175).

This, however, is *not* the sense in which we cannot step into someone else's shoes, take his decisions, live his life, face his difficulties, take away his distress from him and feel it in his place. It has to do *not* with the use of personal pronouns *in their ordinary sense* but with their use in what I call their 'strong sense' – such as in 'He is not *himself* in what he does', 'his decisions are not *his*'. Take the example of a person's decisions. There are two possibilities. In the one case I ask an expert to invest a sum of money for me. He decides where I should invest my money. I trust his judgement and follow his advice. Here the decision to do what he tells me remains mine and I still do what *I* decide. In the other case I turn my problems over to a psychotherapist and am ready to submit to his decisions. If he agreed, then any decision he takes for me would not be *my* decision and what I do as a result would not come from me. That is why a psycho-analyst would not enter into the relationship I try to lead him into, but instead would try to get me to see what I am up to.

Thus, briefly, either I make another's decision mine or I don't. There is no third possibility. Where I do, *he* has not taken my decision, for though I act on his advice I still act on my own decision; and where I don't make his decision mine, the decision I act on is not mine. In neither case has *he* taken *my* decision.

Let me quote a short passage from my book *Love and Human Separateness*, Chapter 7:

> Where I assume responsibility for what you tell me to do, what I do comes from me; and where I do not, the actions in which I conform to your will are not 'mine' in the strong sense under

consideration. We could say that what I am willing to take responsibility for determines the boundaries of what comes from me.

Similarly, you can give me not only advice, but sympathy and
support, put yourself out for me; you may even hold me together
when I am falling apart. But you cannot make me whole.
Whatever it is that I owe to other people [my parents, my teach-
ers, my psycho-therapist], my wholeness, like my convictions,
has to come from me. And if you wish me to accept something, a
gift or a proposition, then I accept it only if I want to, only when
I am genuinely persuaded. Then and only then am I the one who
says 'Yes' or 'Thank you'. This too marks our separateness.

To be myself in what I say and do I have to accept this separateness; it is only in my recognition of my separateness that I can be
myself. Even where I obey or submit I am myself so long as I do so
from conviction. To renounce oneself in the sense in which spiritual
religions demand from their believers one has to be oneself. There
is nothing paradoxical in this. For in being oneself one acknowl-
edges one's separateness as an individual; but this separateness is
not a form of separation. And neither does being oneself have to be
a form of self-assertion.

Likewise to find togetherness with a friend or beloved I have to
be myself and respect his or her separateness. Our separateness is a
barrier to such togetherness only if (i) I am afraid or do not know
how to be myself in my relationship with him or her, and (ii) if I do
not respect him or her in his or her separateness. Only then does
our inevitable separateness become a form of separation.

The idea that this separateness separates people, makes sharing,
reciprocity and togetherness impossible is a form of philosophical
scepticism which I have combated in some earlier writings. But
where it appears so in one's own life and relationships its source is
personal and affective. To recognize one's 'error' – if it can be called
an error – one has to change affectively in oneself. Labouring under
its shadow any attempt to overcome such separation by trying
either to possess the other or to sink one's identity into his or hers
by stepping into his or her shoes is what Sartre calls 'a project of
bad faith'. It involves conflicting and, indeed, contradictory aims
which cannot be reconciled.

Such a conflict can only be resolved by giving up the project. To
give that up in turn means changing in oneself affectively – i.e. in

one's affective orientation – towards greater authenticity whereby one understands that one's separateness from the beloved or the friend is not a barrier to be overcome. In other words it is not *that* which excludes the togetherness one seeks but one's way of seeking it. In such a change one does not come to settle for less than is possible.

1.2 The Individual's Dual Reality: in Himself and for Others

I referred earlier to an important sense in which our own centre of gravity lies within our own individual lives. It is, of course, a platitude that each person lives his own life. There is a sense in which this is not only true but necessarily so, and a sense in which it is false, since the life that a person lives is sometimes said not to be his life – in the sense that he is not himself in that life. But it is in the life that is inevitably his that he can be himself or fail to be so. In what he 'lives' (I use the verb unusually in the accusative), that is in what he takes into his life, what he 'lives' is not independent of the way he lives it. For instance, the way a married person 'lives' his marriage – i.e. the way he responds to its gifts and its demands, what he makes of it in his life – characterizes the kind of marriage he has. This is not to deny, of course, that what his spouse contributes to it may make a difference to what he can make of it. Of course not. For marriage – like a dance: the tango – is what two people participate in and in that participation *make*. More briefly, it is in the life that each lives that the individual marriage is what it is. Not surprisingly, for, in each case, the life is his or hers and the marriage is part of that life. The husband and wife share the life of their marriage; but as separate individuals. The possibility of this sharing of the life of their marriage depends on their individual contributions to it: the contribution each makes as a separate individual. The contribution comes from each of the individual's life and depends on what each makes of the marriage in his own separate life. If I may put it like this: they achieve something, namely what they can do together, jointly, as a result of what each does singly, as an individual, in the life that is *his* or *hers*.

'The life is his.' This implies that he can take responsibility for it in a way that no one else can do. He can make certain changes in it, he can give up things that are part of it – he can stop beating his wife, he can feel remorse for having done so, he can make amends to her. But whatever he may in fact do or not do, however he may live, what he is like finds expression in it – whether in his authenticity or in his duplicity.

'It is *my* life, I can do what I want with it.' As a logical claim this ignores the limitations imposed by various contingencies outside my control on what I can do. But generally when one uses these words it is not to express a logical point. These words are sometimes uttered by way of staking a claim on licence: 'I can do what I want with it.' One answer to it is: 'Perhaps you can, but that doesn't mean that you would be justified in doing what you want. You certainly would not be justified in doing whatever you want. You could go to gaol for it, you could regret what you have done for the rest of your life. Beware of what you would be bringing upon yourself.' The words may, however, be directed to someone who interferes with one's life, makes constant demands which fail to respect one's autonomy. It is a way of saying: 'You have no right to interfere with what I do here, no right to make demands on me the way you do. What I do for you, what I give you, is up to me.' Indeed, there is asking and asking; and one way of asking is a recipe for driving the other person away when it ignores the separateness which is essential to the maintenance of his individuality – to his authenticity and autonomy as an individual.

Let us consider, for a moment, the diverse affective responses which are such an important part of human life – joy, elation, anger, dejection and despair. Obviously the scope and limits of what matters to people vary from individual to individual. For one person they may be confined to his own individual successes, failures and frustrations, while for another they may encompass those of the people for whom he cares and has concern. But whichever it is, it is clear that for one to be moved to any of these diverse responses that to which he so responds must matter *to him*.

That means that he is only moved in one of these diverse ways by what relates *to him* – relates to him in one or another of *different* ways that are possible. The different things he thus 'lives' in the way he is moved – e.g. the things he celebrates or mourns – constitute 'the world he lives', and in that sense 'his world', that is a world whose existence is dependent on him: on his existence *and* its mode or character. *This* is the world of which he is inevitably the centre. But just as human separateness does not have to separate friends, lovers, people who share the same interest or fight for the same cause, though it can, so similarly our being the centre of the world which each of us 'lives' need not make us selfish or self-centred (ego-centric), though it can do so.

A self-centred person is someone who is only interested in himself. He thinks of others as satellites that revolve around him. In his emotions he takes them as existing for this purpose. Indeed, in his affective apprehension the existence of others is confined to this. They are real to him insofar as they fulfil this purpose; otherwise he is indifferent to them – that is in his emotions they do not exist. They come into existence again if and when he needs them or if they happen to intrude into his life by opposing his schemes, resisting his manipulations, or not falling in with his needs. They stick out in his apprehension then like a sore thumb. In short he has an attenuated apprehension of the reality of other people. Here we need to be clear that our apprehension of other people's reality is affective, that is through our emotions. I mean the reality they have in their own individual lives, separate from mine. For the reality so apprehended – that is affectively – is one which each person *lives* for himself, a reality he lives in his relations with them, in his sympathy and concern for others or in his hostility and resentment.

Before taking this further let me make it clear that reality, what we call 'real' as opposed to 'illusory', 'false' or 'fake', is that with which we engage – the internal object of our engagements. A lake as opposed to a mirage is real – i.e. has physical reality – because we can drink from it, bathe in it. A chair as opposed to a mere shadow or illusion is real in the sense that we can sit on it, pull or push it. It is something *we* can handle, move, etc. Similarly, though I have never visited China, I know that there are really people living there – a very great many of them. But if in the paper I read that one of its citizens has broken a leg, etc., the impact that this makes on me is minimal. For he exists for me at best as a name. I am sorry that this should have happened to *anybody*; but this is the limit of the difference it makes to me in my feelings. Thus his reality for me is severely curtailed by the limitation of my knowledge and sympathies in the near absence of the contact I can make with this total stranger in his misfortune. For the ego-centric person the reality of others is curtailed in the same way even when his life and theirs are interwoven in many ways. They come into contact constantly, but he makes no contact with them.

This applies equally to one's own reality *for oneself*. If others constantly ignored me, wanted to have nothing to do with me, evaded any kind of engagement with me, refused either to give or accept anything from me, I would begin to doubt my own existence as a person. Unless I already had inner resources on which I could fall back, inner resources derived from an earlier time when I was treated with care and regard, I would begin to lose all those convictions which give me substance and a sense of my own reality. Having no reality for others I would begin to feel I was nothing and end up by having no reality in myself.

In short, if others treat me as if I do not exist as a person, I would stop taking it for granted that I do so exist. But then I would in reality begin to stop existing as a person; I would turn into a kind of zombie. Here the relation between conviction and reality is not external. When the sources that maintain my convictions dry up the reality in question disappears.

These sources are originally external and go back to my childhood. They are to be found in my early engagements within the family. If, as a child, I have been given love, care and attention, this will enable me to make giving relationships in the course of my development in which I shall find sustenance. I will then find it easier in later life to develop convictions and to put myself out for others. My sense of being a person or, which comes to the same thing here, my reality as one, will not then be easily undermined in changed circumstances, such as if for instance I find myself in a milieu from which I am estranged or in which I am ostracized. I shall have inner resources to fall back on, inner resources that will sustain me. I may thus manage to maintain my own reality as a person in my inner, spiritual life. If, for instance, I have religious convictions my relationship with God will sustain me. Even if my parents are dead, my interactions with them in my continuing relationship will keep me going in my reality as a person.

The point I am trying to make is that both my own reality as a person and that of others for me in their separate existence cannot be divorced from the way I 'live' them, from what I make of myself and of others in my own life. Both are *lived* realities, realities lived by each individual in his life. As such, therefore, they belong to the world lived by the individual – *his* world. They are thus inevitably *personal* realities – my reality as a person in my own right and the reality which others have for me. This does not mean that others do not have an *objective* existence. Of course they do. When I die their life will continue; they will continue to exist. They have, that is, a life and existence independent of me. But I can apprehend their existence *as such* only in the way I take it into *my* life – my own life. It is *there* that they have reality for me, or fail to do so. This is a matter of my affective orientation and, therefore, of my own mode of existence. They will thus appear in their separate and independent existence in *my* world; or they will fail to appear as such to the extent of my ego-centricity. To repeat, in *my* world others *can* have an independent existence. They do not have to have the existence of satellites there. The fact that their reality can only take shape for me in *my* world does not make it so.

We can compare the existence and reality of other people in this respect to the existence and reality of moral values. They too have an *objective* existence in the culture in which they have developed. They were there before me. I came into contact with them first in the way my parents brought me up, treated me, responded to me, praised and admonished me in various situations. But they assumed reality for me in my life in the way my understanding and affective orientation began to take shape, in turn shaping my life, through my growing active participation. In his way I began *living* the moral values as I made them my own, and in my living of them they became real to me. 'This is what *is called* good, right, etc.' – an *objective* matter, the object of a factual statement, a factual truth – came to be replaced by, 'This *is* good, right, etc.' – a *personal* matter, the object of a *moral* judgement made *by me*, a *moral* truth *for me*. We could thus say that moral values have a double existence: an objective existence which we can characterize as 'social', of interest to the sociologist, and an existence in my world which gives them reality for me, a 'moral reality' which we can characterize as 'personal'.

Human beings too have this double existence and reality for me and for others: objective and personal. Philosophers in their discussion of 'the problem of other minds' have directed their attention to the objective existence of other people. But, engrossed in such an orientation, they have missed understanding what we normally call 'knowing a person' (see Dilman, 1987, Chapter 9). It was Wittgenstein who pointed out that I apprehend a person's reality as a sentient being and intentional agent in 'my attitude towards a soul' – towards a human being (*PI* Pt II, §iv).

No sane person, of course, has any doubt about the existence of people other than himself, about such people's sentience and human agency. He has no doubts on this score when he meets people in the traffic of human life. It is in his unthinking reactions, unreasoned responses to them that he takes them as human beings. Indeed, what these reactions – our attitude towards a soul – thus circumscribe goes to define what we call a human being: 'a human being is a being who, in certain circumstances, can awaken my anger or irritation, in other circumstances my pity, etc.'

It is, of course, as an individual that one comes to *know* a person whom one thus takes to be a human being as a matter of course. Hence Wittgenstein's distinction between fallible beliefs and concept-forming attitudes. Obviously where knowing a person is concerned reasoning, reflection and imagination have a role to play. Also one needs time and opportunity to come to know a person. Furthermore such knowledge admits of degrees – thus we say 'I know him well' or 'I don't know him that well', which doesn't mean 'I don't know all there is to know about him.' Also one can be deceived by him or mistaken in one's judgements. But it is in one's affective reactions – those same ones that constitute one's 'attitude towards a soul' – and in transactions that draw such reactions from one that one makes contact with others and in that contact comes to know them as individual human beings. Obviously these transactions can take different forms: in them the other person may hide from one, deceive one, or he can be trusting and open to one's responses in his. Again just as it takes two to tango, it takes a two-way relationship for one person to come to know another.

In the course of such transactions, people of course exercise their judgement, and in the affective contact which each makes with the other he *lives* the other's reality in its fullness or in a curtailed form. He lives that reality as the reality of a person who is *there* in his separateness or as one that is curtailed by the evasiveness of a person who is not altogether there for one. It is in the latter case that one may say, 'I have known him for a long time, but I don't know him well at all'. In either case the other is there or not altogether there in his responses to me. I, in my turn, take those responses into *my* world in the way *I* live them in my responses.

It is *there* that I come to know the other person, or fail to come to know him, *there* that he has full reality for me or only an attenuated one. His reality is attenuated because our engagements with each other are curtailed. I should point out that a person who opposes me, my enemy, may be fully there for me in his opposition and as such be fully real to me. I shall certainly come to know him then as my enemy in his individuality; but I shall not come to know him as I would if we were friends. I shall not come to know him, perhaps, in his kindness and generosity. I say 'perhaps', because it is possible for this side of him to appear even in the course of our fight.

It is sometimes said, 'you have to live with someone to really know him'. Part at least of what is meant is that this will provide the opportunity for the different sides of each of the two persons to appear in their interactions and so to engage them. But obviously one has to be authentic and continue to be there for the other, not turn away from him or her; and this takes love, faith and patience.

The connection between how well I *know* a person and how *real* he is to me is a complicated one and needs further discussion.

1.3. Summing Up

I have tried to clarify the sense in which one's knowledge of others is *personal*, the sense in which one comes to know others in one's life – one's own life, a life from which one is inseparable. One can say that such knowledge is 'personal' in the sense that the intellect and scientific knowledge are *impersonal*. What one knows in science is independent of the life one lives and of the being one has in it. I have argued too that the reality which people have appear in their engagements with each other. Each person finds it in his engagements with others – engagements to which all the parties involved contribute. These engagements belong to and are part of each individual's life, his or her life as an individual in his or her separateness from others. It is thus a *lived* reality and as such it is not separable from the person who lives it; it comes into being in *his* life. In his apprehension of this reality he, himself, appears in his separateness from others. As Wittgenstein put it in connection with moral judgements: 'here I can only appear as a person speaking for myself' (Waismann's 'Notes on Talks with Wittgenstein', *Phil Rev*, vol. 74, no. 1, Jan 1965, p. 16).

It is otherwise with my knowledge of an object and its reality. I may perceive or experience its qualities for myself by touching it, poking it, experimenting with it, or I may take on trust what others who have done so tell me. Here, in practice, there is little difference between 'It is so' and 'He tells me it is so and I believe him – with good reason'. As far as its being so is concerned here he and I do not appear in our separateness. That is I do not speak as myself in my separateness, but as a qualified judge or witness; and as such I am replaceable by someone else so qualified. I do not have to 'live' what I so judge. *What* I apprehend I do by means of my senses and by the exercise of my intellect, and it has objective reality: it exists independently of my apprehension of it.

People, by contrast, like moral values, I argued, have a dual reality: an objective reality and one that is inseparable from the person who lives it – the person himself and those who come to know him in their engagements with him. My contention has been that as human separateness is no obstacle to reciprocity, sharing and togetherness, so equally the personal character of the reality that others have in human life – one's own life as well as the lives of other people – does not make the interpersonal communication of our apprehension of it in particular cases impossible. If what I live and apprehend in the living of it here is *mine*, in the sense that it appears in *my* life, how can I go wrong in my apprehension, fail in my knowledge? My answer has been that failure here often involves a failure of self. Such failure is intimately connected with the kind of failure which makes our separateness a form of separation: lack of respect, lack of patience, self-absorption, self-centredness. It also involves the contribution of the other person to the interactions in which alone I can come to know him or her – in the form of mistrust, withdrawal, insincerity, deception. These contributions on the part of the people thus interacting are not obviously independent of one another. Each comes from the person concerned in the personality and character he has, but is at the same time inspired or triggered by the other person and is, therefore, a response to his contribution. Their mix is thus seamless and, of course, varies from case to case.

One last question which I have not left myself the room to discuss: if the *life* that I live is the life that *I* live, if I am at the centre of that life, does that mean that I must inevitably come first in my considerations, that for instance I cannot come second even to the person I love in the way I take him or her into my life in my interactions? I don't believe so. For although I am inevitably at the centre of my life in the sense that has been under discussion I can be related to what I live here, as we have seen, in different ways. The life into which I take the person I love does not have to be self-centred; and only when it is so do I always put myself first in my consideration of others.

However, this being at the centre of my life in the sense that the life in question is *my* life is liable to perversion. The logical 'my life is mine' can turn into 'I have only one life to live, so I mustn't compromise with anyone on how I live it.' Equally 'nobody else can live my life for me' can turn into 'I mustn't give precedence to anyone in the way I live my life'. This perversion then of the sense of the words used to express a logical point becomes a recipe for selfishness.

2

Love and Hate:
Are They Opposites?

2.1 Mature and Immature Love

In a paper 'On Love and Hate', read at the 17th International Psycho-Analytical Congress in Amsterdam in 1951, Michael Balint describes a woman, a patient of his, whose 'whole life', as he puts it, had been 'an endless repetition of the same pattern'. She had always been terribly in need of love and affection. She had 'thrown herself away at the first signs of some slight attention'. The person in question became an angel in her mind and for a short while she lived in blissful expectation. Then because the other person had a separate existence from her he could not satisfy her absolute demands. She interpreted this as heartlessness and cruel neglect and the result was a painful disappointment. This then turned into hatred and the person was discarded as bad, heartless, rotten and cruel. She was then overcome with anxiety.

Was the love for the person she came to hate genuine? Balint argues that it was, but that it was a primitive, immature sort of love. In contrast, he says, his patient's hate cannot be called either mature or infantile, or primitive; but then immediately after having said this he adds: 'anxiety, and to some extent hate, exist only in primitive forms.' At first he concentrates on love: what is the difference between a primitive and an adult love? He gives seven characteristics of immature, primitive love which distinguish it from mature love.

(i) The person has a weak sense of self and feels insecure in herself. As a result she needs the reassurance of love, affection and attention. When, in the separateness of his existence the other cannot meet the absolute demands she makes on him the result is cataclysmic. Anything other than fusion is felt by her as a let down, a betrayal. She feels abandoned and condemned to nothingness for having been denied the confirmation of love and affection.

(ii) The more desperate her need for confirmation the less she is able to be realistic both in her expectations and in her assessment of the other's response to her. She expects from the other something he cannot give her, or at least something he cannot sustain, and her disappointment is out of all proportion to reality: her idealization turns into an equally unrealistic disappointment followed by denigration.

(iii) Given her weak sense of self and feeling of inner deprivation she cannot avoid envying those who feel at home and secure in their own skin, and is therefore charged with the destructiveness which belongs to her envy. 'Such people [Balint writes] can only have ambivalent relations ...' and their love is 'easily smothered by their destructive tendencies.'

(iv) She cannot form a realistic picture of the other and tends to split him into two: the loving, caring person who will fulfil all her expectations and the selfish, feckless person who is unable to care. He thus tends to oscillate in her apprehension between these two irreconcilable aspects. Similarly so do her feelings towards him oscillate between love and anxiety, and at times, a defensive hatred. She cannot feel at home with him, nor with herself in her need for confirmation.

(v) Balint points out the possibility of strong narcissistic tendencies in such a person which she has failed to outgrow. She loves herself in him. This makes her intolerant of any fault or blemish in him and also makes her demanding: he must be perfect in his love and attention towards her.

(vi) A sixth possibility is what Balint, after Freud, calls 'oral greed'. She looks for sustenance in the love she expects and demands, and she can never have enough of it. Such greed is rooted in her absolute dependence that goes back to her very early childhood – indeed babyhood. This is dependence which she has been unable to grow out of and which in the way she has approached personal relationships she has perpetuated. On the one hand it makes the other person all-important to her and, on the other hand, it stands in the way of her considering his interests, needs, sensitivities and well-being. He is seen as being there to cater to her needs.

(vii) A seventh characteristic of this primitive, immature love relationship from which she cannot escape is her need to control it unconditionally. This need to control the relationship, to impose her own terms on it, is a defence against her own helplessness.

What Balint gives here is a characterization of the only kind of love his patient is capable of and of the kind of person she is. It is the kind of person she is which confines her to this kind of love and its consequences. Some of these characteristics are to be found in most love relationships, to a certain degree, on one side or the other. The love in question is a very early form of love, the love of a young child for his or her mother, where the child's sense of herself is precarious, she is dependent on her mother for the satisfaction of her needs, her world is limited and only marginally coincides with the world of the adult members of the community in which she will grow up. It is a world defined by significances determined to a large extent by the child's emotions and phantasies. To the extent that she fails to outgrow these emotions and grow up affectively her contact with the adult world remains precarious – especially in situations which bring such emotions into play.

Adults, on their part, who have lost touch with such emotions in themselves, either because they defend themselves against these or because their imagination has remained stunted, will have only a tenuous contact with the world of the young child. Yet because so often this is a world which intrudes into the relationships of adults they will be helpless and impotent when faced with it in others. They will be unable to help their loved ones and only exacerbate their anxieties.

Let me emphasize: to outgrow such a world is not to lose touch with it. It is often people who fail to outgrow it and cannot tolerate facing it in themselves who lose touch with it. Consequently their contact with others comes to be limited and their life is impoverished. These are the two sides of the same coin: on the one side we have the woman who is incapable of adult love, on the other side the person who has not outgrown what she lives. He moves within a well-mapped pattern which at best sterilizes their give and take and impoverishes their life together.

To return to the kind of person exemplified by Balint's patient: she lacks self-reliance, she needs confirmation, in any intimate relationship she cannot tolerate the other person's separate existence; it poses a threat to her. She cannot appreciate the other person in his independent existence: she cannot allow him an independent existence and what he lives independently of her she takes to be neglect or treachery and hates him for it. Her love is thus narcissistic or possessive (not the same thing); it is demanding and draining. What she is capable of giving she gives on her own terms; it is therefore conditional on his being just the way she wants him to be.

It is thus to be contrasted with a love where care and giving is unconditional and directed to the person in his separate existence. It is a love that is considerate, one that is capable of appreciating the other's pains and difficulties and responding to these. It is capable of appreciating his differences and tolerating his foibles and, indeed, his defects. It is mature in the sense that what makes the person capable of it is his having outgrown the very features from early life which stand in its way. Those features – patience, tolerance and respect of the other, unconditional care, appreciation and active concern, the ability to give emotional support, to bear his pains and share his sorrows, to forego thinking of oneself – are themselves a mark of *moral* maturity. A person comes to them by growing out of what belongs to his early affective life and through inner work. Just as a plant needs time to mature, in a very different way these qualities are qualities that need and take time to develop. Just as, it has been said, one cannot fall into goodness, so similarly one cannot be granted these qualities at one go with the wave of a magic wand. It takes time, inner work, letting go, and a certain kind of faith for a person to be able to move, to grow, so as to come to them.

2.2   Asymmetry between Love and Hate

What is philosophically interesting is the asymmetry there is between love and hate in this respect, which Balint himself points out. I should like to develop this point and, indeed, to point out that while love certainly comes from the heart, it is not an emotion, whereas hate is.

We have already seen that Balint says that the distinction between infantile and mature which applies to love does not apply to hate. But then he adds that to some extent at least hate exists only in primitive forms. Let me first help to resolve this contradiction and explain what it is that makes Balint waver.

Fear is certainly an emotion. There is such a thing as phobic and irrational fears and also what one may call a realistic fear. I would not wish to speak of mature and immature fears, even though phobic fears are, I believe, rooted in unresolved conflicts that go back to one's childhood. What is mature in the case of a realistic fear is the courage one exhibits in the face of it. It is the mark of a mature personality. I spoke of patience as a mark of moral maturity; I would put courage together with patience in this respect. Courage is a quality of character and not an emotion, of course.

Similarly, hate is an emotion. But unlike fear I would not speak of a realistic hate. Fear is generally directed to danger. It is difficult to give a general characterization of the object of hate. But I would distinguish between a hatred charged with animus and an impersonal hate. Thus I may come to hate someone who constantly treads on my tail, humiliates and ridicules me in a sneaky way without giving me a chance to defend myself. That is, he may do it in such a way that any proper response to it would aggravate the situation into which he puts me. It is the pain of having my tail trodden on and having to take it that turns into hatred. If I could I would bite him. I have to swallow the pain; therein lies the animus of the hatred I feel for him. Such hatred may be understandable, but it is neither realistic nor unrealistic, neither rational not irrational. I would use neither of these terms to characterize it.

Now, in contrast, I might say, 'I hate corruption and the person who takes bribes.' This applies to any person who takes bribes. It is not because I have had to pay bribes or because my refusal to do so has cost me dear that I hate anyone who takes bribes. It is because of the moral significance I find in it that I hate bribe-taking. I might say, 'It nauseates me.' Here the hate is *impersonal*. The distinction I have in mind is similar to the one between revenge, which is personal, and retribution, which need not be. This is something which people who discuss the rationale of punishment don't always appreciate.

Now to return to my first example – the person who treads on my tail. Here my hatred is not impersonal; indeed its source lies in my inability to take revenge which I characterized as personal. If I can get my own back on him in such a way that he stops, my hatred may go, evaporate. Here my hatred stops, but I don't change in myself. If he stops of his own accord and says he is sorry, I may forgive him. Here I change towards him. But it may so happen that although he continues, my perspective changes; his constant needling me or ridiculing me no longer matters to me. I say to myself, 'That is the kind of person he is; I must be touching some sore spot or vulnerability in him because of the way I am'. I may even be more specific about this. We find what I am trying to depict in Spinoza. He calls it detachment. Now the detachment he has in mind is a mark of maturity.

We find the same kind of maturity in the person who wants the punishment of a criminal without any sense of vengeance. Thus Socrates in the *Gorgias* when he speaks about punishment. When I say that bribe-taking nauseates me and that I hate the bribe-taker my hate may be similarly empty of my ego, devoid of ego-centricity. Having outgrown one's ego-centricity is the other face of the detachment of which Spinoza speaks: they are the two sides of the same coin.

In the former example hatred is something I suffer; it is what Spinoza calls a 'passive emotion'. I am passive in receiving it; I *yield* to it. In the case of the bribe-taker my hate is not an emotion to which I yield. I own it; it does not own me. It is an affective, moral response to bribe-taking in which I am myself. By contrast I am not myself in my hatred of the person who treads on my tail and forces me to swallow the pain and humiliation without being able to do anything about it. It is precisely in my passivity that I hate him. When I can detach myself from it I am myself and exhibit what Plato calls 'self-mastery'.

2.3   Richness of Love and Poverty of Hate

It is precisely this kind of self-mastery which Balint's patient lacks. In Socrates' language from the *Phaedo* her love is a form of 'self-indulgence'. Put it like this: she gives her heart to someone whom she expects to satisfy her needs – needs that she has because she has failed to come to herself, because she has been starved emotionally in one way or another or has been unable to accept or assimilate what she has been given, because she has been unable to outgrow her narcissism, etc. She gives her heart conditionally; she has unrealistic expectations. Her giving is qualified; her love is a qualified giving. Spinoza's distinction between 'active' and 'passive' is applicable here.

The more active a person's love for another the more her love is a mode of being in which the person is herself. No doubt it is an affective mode of being, one in which a person is affectively directed towards the loved one. Loving a person is not being in an affective state. Perhaps one is in such a state when one is *in* love. The person in love is attracted, consumed, 'star struck'. She is in the grip of an emotion. The person in love can think of nothing but the beloved, wants nothing better than to be with the beloved. She glows with the reciprocation of her feelings. But though she can think of nothing but the beloved, she finds a great deal of pleasure in thinking of him. She lives as in a dream; the lover and the beloved share this dream; they indulge themselves in the dream they share.

It is only when they can pass the test of coming to know each other and bearing each other's difficulties, entering into each other's problems constructively, learning to give each other a space in which they can be themselves, have independent interests, that they will come to love each other. They will no longer be *in* love, though not because they have fallen out of love. Their love for each other will be transformed into an active love – that is into care and devotion. They will be free to think of all sorts of other things, but in what they do they will always consider each other. Here 'thinking of the other' takes on a different meaning; it is not pleasurably dwelling on the other in one's thoughts.

A love that is devotion to another, one that finds expression in the way one cares for the other, in one's warmth, in the friendship one gives to the beloved, the support and protection when it is needed, and the unspoken loyalty, is not a state; it is not an emotion. It cannot be compared with hate to be its opposite: they are not in the same grammar.

One may hate another person, resent the way he has been towards one – even for the rest of one's life. This is something one feeds or sustains; at least one is unable to let go of it in forgiveness. In some ways it is like being in love; it is a form of passivity. It is something one suffers; and what one suffers has 'genuine duration' to use an expression of Wittgenstein. An intention, or knowing something, he said, does not have genuine duration; it has no substance of its own. This is equally true of active love, of care, loyalty and devotion. If I love her I certainly will have feelings for her; but my love itself is not a feeling or an emotion.

Compare loving someone with liking him or her. Liking someone is finding him agreeable, enjoying his company, finding in him qualities that give one pleasure or which one admires. If I like him I would seek his company and, of course, he would inspire warmth and friendship in me. If I spend time with him and the give and take between us increases we may become friends. Friendship is a bond which involves loyalty and trust.

I like him because he is the kind of person I enjoy spending some time with – talking, joking, doing together something we both enjoy. We may have common hobbies or common interests. Enjoying someone's company is one of the innocent pleasures of life. When one simply likes someone one is detached from him or her, which doesn't mean that one is indifferent. Love by contrast engages one's emotions without itself being an emotion.

If I love someone I shall be attuned to his or her pains and pleasures. Her pains will be mine; her pleasures, successes will give me pleasure: I shall be pleased for her. The more mature I am in my love the more selflessly will I enjoy her pleasures: that is I shall be pleased for her. My pleasure will not be the vicarious pleasure of identification. That is I shall accept her separateness, her independent existence. This is not detachment; it characterizes the form of my attachment. I am thinking of personal love, such as the love of a man for a woman, of a parent for his or her son or daughter and *vice versa*, of love between brothers and sisters, etc., as opposed to compassion which is impersonal in the sense that anybody can be the object of my compassion.

I was speaking of the way the beloved's pains are mine and the way I share her pleasures and her good fortune. Thus I will defend her, protect her, support her, put myself out for her, remain loyal and faithful to her during periods of trial – when my love is tried or tested. I shall also trust her, forgive her, accept things from her which I could not accept from others, and even ask things which I would not ask from others. All this engages me affectively, in my whole being. But I must be whole in my being to be so engaged. As it is put colloquially, I have given her my heart. This is itself an act of trust and faith which exposes me in my vulnerability: it is up to her whether she cherishes it or breaks it. If she breaks it then it will cut me to the core. This is one reason why people often shun love and are afraid of it. It takes a certain courage to love someone, to commit oneself to another. I am speaking especially of sexual love, the kind of love there is between man and woman. How I shall respond in such an eventuality will be a measure of my love for her. Forgiveness certainly, but compassion too have a role to play even in such a personal matter. They are a part of love.

This is all part of the complexity and richness of love. It has many dimensions, and the primitiveness and maturity which Balint was speaking of are a pair of poles which define one of its dimensions. It has been said, 'each kind of person loves in his own way; what he is his love is.' This cannot be said of hate, nor of fear. And while it is true that what a person is his love is; it is equally true that a person can grow and come to himself in love. This too cannot be said of hate, nor of fear.

Certainly hate or fear can change a person; but this can never amount to growth – unless a person learns to turn away from his hate through forgiveness or detachment, or he finds courage and overcomes his fear. But in either case it is something he values or loves that makes this possible; it is through love and faith that he is able to forgive, to let go of resentment, and to find courage in himself to conquer fear.

Thus in love one finds sustenance and growth, though not when one seeks them, makes love a means to them. Indeed the sustenance people seek in love and the sustainment they find gratuitously when they genuinely forget themselves are not the same thing at all. The sustainment they seek is the sustenance of the ego. As Florida Scott-Maxwell puts it in a little book entitled *Women and Sometimes Men*:

> The longing for love that both men and women feel, the clamour and grasping for love, obviously does not come from full hearts that must give; full hearts usually overflow quite simply and with little fuss. The great do about love is more like the starveling bay set up by hunger. Our emptiness must be filled, our nothingness must be denied. We thirst for love's denial that we are small, we want its reversal of truth, its enhancement of value, its turning of aloneness into uniqueness. We crave to be given ourselves.
>
> (Routledge, 1957, p. 185)

This is precisely what Balint characterizes as primitive, immature love.

By contrast the sustenance which love gives comes through the way in it we learn to forget ourselves and put the loved one first. In losing our ego we find ourselves; we can no longer then need to be given ourselves; our smallness stops to matter; our emptiness is not filled, it disappears.

In love, I said, we grow to greater maturity. Hate, on the other hand, immobilizes, it arrests us: we hold on to things, we repeat the same pattern. This itself may bring a change: bitterness, isolation, withdrawal. Hardly anyone would characterize this as growth or development. It is what I would call a deterioration of the person – a deterioration that comes from the starvation of isolation and withdrawal. In *this* respect one can say that love and hate are the opposite of each other; but they are *not* opposites in the sense that black and white are opposites – opposite colours, opposite emotions.

2.4 Love and Hate: Goodness and Evil

I want to finish this chapter by linking love and hate with goodness and evil. I shall be brief and only indicate the link.

We are familiar with goodness as a virtue; we know what it means to speak of the goodness of a person. A person who possesses goodness is kind and considerate towards others. He treats them with justice and respects their rights. He would not lie to them, cheat them, use or exploit them. When they need help he helps them if he can. He is ready to put himself out for others. He is forgiving. In the face of provocation he controls himself; he is not easily provoked. He shows courage when he has to defend what he cares for and values. These virtues – compassion or charity, justice, honesty, generosity, forgiveness, courage, patience and self-mastery – form a unity and together belong to or constitute goodness.

Goodness is an ideal, a value and virtue at the centre of a kind of morality we find in Plato's ethic as well as in Christian morality. The virtues it unites all have their source in the loving side of our nature. We come to them, or move towards them, through the purification of the love of which we are capable – its purification from all ego-centricity. The purer our love, the more we are able to consider others, to put ourselves out for them unconditionally and without the expectation of any return. Our justice towards them springs from our ability to put ourselves in their place. The same is true of our honesty towards them of which our trustworthiness is a part. The courage it takes to remain loyal to the trust others put in us is also made possible by our selfless concern for them. Finally our ability to surmount the grief others may cause us and to forgive them for the harm or injury they inflict on us, instead of returning it in revenge, is again made possible by the degree of selflessness we have reached.

Not all love is selfless of course, but there can be no selflessness without love. It is by means of the purification of our love that we become selfless; it is in our love for others that we find selflessness. It is to the degree to which the other becomes important to us *in himself*, in his own independent existence, regardless of any way in which he may serve us, that is in what Plato calls 'decent indifference for ourselves', that we become selfless, turn away from our ego in such a way that it withers. The other, however, can become important to us in this way only in the kind of care, concern for, and interest in him which belong to love. Indeed his importance in this sense is internal to the object of our love and compassion in its purity.

What is of interest is that the development towards the capability of a mature love, in Balint's sense, coincides with its purification from all ego-centricity. The development in question thus is at once towards greater goodness and towards greater self-knowledge and self-mastery. What unites them is the purification of the soul from the kind of ego-centricity which inevitably characterizes all infantile modes of being and orientations. If such ego-centricity is equally prevalent in adult life that is because it is so tenacious; indeed so much so that ego-centricity can be said to be one of the poles of the human soul – or at any rate a natural perversion of one of its poles.

Just as all the virtues that are part of or, indeed, constitute goodness are characterized by their purity in selflessness, by the degree of selflessness which the person has reached in the love and concern he is capable of for others, so, on the other side, everything which by contrast is considered evil in a morality of love is characterized by ego-centricity. The evil person thus is someone who only thinks of himself and for whom others are either obstacles to his schemes or instruments to be used to further them. They are to be exploited, preyed on, discarded. If they enhance the ego they are sought; if they make him feel small in the ego in any way or stand in the way of its expansion they are hated and 'punished', 'taught a lesson' whenever this is possible.

In one word evil is the total disregard of others; it is an aggressive form of ego-centricity – such as is to be found in malice, greed unrestrained by any moral consideration, envy, strong lust, vindictiveness. Such disregard is the opposite, the very antithesis of love. Hate in this context is the ego's response to any threat to its expansion and to the boundless sovereignty for which it craves. It wishes and seeks the pain and destruction of anyone and anything that stands in its way. But in such hate the ego already finds compensation for its sense of diminishment in having been ignored, obstructed or insulted. For in hatred it finds a sense of power and being.

It is worth pointing out that what I have described as constituting evil has that character, significance and identity from the perspective of a morality of love. If asked, 'What is evil about these things?', I can only tell the person who asks me if we agree on what goodness is. I repeat, it is only from the perspective of a morality of love in which goodness has its identity that the things I mentioned, such as malice, vanity, unrestrained greed and a lust that rides rough-shod over the other are evil.

3
Forms of Love: Emotional Maturity and Reciprocity

3.1 Love and Reciprocity: Troubadour Love

I have spoken of reciprocity as at once something to which one contributes and at the same time a gift. For obviously reciprocity is something one finds in a relationship and it is part of the harmony between two people to which both contribute. Two people are sometimes said to 'hit it off' with one another in a co-operative relationship, in love, friendship or work. Sometimes they are said to 'rub each other up the wrong way'. That two such people should come together, that their paths should cross, is a matter of chance – of good or bad fortune. But in either case there is something each can do, within the limits of their circumstances and personalities, to consolidate and sustain the harmony in one case or to minimize the grating and perhaps elements of destructiveness in the other. The relationship may be one between two colleagues having to work together or engaged in a joint project, or it may be one between two lovers entangled with one another in their love.

Each obviously has a responsibility for the way he is shaping the relationship, and what he offers to and brings out in the other. Unless his interest is confined to either getting something out of the other or establishing a mere working relationship with the other he will want to be himself in the relationship, to be allowed to be himself by the other and to be accepted as such. Indeed each may learn to be himself in the relationship and be grateful to the other for making this possible. This may involve being able to express anger, irritation and resentment without fear of injuring the other or being rejected, being able to be depressed or disappointed in the other's presence, indeed putting a strain on the relationship while relying on the other's ability to tolerate it. This need not be a form of thoughtlessness or selfishness and he may be grateful to the other for being able to tolerate it. Where this is the case there will be movement in the relationship as opposed to what is in question

24

being a constant repetition of the same thing. The person will then be able to move towards being himself in the relationship and in the gratitude he feels to be more giving.

In such a case we have an instance of reciprocity leading to greater reciprocity. The reciprocal contributions have their source in love and in the faith and trust that belong to such love. The behaviour which puts a strain on the other and on the relationship, I said, may or may not be selfish, thoughtless and irresponsible. When it is not, then there is love in the relationship on both sides and trust and gratitude which are part of that love. In such a case, of course, none of this is the result of any calculation; certainly here reciprocity is not something that is being aimed at. That would be to subordinate love to its possible fruits.

In this respect Balint sails too close to the wind when he writes: 'we must accept the fact that we have to give something to our object [to the loved one], something that he expects from us, in order to change the object [the beloved] into a *co-operative partner*' (Balint, 1952, p. 146). And again: 'To establish this mutuality [what I have called 'reciprocity'], to change a reluctant and uninterested object into a co-operative partner, means both tolerating considerable strains and maintaining a steady and reliable reality testing. I have called this *the work of conquest*' (p. 147). 'To change the object into a co-operative partner': this sounds like manipulation. But what, I believe, Balint means to say is that if we are selfish and thoughtless we risk alienating the beloved. What we should be concerned with, however, is to care for her, to attend to her needs, without thought for any return. If we are mature in ourselves, in our emotions, then we shall be concerned with this as a matter of course. For such concern is the concern of mature love.

Balint's expression 'the work of conquest' equally smacks of manipulation. Courtship may be described as 'winning the heart' of the person who attracts one. Certainly the person who does the courting 'has designs on' the person courted. We find something similar in animals – e.g. the courtship dances and songs of certain birds. But courtship is one thing and love is another. Love itself is not a permanent courtship. However again Balint here does not express himself well. All he means to do is to point out some of the conditions necessary for the growth of love in a relationship of love, namely tolerating the other's faults, accepting her as she is, loving her without idealizing her. He claims that it takes maturity to do so.

I said that while *personal* love certainly desires reciprocity and the return of love it looks on such return as a gift or favour when it is forthcoming and feels thankful for it. When for one reason or another it is not forthcoming it does not switch off, turn away in a different direction. I believe that T.S. Eliot's wife went insane; but he remained loyal and devoted to her all his life at the cost of a great deal of suffering.

Professor Phillips mentioned to me the love of the troubadours in the middle ages in southern France. They devoted themselves to a lady, were prepared to give their life for her, without expecting any return. Indeed each gave his heart to a lady of his choice; but secretly, without even declaring his love. As I understand it this was the discipline of a troubadour's love; it was the love that made such discipline possible. Why discipline? Because personal love desires its return. But the deeper the love the more it can do without it. Indeed it can make its renunciation food for its growth by devoting itself into the active service of the beloved while hiding itself from her. Certainly it takes character and self-mastery to love in this way, and these surely are marks of a mature personality. Of course this is so, provided there is no senti-mentality and the lover derives no food for himself – no food for his ego.

3.2   Love and Maturity: 'Ecstatic Love'

Phillips, in argument with me, said that maturity is a moral concept and it belongs to a certain conception of love, one that is shaped within a particular kind of morality. He could have added: there is no such thing as love *as such*; there are different forms of love, dif-ferent conceptions of love. To characterize an instance of love as mature or immature is to take a certain conception of it – perhaps one that belongs to psychoanalysis. Love can be beautiful or terrible without being mature or immature. He asked me to consider what he called 'ecstatic love': would you describe it as immature?

He quoted a poem by Edna Vincent Milais called 'The Candle', to give me some impression of the kind of thing he had in mind. The poem is just four lines and goes:

> My candle burns at both ends
> It will not last the night

> But ah my foes and oh my friends
> It gives a lovely light.

From the first line I take the impression of a love that is brief – possibly lasts only one night as Phillips said – and is lived breathlessly. It carries no commitment: you give yourself, you are grateful for what you receive, and you move on to another love. As an old Turkish song puts it:

> My mad heart, you spend your time wandering,
> You stop only where you find a beautiful woman.

Let us try to put the best interpretation on this and see how far we can go with it. The wandering is the restlessness of life for such a person who is, as it were, a poet in the sphere of love and sexual passion. What moves him is the beauty he finds in women in their variety: 'My candle … gives a lovely light' (see Milan Kundera's *The Unbearable Lightness of Being*). He is genuinely moved and excited by the beauty he finds in women, in the individual women he seeks and encounters. In the ecstasy he finds in savouring their beauty he forgets himself.

I shall mention some questions which will need to be answered in particular cases. Why does he not stay where he finds beauty in a woman? Why is he restless? Is he, perhaps, unable to grow roots? Wherefore this 'lightness of being'? Is he a Peer Gynt? a Don Juan? Let me grant that none of these need be the case. He need not be motivated by sexual greed or by the desire for conquest. His non-attachment need not be a consequence of his rootlessness. He may be a seeker of beauty in women. Whether credible or not, let us admit this reading which I am offering for examination.

I am comparing our 'ecstatic lover' to a poet or an artist: someone devoted to beauty. So let us imagine someone with a great capacity for appreciation of works of art and natural scenes. He falls in love with the view of a mountain; he sketches it, paints it and paints it again – as Cézanne did with Mont St Victoire. This is his way of caressing it, savouring the beauty he finds there. Or he hears a piece of music and falls in love with it, even with a phrase in it, finds it full of significance – as Swann did in Proust's novel with the little phrase in Vinteuil's sonata.

Similarly with a painting he comes across in a museum. He stops in front of it and admires it for hours. Even if at some later date he returns to it, he moves on, looks at other paintings and derives much enjoyment in contemplating them. If he did not move on, if as an artist he painted the same object again and again, never painting anything else, people might describe him as 'obsessed'. But it may well be that what he finds in this object or natural scene is inexhaustible. However, if he really never had eyes for anything else then people would be justified in describing him as 'obsessed'.

By contrast, if a lover had only eyes for his beloved we would not speak of obsession – not necessarily any way – but of faith and loyalty. There is a radical difference between human beings, even in their attractiveness and beauty, as objects of love, and works of art and the objects they depict in their particularity – whether in their beauty or not. It is notorious that someone who is interested in human beings as a novelist, however deeply he may see into their souls, will fail to engage with them as fully as he might otherwise have done – that is insofar as his interest remains confined to the 'voyeurism' of a novelist. I suspect that something similar is the case with the lover whose interest in the women he loves is confined to the ecstasy he finds and shares with them.

'Lightness of being', perhaps shallowness of emotion, but immaturity: can we speak of immaturity in connection with such a man's love? I do not know: what he finds in love is all that he wants. If it were the case that he *could not* stay long with the same woman, that if he did not move on he would get bored, it would be different. But I have not established the 'psychological necessity' of *that* in the personality I have sketched or imagined for our 'ecstatic lover'.

I certainly am not saying that one cannot make contact with a person, of a sexual or other kind, in a single brief encounter. I am now turning from our 'ecstatic lover' to a character and incident in a film. The film is an Argentinean film *Sur*, which means 'south', directed by Solanas, and the character in question, the main character in the film, is Floreal. His path crosses with Maria's, a young attractive woman, in dramatic circumstances. They find themselves taking refuge in a room where they spend the night together. He is being chased by the police, with live bullets, for his involvement in industrial unrest in the workplace. He knows that he may not be able to return to his life, his work, and his wife. He is in fact soon going to be ruptured from all this by being arrested and sent to prison in Patagonia, far away from home. Maria has already lost everything and broken up with her boy-friend. She wants to get away, to go South to start a new life. Where exactly there and how, she doesn't know. She has no money, not even to buy a ticket with on the bus to go South, and no idea as to what the future holds for her.

It is pure chance that they find themselves together, both thus on the verge of leaving behind everything they know and love. They are kindred spirits in their desolation. They are attracted to each other, and have very little to lean on or hold on to at the time. They are exposed to each other in their vulnerability. They make love and in their openness they touch each other in their very souls. In that short night they love each other with all the yearning that comes from the transience of the occasion in the midst of their rupture from all that is dear to them. I will translate the song, played in the background, which puts into words Floreal's feelings and perspective on the occasion when Maria thus steps into his life for one night.

> Perhaps you were simply called Maria
> You may have been the echo of an old song
> But long, long ago, you gave yourself to me
> In a desolate landscape, heavy with love.
> An autumn day brought you to me full of agony,
> Your poor little hat and your brown coat;
> You were like the street of melancholy
> Which was raining and raining on my heart.
>
> Maria
> In the shadows of my room
> It is your footsteps that keep coming back to me
> Maria
> And your sad little voice,
> That of the day you said: 'There is nothing
> more between us!'
>
> Maria
> Mine the most! The far away one.
> If only one morning you were to come back to me
> Through the streets of our good-byes.
>
> Your eyes were harbours
> Longing for the horizons of dreams and
>   the silence of flowers

But your tender, generous hands, painted
    with love
Will always return to calm my fever.

An autumn day brought you to me
Your name was Maria
But I never came to know anything of
    your unhappy destiny
It was like a landscape of melancholy
Which rained and rained on the grey afternoon.

Now this is a one-off occasion and it is charged with a haunting significance. Yet repeat it and it will change character completely. It has not been sought. What we have is a purely chance encounter between two people in their spiritual nakedness, their futures totally in the melting pot. Severed thus from their past, their future unknown, they are able to give in to their attraction for each other without reserve. They live each other in their short-lived ecstasy and they find full reciprocity in their short togetherness – a togetherness that goes well beyond their ecstasy. Each lives the other without any thought for the morrow. But when tomorrow comes, with it comes the agony of good-byes through which Floreal remembers Maria and the way she gave herself to him.

When much later, after five years of prison, he returns to his wife and is reconciled to her after her forgivable infidelity, through which she never ceased to love him, Maria's name is a distant echo. But what he has lived with her remains with him, inarticulate, and part of him for the rest of his life. It is never forgotten.

Everything that can be said about what went on between Floreal and Maria has thus been said. Have they loved one another? Of course. What they gave one another was love pure and simple. To ask a 'clinical' question in our quest to grasp its character: were there any traces of immaturity in their love or in their loving?[1] In the case of real, live people only the future can provide the answer; but in the film there is no such suggestion. What it portrays are two people who meet as mature adults. In real life, however, I should add, there is a difference between meeting a situation as an adult,

---

1. For the sense of 'clinical' in this context see Dilman 1987, Chapter 10, section 3, pp. 155–8.

responding to it with maturity, and sustaining that maturity through time in the course of a relationship.

3.3 'La Folie de l'Amour'

The madness of love: this is an expression used by Simone Weil. She is thinking particularly of the love of God such as is to be found in a saint. But it would apply also to any great love, sexual or otherwise, for another human being – such as Romeo's and Juliet's for one another for instance. The madness in question is meant to be the antithesis of reason and reasonableness. I mention it because it could appear to be incompatible with the maturity of which I have been speaking. Indeed one might think of it as more compatible with disorder and chaos. The love of Romeo and Juliet turns their lives upside down and brings upheaval to their families. But here clearly it is their families that are to blame. And while it is true that Romeo and Juliet are adolescents, their love for each other is pure. It is incompatible not with maturity but with the politics in which their families are enmeshed. I am almost inclined to say that if there is any immaturity to be found here, it is to be found on the side of the families – the members of both families who are so engrossed in their feud with one another that they have lost sight of their children, in their individuality, and are unable to consider them as such.

What I am saying is that the trouble that love brings to Romeo and Juliet has to do with their external circumstances. Had those circumstances been different there would not have been that trouble. There is certainly no suggestion that the trouble is sought, or that their love feeds on the circumstances in question.

Reasonableness is at least in part connected with prudence. There are, certainly, circumstances when a mature person would err on the side of caution and choose to be prudent. This, of course, is a matter of individual judgement. But there are equally circumstances when a mature person would disregard considerations of prudence. There is nothing immature as such in this. Indeed it may take certain qualities of character such as deep conviction and courage to be able to do so which together may themselves constitute a mark of maturity. From the outside such a person may appear 'unreasonable' and, given the direction in which he is moving, people may say that he is acting 'madly'. I am not saying 'No, he is reasonable.' Rather, I believe, it is this distinction that confines our apprehension of what we have here. Indeed, one may turn what they are saying on its head by replying that love *is* mad.

This is precisely what Simone Weil does when she characterizes the saint's love of God as 'mad'. In so describing it she expresses a moral judgement on our worldly concerns and preoccupations.

The idea that maturity is something that always finds expression in order, adjustment, reasonableness and even self-preservation is a misconception. Sometimes what appears as self-control is the inability to let go; the person is not in control but is being controlled by a part of himself he doesn't really own. Likewise while it is true that abandon may be a precursor to disintegration, sometimes the ability to let go is a sign of conviction and confidence. Thus we have the person who out of devotion to a cause gives up everything in which he has found security, solace and satisfaction. Similarly this occurs for a great love even when it rips one's life apart. Not to turn away from it takes strength and character, and it is foolish to suggest that giving oneself to it must be a sign of immaturity.

Here we may ask: can love itself, when it is mature, that is when it is the love of a person who is giving and thoughtful of the other and puts him or her first, can such a love be destructive in itself? My very short answer is that it is not so when it is mature. I shall return to this question further down in my consideration of Lady Macbeth's love for Macbeth. Certainly it can *bring* destruction – the destruction of the lover or the disintegration of the loved one. The lover may, for instance, be unable to recover from his loss when the loved one dies. Or it may bring disintegration to the loved one when she is swept off her feet and opens herself to a great love which she cannot contain. But in neither case does it follow that the love itself was therefore destructive. In the latter case it was the loved one who could not measure up to it.

Again, a mother's love for a son who turns to crime or goes to the dogs may cost her heartache and her health and perhaps ultimately her life. But this does not mean that there was anything the matter with her love, or anything wrong with her for not thinking of protecting herself. Her mother's love was pure and I would not for a minute describe her as foolish or immature for continuing to love her son when he let her down so badly and did not give any thought to her in the suffering he caused her in her love for him.

Sometimes a mature love is a love that can survive such a lack of reciprocity. But sometimes continuing to love someone in the face of its absence is foolish and, indeed, an expression of the person's immaturity. Here we need to consider each case for itself and on its own merit.

Let us return briefly to Simone Weil's characterization of the saint's love of God as 'mad'. Her point is that such love is a turning away from 'the world', a detachment from its concerns, preoccupations and measures. In certain circumstances it involves, as I said, turning things on their head, such as when someone gives up all he owns and has aspired to and chooses to live a life of poverty. Tolstoy gives us a penetrating portrait of such a person in his story of Father Sergius. From the perspective of the concerns and measures of the world such love and behaviour is mad.

In this connection Simone Weil speaks of *'une fidelité à vide'* – a loyalty in the total absence of all reciprocity or return. She finds it exemplified in Christ on the cross by contrast with those martyrs which the Romans threw to the lions for their belief in Christ. They linked arms and went to the lions singing. In his love of God Christ by contrast did not only die on the cross but remained faithful to God while believing that God had deserted him. This, of course, is the very peak of love.

Let me add that when we speak of maturity we need to distinguish a child-like trust and faith from childish behaviour. And if we speak of dependence we need to distinguish between 'mature dependence', which involves humility and the recognition of one's insufficiency on the one hand, and immature dependence in which one relegates responsibility and seeks a symbiotic relationship in which one expects to be taken care of as by right by the other.

3.4 'The Terribleness of Love': Lady Macbeth

Phillips reminded me of David Sims's reading of Macbeth which I came to know when his wife Joyce Sims read her husband's paper in a lecture in Swansea in a series on 'Great Characters in Literature'. On his view, which I shall enter into, what moved Lady Macbeth to make it possible for Macbeth to murder Duncan the King, was her love for him. For what she did – I am putting it in my own words – was to help Macbeth to realize his dream, even though she knew that it was a terrible dream. In this she thought of *him*, made herself into a vehicle to the realization of *his* dream. Intent on this giving of herself to it she threw caution to the wind and was unable to think and perhaps to care about what consequences this might have for him or for herself. Thus love beckoned her to help him have his dream and in it find the togetherness which love craves. She could see what he longed for more clearly than he did because of his qualms. She encouraged him to make his own a secret dream which he struggled to deny and disown. So, more briefly, it is her love that says: 'let him have his dream; let me help him make it his own; let us make it something we share.' Thus upon learning from a letter from Macbeth what the witches have prophesied for him, she says:

> Glamis thou art, and Cawdor; and shalt be
> What thou art promis'd. Yet do I fear thy nature;
> It is too full o' the milk of human kindness
> To catch the nearest way; thou wouldst be great,
> Art not without ambition, but without
> The illness should attend it; what thou wouldst highly,
> That thou wouldst holily; would not play false,
> And yet wouldst wrongly win; thou'dst have, great Glamis
> That which cries, 'Thus thou must do, if thou have it';
> And that which rather thou doest fear to do
> Than wishest should be undone. Hie thee hither,
> That I may pour my spirits in thine ear,
> And chastise with the valour of my tongue
> All that impedes thee from the golden round,
> Which fate and metaphysical aid doth seem
> To have thee crown'd with all (*Macbeth* Act I, Scene V).

She is clearly impatient for him. Macbeth thinks: 'If chance will have me king, why, chance may crown me, without my stir' (Act I, Scene III). But she wants him to 'catch the nearest way'. She has no respect for his moral qualms; indeed her attitude towards them is one of contempt:

> Art thou afeared
> To be the same in thine own act and valour
> As thou art in desire? Wouldst thou have that
> Which thou esteem'st the ornament of life,
> And live a coward in thine own esteem,
> Letting 'I dare not' wait upon 'I would',
> Like the poor cat i' the adage?

I shall quote Macbeth's answer:

> I dare do all that may become a man;
> Who dares do more is none.

I agree with David Sims that it is a kind of love that moves Lady Macbeth to catch onto Macbeth's secret dream, voiced and stirred into the twilight of his soul by the three witches, to bring it into clear consciousness, to force him to own it and then to seek to realize it. That what moves her is a kind of love rather than simple ambition is, I believe, the deeper reading of the play. But what kind of love? Phillips says: a terrible love. Indeed, it brings with it and embraces a trail of destruction of which the loved one is the author and the beloved the main participator, the *éminence grise* – that is the source of its author's inspiration.

Yes, but what kind of a person is it that loves in this way? I had quoted a line from a little book *Women and Sometimes Men*: 'each kind of person loves in his own way; what he is his love is' (op.cit. p. 186). How is Lady Macbeth's love marked by the kind of person she is? She has taken Macbeth for a husband and has thrown in her lot with him in her love for him. She brings into their relationship what belongs to her love.

She is the dominant party in that relationship. She wants him to be great – as *he* wishes this with *part* of himself – a secret part and until the beginning of the play, we understand, dormant. We hear of him first in Act I, Scene I, as a captain in the King's army fighting 'the merciless Macdonwald – worthy to be a rebel':

> For brave Macbeth, – well he deserves that name –
> Disdaining fortune, with his brandish'd steel,
> Which smok'd with bloody execution,
> Like valour's minion carv'd out his passage
> Till he fac'd the slave;
> Which ne'er shook hands, nor bade farewell to him,
> Till he unseam'd him from the nave to the chaps,
> And fix'd his head upon our battlements.

The king's response is: 'O valiant cousin! worthy gentleman!' We are led to understand, he really was. The violence he is capable of is in the service of his king and country, of maintaining order by crushing a rebellion.

I said, she wants him to be great, as she understands greatness. She wants it *for him*. She is not satisfied with what he is – with what the king calls him. She wants him to be great so that she could share in his greatness, share his greatness with him. This is a perfectly intelligible object of love – 'object' in the sense of 'aim'. To elaborate further, she is not prepared to love and accept him *as he is*. Though valiant in battle, she sees him as weak: a weakness that belongs partly to his goodness. His bravery is in the service of the King: I mean it is exercised in his willing service to the King. He is genuinely brave. She wants him to put it into her service; she wants it to serve her – to serve her in what she wants for him. She wants to mould him to her *ideal* of the kind of man she can love. She wants to make her fantasies of love come true in him. What is best for him is only what *she* thinks is best for him. She loves him, yes, but only on her own terms.

To qualify this: what she loves in him *is* in him and it accords with the fantasies of her love, what she longs for him as her lover and her beloved. It *is* in him, but as I said it is only part of him – a part that is secret, unowned and dormant. She wants to blow life into it so it can take over, but without regard to consequences to which she cannot give her mind. And she wants it now: immediately, quickly, all at once. This belongs to what in my book *Freud and the Mind* I called 'phantasy thinking' – see Chapter 3, 'Unconscious Phantasy: Reason and Emotion'. It is the expression of a mentality we all can regress into; but the extent to which it rules a person is a measure of that person's immaturity. I submit that that immaturity characterizes Lady Macbeth's love.

Let me repeat, what moves Lady Macbeth is love and not simple ambition. If it were the latter Macbeth would have been merely a tool, a means to her ambition, discardable if that were possible – that is if she could be Queen of Scots on her own. But that is not the case. She manipulates him, yes, but for something she wants to share with him: it is part of a relationship, a relationship of love. What she wants to share is something to which she has come in her relationship with her husband. He is indispensable to what she wants.

If she had been more mature her love for her husband would have been different. She would have cared for and considered him in what she wanted to share with him. She would have sided with his other side, with his goodness – his kindness and restraint. These two sides of Macbeth, in conflict with each other, do not lie on the same plane, so to speak; there is an asymmetry between them. From one side, with patient nurturing and inner work, can come wholeness. This is the only side from which wholeness can arise. The other side, by contrast, can only breed disintegration and destruction. This is precisely what is depicted in the play as ensuing from the alliance between Lady Macbeth and her husband.

What Lady Macbeth lacks is the maturity of wisdom and the capacity for patience, judgement, consideration and restraint that belongs to wisdom. This lack characterizes her personality and through it her love. It is not love that makes her impatient, without wise counsel and restraint. Rather it is her personality that gives her love these characteristics. Indeed the wisdom she lacks characterizes her mode of being. Without it she lacks the wholeness and collectedness of being which are marks of maturity.

3.5 Conclusion

Love, at any rate such as we find in sexual passion and friendship, naturally desires the good and welfare of the person to whom it is directed. But at the same time, and equally naturally, it desires some response from the other, some acknowledgement and, if possible, some reciprocation. If it is forthcoming, the lover or friend may consider it a gift and accept it in gratitude or, if his love is dominated by need, he may consume it in gratification and expect more of it. In the latter case, clearly, the side of love that desires its return is in conflict with its giving or caring side which is at risk of being choked by it.

That is why the caring side of love calls for the abandon which itself belongs to love to be combined with discipline, self-discipline, so that (i) its giving is informed with a caring contact with the loved one, and (ii) in the pleasure found in what is received the other is not forgotten or taken for granted, that the pleasure takes the form of appreciation. This cannot be attained at will and takes emotional maturity to which it takes self-discipline to arrive. Only when one has reached such maturity that the abandon of love poses no threat of disintegration on the one hand and no danger of self-indulgence on the other. But the maturity in question is not a static resting place; it needs to be maintained by active work. Even those who come anywhere near it are subject to the inclination to regress to immature forms of response in the face of frustration and disappointment. They have, therefore, to remain vigilant. Such vigilance – not self-conscious vigilance, but rather an appreciation of their own weaknesses which gives their response a certain moderation that is a mark of humility – is an important part of self-knowledge.

A person's ability to love, in a broad sense of the term, is one of his most important assets in the sense that it affects almost all of his other abilities: his ability to work, to co-operate, to persevere, to endure pain, to face danger, to resist temptation. It affects them favourably, of course, to the extent that he is capable of mature love and so is himself mature and wise. His ability to love with maturity, to give and to receive with gratitude, that is without wanting more or feeling demeaned, calls for inner resources in him, and the exercise of this ability develops those resources – patience, courage, humility, generosity, honesty and justice, which are virtues in a morality of love.

Earlier I quoted a line from the book *Women and Sometimes Men*: 'each kind of person loves in his own way; what he is his love is.' I also quoted a short paragraph in which the author refers to the compensations and consolations most people, men and women, seek in love – 'we thirst for love's denial that we are small, etc.' – and alludes to other immaturities that find expression there. Are these not the same weaknesses and immaturities which go to mould our moral behaviour and the character of our relationship to the moral values in which we believe? Just as our moral concerns provide us with the opportunity to grow to greater emotional maturity, in the same way the commitments which our loves exact from us equally provide us with the challenge to grow into more mature individuals. Thus if it is true that what a person is his love is, it is equally true that he becomes what his love gives him the opportunity to be in meeting its challenges.

No doubt conceptions of maturity differ with moral perspectives. But certainly maturity is a developmental concept: people grow to maturity, by degrees, through time and as they learn from their experiences. Maturity, like goodness, is an ideal limit – 'limit' in some ways as this term is used in mathematics. This, as I understand it, is the meaning of 'maturity' as the term applies to human beings.

What is perhaps unique about the psycho-analytic conception can be summed up as follows. Our very early experiences are formative and our early character, though subject to change, tends to stick with us and resist change. In doing so it retains early modes of thought, behaviour and response incompatible with our grown-up apprehension of what we meet in the grown-up world. An immature person thus is someone who carries with him these early modes of thought and response. These may, however, so blend with his grown-up mode of apprehension, calculation and behaviour, so much become part of them, as to be difficult to detect. They become visible when in extreme situations they gain the upper hand. Indeed, in such situations a person may abandon his grown-up behaviour, he may no longer retain it, and 'regress' to modes of thought and apprehension which have always been with him though in grown-up clothes.

This is a thumb-nail sketch of the psycho-analytic conception of immaturity. I have already said something about its content, that is about what characterizes it: what I called phantasy-thinking, lack of respect for reality in the way a person seeks the fulfilment of his desires, pursues his aims and objectives, impatience, ego-centricity, global and undifferentiated reactions to obstacles and frustrations seen in black and white terms.

Having said this I turn once more and briefly to Lady Macbeth. I asked what kind of person is it who loves like her. Someone may answer: 'She is one who is open to love and is prepared to risk all for love. She is inspired by love, albeit a daemonic love. No doubt she lacked wisdom. She did not have wisdom to direct her love to love wisely; but this does not mean she did not 'love well'. Othello's love was a jealous love, the love of a jealous person. This jealousy was an expression of the strength of his love for Desdemona. Lady Macbeth's love was one in which she gave herself wholly to her husband's heart's desire. She may not have been wise but it was the strength of her love that impaired her judgement. Even if her ambition for her husband was a form of identification with him so that her love may not have been pure, lack of maturity does not come into it.'

I have given my reasons for not accepting this answer. There is all the difference in the world between what Shakespeare depicts here and what Simone Weil calls '*la folie de l'amour*'. She is thinking of a totally selfless love, ignoring considerations of prudence in its commitment to goodness. She is thinking of a love in which a person is ruled by his heart, but a heart that is at one with goodness. In its directedness to the loved one, such love is mediated by goodness. Kierkegaard, as we shall see, describes such a love relationship as triangular. The lover in his or her relationship to goodness maintains his or her integrity.

What Lady Macbeth lacks in her love is not prudence but wisdom. She knows how to arrange things so that the murder of Duncan, the king, cannot be attributed to Macbeth. Prudence is concerned with self-interest, wisdom is committed to goodness. Lady Macbeth's love for Macbeth is thus by no means selfless. She is not willing to let Macbeth be; she does not respect him. She wants to be able to 'respect' him so as to be able to identify herself with someone she can respect for his strength and ruthless determination. Her love longs for Macbeth to realize those ideals in which she would be at one with him if only he would share them. But he does not share them whole-heartedly until she makes him do so. Her love thus is a manipulative love, one that is intolerant of any imperfections in the loved one. I argued that this whole mode of wanting, thinking, apprehension and relationship characterizes the love in question as immature.

I spoke of the conflict between love's desire for its reciprocation and the giving, caring side of love and I suggested that this conflict is reduced with maturity – that is as the person comes to a greater unity in the course of his emotional and moral development. But in a love that is centred in sexual passion can this conflict be ever resolved? How is sexual passion to co-exist with emotional maturity? This is the question I turn to in the following chapter.

4

Conflicting Aspects of Sexual Love Revisited: Can They Be Reconciled?

4.1 A Problem for Love

It is a truth, though only a half-truth, that love brings people together. Of course it is not only love that does so. Common interests too, work, common convictions and also, in a different way, common enmities bring people together. One difference is that in love and its reciprocal response, whether of the personal or impersonal kind, in mutual love or in compassion and, gratitude, it is two people who come together and their attention is directed to one another. Whereas in joint work or battle the interest of those that are brought together is directed to something outside them – except in so far as the battle is a conflict of personalities as opposed to a struggle over something the battling parties cherish.

This, however, is not so much what interests me now. The other half of the truth with which I began is that love, at least sexual love, the kind of love that a man and a woman may have for each other, can also divide those that are in love, separate them, indeed break them. This can and does, of course, happen in other forms of love too, in friendship and in the love that parents have for their children and children for their parents. Such love can be equally possessive, dependent, jealous,[2] and it can play havoc with people's lives, devastate their relationship with one another. So much so that Simone Weil speaks of friendship when it is pure, that is when it is unsoiled by the wish to please or the opposite wish to dominate,

---

2. The fact that love can bring jealousy when the loved one gives her love to someone else does not make it necessarily into a jealous love. After all the lover may be unable to trust the beloved and suffer on this score not because he is incapable of trusting anyone in that position but because he has been deceived.

as a miracle. But she does not doubt that such friendships can exist (Amitié in *Attente de Dieu*, Weil, 1960, pp. 154–61). The question that interests me is whether the same is true of the love between man and woman, that is of the kind of love that finds expression in sexual passion.

There are some considerations that make this seem doubtful. Certainly Plato thought so. Simone Weil thus contrasts Plato's conception of love with that of Freud. She points out that for Plato 'carnal love' is a degraded form of chaste love, whereas in Freud chaste love is a sublimated form of carnal love (Weil, 1948, p. 69). My question now is: why should Plato, or anyone else, think that when love is carnal it takes on an aspect that cannot be reconciled with other aspects that belong equally to what we understand by love? Plato's view about how attachment to the body inevitably corrupts is at the centre of the *Phaedo* and is well known. How this view applies to love is expressed in the *Symposium* through the words which Plato puts into the mouth of Diotima. It is not Plato's view, however, that I am specifically concerned to examine in this chapter. For I find certain difficulties, philosophical difficulties, which pertain to sexual love in particular, and I would like to clarify these for their own sake.

There is one matter, however, which I should like to get out of the way at the start. It is this: love, in its various forms, is what each person brings to it, makes of it, so that whatever difficulties there may be in love are the difficulties of the person or persons and their relationship. If so, how could these be regarded as *philosophical* difficulties, and why should they be thought of as having to do with what *love* is when it assumes a sexual character? The very short answer to this is that while the difficulties in question do indeed come from the person and his relationship with the beloved, they are difficulties that are confined to those responses, tendencies and inclinations of his that are expressions of love. That is, the person's difficulties come from the kind of passion and longing which belong to love and they mirror conflicts and tensions within what we understand by love in its sexual form. They throw light, therefore, in two different directions: on the person and his individual psychology and, secondly, on the character of the passion and longing that have taken possession of him, seen as a form of love. Therefore turning from the person and his problems to the concept and the strains within it which throw our understanding of it into confusion is to turn from psychology to philosophy.

One of the questions that confront us when we do so is this: when love takes on a sexual form, finds expression in sexual passion, does the contribution which sexuality makes to it introduce an element which is inevitably in conflict with what else there is about it which gives it its character of love? Sartre seems to think so. He does not, like Plato, think of carnal love as a degraded form of love, since, more like Freud, he sees in sexual love, which he takes to be necessarily carnal, a paradigm (or 'skeleton' as he puts it) of all human relationships. Not recognizing an alternative to the kind of relationship he finds in sexual love he does not have a norm against which what he finds there can appear as degraded. He simply speaks of '*les échecs du désir*' and '*les échecs de l'amour*', seeing the very special character of sexual desire, but failing to distinguish it from love.

The main point that he argues is that the aim or object of sexual desire cannot be attained, or at any rate maintained because it hides a contradiction. For its aim is to conquer another person from inside, from the side of his consciousness or subjectivity, to make his vision and will a captive, without interfering with his or her freedom or autonomy. And this, Sartre argues, is impossible. The attempt to realize the impossible brings frustration and conflict. Even when the beloved does respond, so that the love she returns is freely given, Sartre argues, such reciprocity cannot sustain itself. If there is nothing else to renew it the lover will soon lose interest in the beloved. If her wish to please the lover becomes the centre of her life, if it becomes a receptacle into which the rest of her life flows, she will stop being an independent person and will cease to offer a challenge to the lover's desire. He will consequently turn away from her, leaving her with the desire to reclaim him, but to no avail. In the opposite case, where an aspect of her life remains aloof to the intercourse, in the wide sense, she will present him with a mystery and will continue to interest and attract him.

Sartre's contention is that complete reciprocity in love is unstable and short-lived, and it is only a certain kind of discrepancy between the feelings which the lover and the beloved have for each other that keeps the relationship going. As Sartre puts it: 'The other is in principle out of my reach. When I try to reach him he runs away from me, and when I turn away from him he pursues and tries to possess me.' ('*Autrui est par principe l'insaissisable; il me fuit quand je le cherche et me possède quand je le fuis.*')

Thus for Sartre love is a dance of hide and seek, if I may mix my metaphors, and it is only the mystery which the lover and the beloved present to each other, the right degree of natural elusiveness, which sustains the different movements or moods of the dance. Otherwise there are some men for whom the mystery of women is soon exhausted. They flit from woman to woman, attracted to each in turn like a bee to a flower; they enjoy the nectar, take what they want and then move on. Because women have no hold on them they remain attractive to women who fight over them. Such men pass as great lovers, though the term 'lover' here is a euphemism. The question is: if, as it is said, such a man 'loves them and leaves them', can what he feels for them and what he gives to them add up to an expression of love? Surely there is more to love than this, and such short-lived encounters cannot afford the logical space for this 'more' to be realized or come into being.

Sartre does see clearly the very special character of sexual desire, and he makes clear that it is not a desire like any other desire. But he identifies love too closely with sexual desire, or at least he sees sexual desire as determining the character of sexual love singly and on its own. Thus the contradictions he finds in the object of sexual desire become the contradictions of sexual love itself. These contradictions stem from Sartre's view that the object of love, conferred to it by the desire that lies at the heart of love, is the *appropriation* of the beloved. Such a desire involves a lack of regard for the fact that the beloved has a life of her own, a lack of respect for her separateness. Her autonomy becomes at once the centre of her attractiveness and also what must be taken over. In other words the lover cannot leave alone that in the beloved which makes her attractive to him. Yet to tamper with it is to destroy it – unless the beloved resists the lover's attempts, fights back or withdraws to a safe distance. But to do so is to refuse to reciprocate the lover's love and so to frustrate it.

For sexual love seeks intercourse with the beloved, physical and otherwise. It finds delight in the beloved through such contact, it seeks and thrives in reciprocity. The kind of intercourse that brings delight, a delight that dwindles to nothing more than mere sexual gratification when it is not shared, presupposes the return of love. This need for reciprocity which is built into what we mean by sexual love raises many questions. One of these is whether it can be identified with the desire for appropriation. Since, as Sartre rightly points out, the desire for appropriation cannot be reconciled with respect for another person's freedom, our question is whether the desire for reciprocity can be so reconciled.

There is no doubt that there is a problem here, and I do not mean only a philosophical problem. Love does pose such a problem for people when they fall in love. This is a *personal* problem which each must resolve for himself, a response to which brings personal growth. It is expressible only in the first person: can I reconcile my need to have the beloved's love with a respect for her freedom and autonomy? The *philosophical* problem is: are these two needs *compatible*, can they ever be reconciled by *anyone*? In other words, are they reconcilable in *themselves*? In this second question the problem is lifted from a personal plane where it has a contingent 'answer', a possible personal resolution, to an *a priori* plane where it brings our understanding of certain concepts and their relations under scrutiny.

Sartre's answer to this second (philosophical) question is in the negative and it must not be taken lightly. We have noted that Simone Weil speaks of friendship, when it is pure, that is when it is unsoiled by the wish to please or to dominate, as 'a miracle by which a person consents to view from a certain distance, and without coming any nearer, the very being who is necessary to him as food' (Weil, 1959, p. 157). 'It is in a sense impersonal' (p. 158). 'The essential thing about love is that it consists in a vital need that one human being feels for another. Because of this the problem is to reconcile this need with the equally imperious need for freedom' (1951, p. 35). This latter is the double need to remain autonomous, for one's own sake as well as for that of the beloved, and also not to interfere with her freedom and autonomy. Simone Weil speaks of this as the need to 'respect the distance which the fact of being two distinct creatures places between them' – between two friends or lovers. I call this distance 'human separateness' or 'the separateness of human beings'. Now the question I am asking may be put as follows: How can a man who is passionately in love with the woman consent to view her 'from a certain distance'? How can sexual love be in any sense impersonal? Does not the longing for reciprocity and for intimacy which is at the heart of sexual love work against such consent? It is, I think, because Plato thought so that he regarded carnal love as a degraded form of spiritual love.

Surely there is at least this truth in Plato's view: there is more to love than we have so far seen in sexual love, and what we have commented on threatens to corrupt such love when the rest becomes subservient to it. We asked whether the need for reciprocity which belongs to sexual love is nothing more than a desire for appropriation.

We agreed with Sartre that the latter is not compatible with respect for the other's freedom, and we asked whether this is equally true of the need for reciprocity. If it is not then we will have found at least a distinguishing mark between the two and we will have moved away from an analysis which closes our question too soon.

4.2   Are Sex and Love One Thing or Two?

I suggested that sex and love are not the same thing. For the word 'love' covers a wide variety of human phenomena from friendship to compassion, and from love of one's country to the love which lovers have for one another. However when sex is at one with love, so that the two are one, sex becomes a vehicle of love. Sexual love thus is more than sex on its own. Love brings to it giving; the lover puts himself into and gives himself to the loved one. His interest centres in the beloved as a person and in making contact with her, person to person, and not in sexual gratification. The way he touches her is an expression of the tenderness he feels for her; the very sensuality she awakens in him becomes part of his tenderness for her.

It is true that a man who lusts after a particular woman may become so obsessed with her that he has no eyes for any other woman. But this is very different from the active commitment of love. Here the passion in question is purely sensual and shows little interest in the person who excites it. She is no more than 'an object of perfect excitement'. He is neither fond of her nor cares for her; he has no regard for her as a person. There may be different reasons why the wanting here remains thus curtailed. It may be, for instance, that the person in question is incapable of attachment and finds affection debilitating. It may be that the women who excite him do not inspire affection in him, or they inspire a kind of aggressive passion which excludes affection. We are not here interested in these reasons. My point is that in lust there is something lacking, something that is either absent or excluded.

Before contrasting such lust with sexual love let me point out in passing that the love that finds expression in sex can be subordinated to a quest for power, for instance, to which it may become a vehicle. Or again sex can become a vehicle of self-seeking. I mean that a man or woman may seek power and domination in sex, that is through the medium of sexual relationships. Freud referred to this as the 'plasticity' of human sexuality.

To return to sexual love in contrast with lust; here the lover is captivated by the beloved as a person, however transformed by his imagination and sensibility, and waits on her response. Her response as a person is of paramount importance for him. Whether or not he loves her selfishly, jealously, possessively, there is a place in it for trust and concern. Indeed otherwise it could not be a jealous or possessive love. It is because in such love the lover gives his heart to the beloved that it can be broken, and because this is so painful that a person can turn away from love. But the person who gives his heart to the loved one and puts his trust in her not only wishes to see the beloved flourish and is pleased to see her happy, he is prepared to take responsibility for her welfare, to care for her. This is where the commitment which love makes possible, and is indeed at its very heart, is different from the attachment of affection – though there is no sharp line between the two. For affection itself is a form of love, a component of love which in different surroundings adds up to different forms of love.

I mentioned trust as belonging to love. The breaking of it by the loved one is an injury to the lover in his love. His feelings of being let down, of his trust having been betrayed, which are moral responses, are responses of love itself, of a love that has grown and been nourished in the give and take of his relationship with the beloved. It is not surprising, therefore, that such notions as 'regard', 'loyalty', 'trust' and 'responsibility' are notions which we employ in characterizing the lover's attitude towards the beloved – an attitude that belongs to love itself. It is not superimposed on the wanting which belongs to sexual love, it is part of that wanting, an aspect of its character.

Thus there is a moral core to what we mean by sexual love. I stress this because although this is something we know and appreciate, it is not something that we always articulate. Thus where there is love, adult, mature love, there is not merely a passive attachment, but an active commitment to the person loved.

To repeat, while sex and love are, or can be, one, or at one, in sexual love, the sexuality which is thus at one with love is transformed by the love. Love gives it a new dimension or dimensions which come from its moral core. This moral core is bound up with the fact that sexual love is directed to a *person*. It is a longing for intercourse with a particular person – physical, sexual, and otherwise: a person to person intercourse and communication. The very possibility of the moral impulses and attitudes which belong to or come from such love presupposes the full participation of lover and beloved in a moral life outside their love. That is why beings whose life lacked such a dimension could not love in the way we do, they could not be subject to the kind of sexual passion we are discussing.

Such love comes from the individual, of course, from the adult individual. It is a matter of what sex means to him, of what, given his past, he is able to bring to sex, what part of himself he can give to it. But it is equally a matter of what lies outside him, what kind of possibilities the life in which he has grown up make available to him – the language he speaks, the literature that belongs to this language, the categories of thought and judgement with which that language provides him. His whole emotional growth would be impossible without all this, his sexual development being an aspect of it, something that cannot be isolated from it or prized apart. I said, such love comes from the individual, but it is equally a matter of what lies outside him, the form of life in which he participates. But these are not two different things, for it is the kind of life and culture in which he has grown up that makes him the individual he is. He becomes that individual in interaction with that life. The relationship is a two-way one: in learning and developing, intellectually, affectively and morally, through his participation in that life, he actually contributes to it. He is not a mere product of his culture; he gives something back as he grows towards greater autonomy.

We see then that the wanting in sexual love is a desire to form a relationship with another person, one who has become a magnetic centre in the lover's life. It is a desire to be with, to savour, to give as well as to receive from this person, and to find delight in this give and take. This is what the lover wants: proximity and contact with the beloved, sharing his pleasures and his cares, togetherness. The physical expressions of love are expressions of this same longing; they form part of this contact and togetherness. At the height of such contact each person's consciousness is so filled with the thought of the other that he can scarcely think of himself and she of herself. This is perfect reciprocity where this is true of both lover and beloved. But the question is: Can it be sustained? How? Does sexual love contain what it takes to sustain the reciprocity for which it craves, seeks and needs to flourish?

4.3   Sexual Desire and the Caring Aspect of Love

We have seen that sexual love desires, seeks and grows in intercourse with the beloved and that such intercourse involves some
reciprocity. Love thus seeks its return, it seeks to inspire love. It is
active; the lover is not content to contemplate the beloved from a
distance. It is not disinterested; the lover is not satisfied simply to
see the beloved flourish. He wants to be the vehicle or means by
which she flourishes. His direct contribution to her welfare and
pleasure is part of the give and take which sexual love seeks. The
response which this inspires in the beloved brings him in contact
with her, and through such contact he finds delight in her. The
delight which her attractiveness gives him is received through contact and not mere contemplation – as in the case of a work of art.
He finds delight in savouring all that he finds attractive in the
beloved. Thus there is in sexual love a propensity to touch, to
caress, to savour the beloved in motion, to drink her words, a
movement towards closeness, physical or otherwise.

Where this is absent love becomes pure affection or compassion,
it loses its sexual character. There are, of course, chivalrous forms
of love which do not exist in our age, though their ideal may fuel
the love and imagination of a few solitary individuals, and these
are recognizably forms of sexual love. For here the lover who is
actively engaged in promoting the beloved's welfare, even if only
in secret, has intercourse with her, in the broadest sense, and from a
certain distance. It is still *he* who is his beloved's knight in shining
armour. It is he who protects her and watches over her, and it
would be deeply disappointing to him if she did not need him,
or if she elevated someone else to this special role and position.
Occupying this position, being recognized and accepted as occupying it, is the form which his intimacy with the beloved takes. The
conferring of such a position to the lover is an important aspect
of the acknowledgement which sexual love gives to whom it is
directed, and as such it constitutes a return of the lover's love. This
is the nearest I can think of where sexual love loses its carnal character, or becomes 'chaste', without losing its sexual character.
However its sexuality is not consummated, it gives up its aim out
of love.

You might ask: why should it ever want to do so? The short
answer is that within the culture where the institution of chivalry
exists ideals flourish which inspire certain individuals to want to

do so. They see the consummation of sexual passion as destructive of what they equally long for as part of their love. These ideals which they make their own enable them to transform their sexual passion while remaining accessible, even vulnerable, to the beloved's sexual attraction. This is still an attempt to reconcile what seems to be irreconcilable in sexual love.

The other aspect of sexual love is, of course, the wish to seek and work for the good and welfare of the beloved – what one might call its *caring* aspect. This is the caring that can take an impersonal form, as in compassion, or a personal one, as in friendship. When it is personal it involves fondness, affection, attachment. Thus sexual love is personal and selective. Further, where there is love the person loved inspires generosity in the lover, so that love is outgoing, giving and considerate. The lover, in caring for the beloved, respects her, and this includes having regard for her autonomy.

These two aspects of love are interconnected; they require and interact with each other, determining the character of love in each individual case. For the giving and caring find expression in what constitutes the intercourse between lovers, and it can give the desire for reciprocity a generous aspect. When this is the case the desire for reciprocity is far from being a desire for appropriation. But can it actually move the lover to a regard for the beloved which enables him to consent to view her 'from a certain distance', with all that this implies? Is there not something in sexuality which resists such a transformation? When, on the other hand, sexual passion is transformed into a calmer love can it still retain what is distinctive of it? In his portrait of Prince Myshkin's love for Nastasya Philippovna in *The Idiot*, Dostoyevsky seems to suggest a negative answer to these questions. For the saintliness which characterizes the Prince's love seems to leave no room for the earthliness of sexual passion. The view suggested seems to be that nothing that is not both earthly and saintly can be sexual love, yet nothing can be both, so sexual passion can never amount to real love. Whether or not this is true is our question and needs to be further investigated.

Before doing so, however, let us take stock of what we have seen so far. I have suggested that sexual love has two aspects which at once require each other and yet are in conflict. Under one aspect the lover pursues a quest for delight of the beloved; he feels a kind of thirst or hunger for her. Under the other aspect he pursues her good. That is what I called the giving or caring aspect of love. Where the pursuit of the beloved's good has been subordinated to the lover's need the pursuit of reciprocity turns into a pursuit of appropriation. This is where the taking aspect of love gains ascendancy over its giving or caring aspect. Even then, however, the lover seeks delight in the *person* of the beloved. Where he is indifferent to that, love turns into lust and the beloved becomes a means to the satisfaction of this lust. There are, of course, other possibilities on which I have not commented.

4.4 Exclusive Love and Regard for the Beloved: Are They Compatible?

We have noted that sexual love, in contrast with some other forms of love, is personal and selective. It is also *exclusive*. Not only does the lover seek contact, including physical contact, with the beloved, and craves for reciprocity, he also wishes this to be his exclusive privilege, one that is willingly accorded to him by the beloved. Indeed he regards this willingness in the beloved as an expression of the return of his love, a proof that she feels towards him the way he feels towards her. He is not interested in this very special way in anyone else, and he hopes and wishes that this is true of the beloved too. That is, sexual love does not wish the beloved to share this privileged relationship with anyone else, it is intolerant of such a possibility. It wishes the innermost aspect of what the lover gives to the beloved to be something which she does not want to have and would not accept from anyone else. He hopes that she views the innermost core of their relationship as in some ways something sacred, as he does too. For the lover and the beloved thus their relationship is not one relationship among others. It is thought of as having and is given a special, and even unique position in their lives. It becomes their centre, the single centre of two lives. For one party to share its fruits and privileges with someone else is for the relation to be wrenched from such a position and would be seen by the other as a debasing or downgrading of it.

The relation between the lover and the beloved can, of course, be maintained in such a position only by mutual consent and commitment. Where one of the parties ceases to give the relationship this position, or stops thinking of it as unique, we would say that his or her love has died. This would be something which the lover mourns. And if the beloved were to fall in love with someone else, wish to accord the privilege of such a relationship to this other person, the lover, however understanding he were as a person, taking the view that the beloved cannot help what her heart wills, might nevertheless, and equally understandably, feel betrayed and think of his love as rejected. My main point is that however much the lover may, as a person, be capable of accepting such a state of affairs without bitterness, love itself *as a sexual passion* cannot do so. When, through mourning, love comes to accept the loss of its object, it ceases to be what it is, it changes character. Whatever friendship, affection and compassion the lover may retain for the beloved, he would have stopped loving her as a man in the sexual sense.

It is true that the caring aspect of the lover's love may give him the strength to resist thinking of his love as betrayed, and his loss may leave him unwilling to enter again into such a commitment with anyone else. We then say that he has remained faithful to the memory of his love. This is itself an expression of love, and its sexual character comes from the continuity it has with the love that was once requited. But it is no longer an active passion.

Thus the exclusive character of sexual love need not be a form of possessiveness. It could be the exclusiveness of the mutual commitment of sexual love and nothing else. It is true that it is only for *this* person that the lover reserves what flows out of his love, naturally and as part of his loving. He feels injured in his very wish to do so if the beloved does not appreciate the sense it has in being meant just for her, in not valuing it as such, perhaps in treating it as a commodity she could receive from someone else. But this does not make it a form of bondage to someone who reciprocates such love. It will be that only if the beloved falls out of love, or if the values she embraces make her unwilling to maintain her commitment. In the latter case her retractation may find expression in some such words as: 'My life is my own; hands off it.' Such an attitude contrasts starkly with what earlier I called an attitude of love. It excludes the ability to reciprocate the kind of love for which the lover craves. Thus we could say that the exclusiveness of sexual love is not a form of possessiveness provided (1) that it is mutually willed and (2) that it does not insulate the lover and the beloved from what lies outside their love.

An exclusive love, then, is not one that will not tolerate the beloved's independence, her having a life of her own. What it will not tolerate is her sharing with someone else or others what belongs to the intercourse of love. For where it is thus shared, that intercourse can no longer be what it is, what it is meant to be. It is the mutual unwillingness of the parties to share it with anyone else that preserves the *intimacy* of the relationship. This intimacy comes from the fact that the lover and the beloved give themselves to each other without reservation. Each is willing to entrust to the other what is innermost to his or her soul. This trust belongs to or is part of the love each feels for the other. It is the inability to trust that turns sexual love into a jealous and possessive passion.

Indeed the willingness to be oneself in the presence of the beloved and to offer what is innermost to one is part of the giving of love and involves risks which some people are unable or unwilling to take. Yet without such willingness, and the trust which makes it possible, love cannot grow. Ultimately a person who will not surrender anything of himself for fear of losing his identity and of being engulfed or exploited, will be incapable of giving or receiving tenderness. One who attaches too much importance to individuality and personal freedom will, therefore, regard with suspicion this boundary-breaking character of love and will try to curtail it. Such a person will consider personal enjoyment or ambition and achievement as superior to affection. This is the opposite of the danger which Sartre emphasizes. For just as sexual passion can take a form in which the lover does not consider the beloved's need for freedom, so equally concern to keep that freedom and preserve her separate identity, can make the beloved incapable of reciprocating the love she is offered. Such a concern is destructive of the giving that belongs to love and may come from certain values which put individuality at the centre of life, just as it may come from an inability to trust. Paradoxically for the individualist, there is a willingness to be used, which enhances a person rather than diminishes his or her autonomy, provided that it comes from genuine love and so has no strings attached to it.

4.5 Quest for Reciprocity and Unconditional Giving: How Can They Be Reconciled?

We have seen that the desire for reciprocity which belongs to sexual love is not, or at any rate need not be, a desire for the appropriation of the beloved. We have also seen that the exclusiveness of sexual love does not necessarily give it a possessive character. But other problems remain. How can the desire for reciprocity leave intact the unconditional character of the lovers' engagement with each other? How can there be no strings attached to what lovers give one another when they crave for their love to be returned? How can the lover seek to inspire or awake a reciprocal response in the beloved and at the same time hope this response to be 'freely given' – that is to come from the beloved and not to be the result of what he, the lover, does?

The short answer to these questions is as follows. True, the lover is active in his relationship with the beloved and he seeks to awaken a like passion in her. But if the caresses and gifts that are directed to awakening this passion are inspired by his love of her, if they are not tainted by any ulterior motive, if they are an expression of his love and nothing else, then they will not be a form of manipulation. That is even when his caresses and gifts are directed to awakening a like passion in the beloved this may be for no other reason than that this is what his love demands. As such, however much the lover craves for the return of his love, he will continue to respect the autonomy and integrity of the beloved, and be prepared to accept her response, whatever it may be. If the response is one of pleasurable acknowledgement he will consider this a gift which he will cherish; if it is one of rejection he will resign himself to it. The problem for him may be in knowing where to draw the line. At what point does withdrawing in dignity and respect turn into a lack of ardour or a lack of persistence which hides a fear of being hurt? At what point does perseverance turn into interference or pushiness? These distinctions cannot be drawn in the abstract; but the right attitude requires a peculiar combination of activity and acceptance on the part of the lover.

If the lover's responses are genuine expressions of love, then what he does will be an expression of what he is, so that if the beloved responds positively she will be loving him for what he is. If, on the other hand, they are mere attempts to obtain a certain kind of response from her, in taking these as expressions of love she will be deceived. If she loves him then, she will not love him for himself. Here in what he does to obtain or keep her love he does not give or surrender himself; rather he makes himself into an instrument for obtaining something he wants.

So where there is genuine love the lover does not act with an eye on love's reward which is its return. He seeks that only as part of his engagement in the intercourse which flows out of his love. His actions are dictated by his love and not by any wish external to it. His wish is for his love to be returned for no other reason than that he loves the other person and so wants what that love itself demands.

What about the fact that love possesses, captivates and enchants the person who falls in love? In engaging in courtship therefore is he not engaged in captivating the heart of the beloved, and is this not a tampering with her autonomy? Does it not show a lack of regard for her freedom? If courtship involves some kind of mesmerism how is the lover engaged in courtship different from Svengali who had to obtain his beloved's heart by hypnotism and consequently continued to feel his love to be unreciprocated? On the other side of the coin, if in the hope of receiving a love that comes from the beloved and is freely given he remains wholly passive, will this not itself be an expression of unwillingness on the lover's part to put himself out, to take the risk of opening up to the beloved? As such would this not show a lack of ardour in his love? So if the lover acts as a Svengali, the love with which the beloved responds to him does not come from her, it is something put into her by him; and if, like the prince in the legend, he takes on the guise of a frog, so that what love he receives is pure, that love will not find him, since it will have been inspired by the disguise. It seems then that whether the lover is active in courtship or passive, whether he displays himself or hides, he will not have his love reciprocated, what he receives will not be what he longs for, namely a love that is at once freely given and inspired by him. This paradox, or rather dilemma, brings to the fore certain strains in the categories to which we resort in our attempt to understand what is involved in genuine reciprocity between lovers.

What is involved in such a relationship is a genuine interaction between two people who begin by being attracted to each other, quite spontaneously, and end by caring for one another.[3] Each responds to, puts himself out for and gives himself to the other, and he does so because of what he finds in the other and what this means to him or her. It touches something that lies in readiness in each, something which the other is able to bring out, sustain and

---

3. The destiny of such love, whether what the lovers bring to it can sustain it, whether it can survive time, and the trials and temptations of love, is another question.

sometimes transform. What is crucial is that each is open and himself or herself with the other and that the other's response, in consequence, is not based on some deception or illusion. What is crucial, equally, is that these responses are inspired by the love which each awakens in the other and not by any motive to please or to dominate (*pace* Simone Weil). Only in the latter case is the love received the result of manipulation.

4.6   Sexual Passion and the Restraint of Love

I want to finish by returning to where we started: does the delight which the lover finds in the beloved in sexual passion, the delight which makes him long for and seek greater closeness with her, make him unable to care for her properly and respect her separateness, her need for some space in which she can be herself without reference to the lover's wishes?

One may think at first that the conflicts which such love brings are simply the conflicts between the two personalities of the lover and the beloved. This is no doubt sometimes true. But it is equally true that the love itself brings to the personalities in question conflicting longings and desires. Is it not on account of the love which they feel for each other that the lover and the beloved make demands on each other, for instance, feel dissatisfied, hurt and disappointed when these demands are not met? Surely, the greater the passion, the ardour – I do not say the love – the greater the demands, until the space which the other needs to be himself or herself is swallowed up. So the passion, the ardour, has to be purified; it has to learn to hold itself in check out of consideration for the beloved. It has to learn to think of the beloved without reference to the self that finds delight in her. That means the capacity to forgo this delight, when necessary, for the sake of the beloved who inspires it. This is a question of learning to share the delight, as opposed to seeking it for oneself, a question of establishing a pattern of mutual enjoyment of each other, in the widest sense, within the parameters of mutual regard. The lover has to learn to contain the longing which his very love inspires for the sake of the loved one, and he can only do so because he loves her, because his love is more than this longing. Yet the aspect of his love from which the longing comes and the aspect which enables him to learn to contain it are different and conflicting aspects of the same love. Everything in the passion from which the longing comes fights against the containing of it.[4]

Perhaps if the longing is to be contained, what is an ardent passion will have to be transformed into a calm one, and yet not everyone is capable of the discipline and self-knowledge which this calls for. Furthermore, many of those who seem to achieve it do so at a cost of emasculating their passion. Sometimes they achieve a greater harmony only when their passion for each other cools off; or they do so by establishing no-go areas between them from which they agree to keep off. But I am sure that there is a difference between such mutual arrangements of convenience and the genuine consent of the lovers to give one another some space in which each can be himself or herself. The first is inspired by the need to have peace for oneself, whereas the second is inspired by a regard for the beloved which is sustained by love. The question to which we come back once again is: Can such regard transform the lover's passionate longing for intercourse with the beloved in the wide sense in such a way as to enable him to contain and discipline it without emasculating it, without turning it into something less, something tamer? Are passion and discipline compatible in any case?

Let me finish by giving the side for an affirmative answer, however qualified and however tentatively. It seems to me that there are some rare cases where the very passionate love that a husband and wife had for each other at the beginning of their marriage is weathered with age and deepened with the trials it survives. In such cases this love becomes more like a friendship, without losing its sexual character. However, it acquires a new centre. The need of the husband and wife for each other no longer remains as commanding as it was. Each becomes more self sufficient; they can now survive without each other. Each allows more space to the other, and this itself is an expression of trust. Indeed one could describe an important aspect of such a transformation by saying that mutual need has been replaced by mutual trust; at least there is a shift in this direction. The delight they find in each other too changes character, it becomes

---

4. The degree to which this longing has to be contained ultimately depends, of course, on the compatibility between the lover and the beloved – compatibility in temperament, in sensibility, in intelligence, in imagination, etc. The limits of such compatibility stretch in many directions and admit of great flexibility, but when they are stretched too far in a particular case this puts a strain on the maintenance of reciprocity.

more contemplative. Each now finds delight in seeing the other flourish irrespective of whether or not he or she contributes to it. The bonds which attach each to the other are now less fragile and allow each a greater detachment. Paradoxically, such a couple grow closer together in their willingness to accept each other's separateness.

But although what I have sketched is still very much a sexual love, it is one that has been tempered with friendship, a friendship based on common experiences, common cares and concerns, the loyalty that comes from the many years which have been spent together. The bonds here are the bonds of affection and of loyalty. In other words, such a love is more, very much more, than sexual passion.

4.7   Conclusion

It seems then that sex which can bring so much colour and excitement to human relationships when it takes the form of love, drawing two people close together, also brings with it conflict and division. It seems that it cannot *in itself* be the basis of a lasting relationship. For sex alone, however much it may flourish only when the person desired is an independent, autonomous human being, and is seen to be so, is no respecter of the separateness of the beloved. The longing for communion, or union, that is at the heart of sexual love is bound, therefore, to end up either in conflict or disappointment and loss of interest.

If this is to be avoided much else has to come together and the lover and beloved have to grow up in themselves and learn to have genuine regard for each other. Such a transformation in the lover and the beloved is a transformation in their love for each other. There is, unfortunately, much in the ethos of our times which makes clear thinking on this subject difficult, and so muddies the space which lovers need in order to be able to turn around and allow their love to be so transformed.

I distinguished between sex and love, and also related them. Does sex have a character or nature of its own, one which contributes to and delimits the diverse forms it takes in human life – love, lust, self-seeking, and so on – though it cannot exist apart from these? This is what I am inclined to say. Sex, in human life, is an impulse to *make contact* with another human being, normally of the opposite sex, to *explore* the other person in physical terms and to enjoy what one *discovers*. Such physical contact embodies the emotions which the other person rouses in one. Sex is thus a form of affective body language in terms of which one makes contact and communicates with the person who rouses one's interest, curiosity, tenderness, or who baits, taunts or challenges one in a special way which needs articulation. But the person who speaks it does not always say the same thing, does not always seek the same thing. In that sense sex has no specific content of its own; it takes on the character of the contact two individuals make or at least long for and strive after. One could also see it as a form of play. It need not involve any commitment and can bring into play almost any part of the person in his responses to the other.

When, in contrast, it is an expression of *love*, the person in love is happy to stay with what he discovers. He finds a new life in it and sustenance. What he has to say and give is then specifically directed to the individual he loves. It comes from what is innermost to him and engages him as a whole. What kind of love he is capable of depends on what he is like. But that does not mean that he cannot learn from living his love with the person he loves. He can. What he can learn will depend on the contribution of the other, on how things go in their interactions, on his openness and honesty, and on his capacity to stay with the difficulties that come up in the course of his interactions with the beloved.

5

Proust: Sexual Love and its Longing for Union

5.1 Proust and Sartre on the Reality of what our Emotions Reveal

Proust is in some ways close to Sartre and in some ways to Freud. He characterizes sexual love as a subjective state: it is not directed to the real woman but to a creature of the lover's imagination. Sartre on the other hand, in his *Essay on Emotions*, argues that there is a world of the emotions and that it is part of the common world in which we all live, a world – if I may add – that belongs to our language:

> All emotions have this in common, namely that they bring to life the same world, cruel, terrible, sad, joyful, etc., a world in which the relation of things to our consciousness is always and exclusively magical (1948, p. 44).

The qualities which captivate a person in love may not come to life until the person falls in love, but they are qualities of the beloved, transformed in the eyes of the lover by his love. Everything that makes her magical belongs to the world of love, a world into which we enter when we fall in love, depicted in so much of our poetry. Sartre insists, rightly, that this is not a world which exists in our minds. It is a part of the human world in which we love and which we share. Thus, in an essay on Husserl (*Situations* I, 1947) he praises Husserl for having relocated horror and charm *in things*, thus delivering us from Proust – as he puts it.

I said that what Sartre calls the world of the emotions and which he rightly insists interpenetrates the common world in which we live, the human world, belongs to our language. The richness of human emotions, the wide spectrum of their intentional objects, the objects that are the denizens of the world of emotions, are all made possible by the language we speak, together with the literature that belongs to it. Our capacity to feel, our sensibility and imagination, are shaped and given width through our language, its literature and the arts. Those in turn enrich the world in which we live. This is something which Proust not only knows but in fact elucidates in his novel (see my 'Art and Reality', *Philosophical Investigations*, July 1995).

The arts enrich and indeed metamorphose our visions of ordinary things which we often look at and pass by without seeing them – that is as we see them when the artist lends us his eyes to see them with: there were fogs in London (as Oscar Wilde put it) but we did not see them until the impressionists painted them. Similarly our love transforms in our eyes, in the eyes of our feelings, the person with whom we fall in love. The poet in his love poetry gives us a sensibility, a mode of feeling, which opens up for us, when we fall in love, a world in which our beloved is transformed in a light which is the light of the world of love. The fact that those who are not in love do not see in my beloved what I see in the light of my love does not make what I see an illusion or a projection. But that does not, of course, rule out the possibility that what I see may be an illusion or a projection.

It is not easy to distinguish between the two cases. Proust contrasts Rachel as she appeared to St Loup before he fell in love with her and continued to appear to others and Rachel as she appears to St Loup in love with her. Does that mean that in his love St Loup is deceived about her? Does it mean that what he sees in Rachel are the qualities he projects onto her – as a person does in paranoia or in wishful thinking? Proust thinks so and that is how it is in the characters and relationships he presents in his novel. These are his constructions and they are perfectly convincing, that is life-like. But that does not mean that they *have* to be like that.

In the light of the lover's love the beloved may shine with qualities that are not visible in the absence of such love. Her physical features, her character and moral qualities may take on an aspect, assume a significance which they may not have in the cool light of the day. The 'chemistry of sex' has, of course, an important part to play in this 'aspect change'. This does not mean that she does not have these qualities in reality and so that they are an illusion – any more than the colours with which the sea is ablaze at sunset are an illusion because they are not visible at any other time of the day.

The fact remains that the qualities that are revealed by the magic of 'falling in love' also leave in the shade other qualities that are just as important in a lasting relationship. In that respect the first stages of love, the heady days when one is 'in love', are akin to inebriation. One has to sober up for it to be clear whether or not one is deceived in one's love. If one's love can survive the transformation of living the beloved in her wholeness in the sober light of the day and still retain the power to bathe her in its light and integrate what appears in the two lights, then it wasn't a love that was feeding on illusions. Or, even if that were the case, it may so change as no longer to need to feed on illusions. Such a change, of course, is a change in oneself.

Love then, sexual love, has the capacity to cast a light which lights up the beloved with qualities which are visible in its own light, qualities that are denizens of its own world – qualities of magical attraction and loveableness. These qualities have their counterpart in the greater world in which we live, reaching beyond the borders of the world of love, and can be integrated with them. Thus the beloved retains the charm, the sweetness, the liveliness, the sparkle which others also appreciate in her. Where these qualities are simply projections they have no counterparts outside with which to be integrated. In consequence the lover either wakes up and falls out of love, to fall in love again and go through a 'repeat performance' with someone else or, tantalised by the beloved's elusiveness, he remains stuck on her in the trance-like state of his love for a while longer – and this may be a long while.

What we have here, in the latter case, is a fairly common experience of mankind and it is what Proust depicts in his novel: the way the pattern of interaction expressive of the form of love in question sustains a trance-like state in which the lover craves communion with the beloved in her very unattainability. This unattainability is the product of their interaction, given the way it feeds their relationship in their individual personalities. Thus Proust's narrator Marcel wants to possess Albertine without taming her. Her attraction for him resides in her untamed independence. Yet untamed she remains for ever inaccessible to Marcel. This inaccessibility fuels his passion for her, his craving to know her, to enter into and share with her every part of her life. This, in turn, makes her more fiercely independent, secretive and so more inaccessible, and thus fuels Marcel's imagination which turns suspicious. The relationship is thus lived in conflict and a dizzy whirl and what gratification it brings Marcel ends in frustration.

What Proust depicts, as I said, is something familiar. In his talented depiction, as an artist, he makes us see it clearly and anew for what it is. Where he goes wrong is in presenting what he depicts so well as the essence of sexual love: what one seeks in sexual love is unattainable for its very aim or object involves a contradiction. It is in this that what Proust maintains is something we find equally in Sartre's philosophy of human relations: 'conflict is the essence of our relations with other people' (1943, p. 502). 'The other is in principle out of my reach. When I try to reach him he runs away from me, and he tries to possess me when I turn away from him' (p. 479). Where Proust speaks of 'les intermittances du coeur' Sartre speaks of 'les échecs du désir et de l'amour'.

5.2 The Solipsism of Proustian Love

I have characterized the first heady stage of love which we describe as having 'fallen in love' as 'trance like'. This can take one of two forms: either the lovers are in a swoon, engrossed in each other they are affectively oblivious of the rest of the world or, as in the case of Marcel, the lover's phantasies come between him and the beloved veiling her from him. In the first place what stirs Marcel is his perception of the gulf that separates the beloved from him: 'I knew that I should never posses this young cyclist if I did not possess also what was in her eyes. And it was consequently her whole life that filled me with desire; a sorrowful desire because I felt that it was not to be fulfilled' (vol. i, p. 852). This is in part a self-fulfilling prophecy. The phantasies thus have the consequence of consolidating the gulf, of setting up a vicious circle which ensures that it will not diminish and that the lover will remain transfixed, staring into it.

In the first case, however, the swoon is the result of the sudden collapse of the everyday barriers that existed between the lover and the beloved before they fell in love with each other. But such a state is of relatively short duration. It needs to be brought into contact with and integrated into their life and interests outside their love to be sustained. If and when this can be done the swoon will be converted into a stable love. The lovers need outside sustenance to be able to have a giving relationship with one another. In its absence the love will eventually grow stale, the lovers will grow bored with each other and they will fall out of love – as Vronsky began to fall out of love with Anna during their stay in Italy in Tolstoy's *Anna Karenina*. For, because of the social stigma attached to their love on account of its adulterous character, each of the lovers come to be cut off from what contributed to the meaning of his and her life – Vronsky from his career in the army and Anna from her son and her social life.

If one of them remains in love or dependent on the other for the sustenance of his love, as was the case with Anna in Tolstoy's novel, her love will begin to take on a possessive aspect as she comes to perceive the other's detachment and consequently the loss of her power to keep him. In what then ensues, insofar as that love does not turn into hatred, its manifestations will display some affinity to those depicted by Proust in his novel.

There, in the second form which the trance-like character sexual love takes in its initial stage, the lover's phantasies which fill in the space of his relative ignorance about the life and personality of the beloved, are the result of the interplay between the lover's tempera-ment and the beloved's detachment. It is these that come between the lover and the beloved preventing the lover from coming to know the beloved. Consequently his love remains directed to a fig-ure which belongs to his phantasies. So Proust describes the love he depicts in several instances in his novel as 'a mental state' which has 'no real connection' with the beloved. It is thus a *solipsistic* love: 'not so much a love for her [the beloved] as a love in myself'. It brings the lover in touch with himself, with those aspects of his soul it resurrects, aspects that had been active in his experiences in the past, in his childhood. But, as I pointed out, in the way they flood into his consciousness and occupy its foreground, they veil the beloved from him.

The person on whom this love is directed is thus not so much the real person as a creature of Marcel's phantasy. The real person, like a magnifying glass, only serves to focus his phantasies on one point. The image which belongs to these phantasies comes between him and her. He cannot see her independently of this image and so feels he cannot touch her – 'just as an incandescent body that is brought into proximity with something wet never actually touches its moisture, since it is always preceded by a zone of evaporation' (vol. i, p. 90). Consequently, he cannot hold Albertine's interest, find in her the response for which he craves, and only succeeds in touching what is 'no more than the sealed envelope of a person' (vol. iii, p. 393).

In short, the 'direct object' of Marcel's love is a creature of his phantasy, and the real woman only its precipitating cause, a catalyst which serves to start the series of reactions I have tried to summarize: 'showcases [as Proust puts it] for the very perishable collections of one's own mind' (p. 568).

A certain similarity exists, although the type evolves, between all the women we successively love, a similarity that is due to the fixity of our temperament, which chooses them, eliminating all those who would not be at once our opposite and our complement, apt, that is to say, to gratify our senses and to wring our hearts. They are, these women, a product of our temperament, an image, an inverted projection, a negative of our sensibility (vol. i, p. 955).

The love which develops this negative is 'pre-existent and mobile'. It comes 'to rest on the image of a woman simply because that woman will be almost impossible of attainment.... A whole series of agonies develops [then] and is sufficient to fix our love definitely upon her who is its almost unknown object. Our love becomes immense, and we never dream how small a place in it the real woman occupies' (p. 917).

In 'The Fugitive' he reflects:

A man has almost always the same way of catching a cold, of falling ill; that is to say, he requires for it to happen a particular combination of circumstances; it is natural that when he falls in love he should love a certain type of woman, a type which for that matter is very widespread. (vol. iii, p. 512).

In this sense, he writes, 'my choice of a woman was not entirely free', it was 'directed in a manner that was perhaps predetermined.' But it was directed 'towards something more considerable than an individual, towards a type of woman, and this removed all necessitude from my love for Albertine.' Proust's argument is that the object of Marcel's love, what I have called its 'indirect object', was not unique.

She is legion. And yet she is compact and indestructible in our loving eyes, irreplaceable for a long time to come by any other.... The truth is that this woman has merely raised to life, by a sort of magic, countless elements of tenderness existing in us already in a fragmentary state, which she has assembled, joined

together, bridging every gap between them, and it is we ourselves who by giving her her features have supplied all the solid
matter of the beloved object. Whence it arises that even if we are
only one among a thousand to her and perhaps the last of them
all, to us she is the only one, the one towards whom our whole
life gravitates (p. 513).

Proust is arguing that to the person in love the beloved appears
as unique and irreplaceable, but that this is an illusion created by
the affective perspective of such love. The particular combination of
attributes which precipitates the state of soul in us we call 'being in
love' is repeatable. A chance meeting with another woman who has
them could have started in us that same complex process of reactions which could have made her, this other woman, the phenomenal object of our present love.

Proust thus depicts and gives us an analysis of a particular form
of love, one in which while we are in constant interaction with the
beloved person we are not in real contact with her. This lack of contact which takes the form of 'introversion', or turning inwards on
oneself, coupled with a haunting sense of the beloved person's
inaccessibility, is part of the momentum of such love. It fuels the
longing which is at the heart of it.

This is a longing to unite one's life with that of the beloved, 'to
penetrate another life', but Marcel feels that it is doomed to be
defeated by the separateness that characterizes the existence of
human beings as individuals. Thus on his first encounter with
Albertine, whose name he does not yet know, he reflects:

If we thought that the eyes of such a girl were merely two glitter-
ing sequins of mica, we should not be athirst to know her and to
unite her life to ours. But we sense that what shines in those
reflecting discs is not due solely to their material composition;
that it is the dark shadows, unknown to us, of the ideas that that
person cherishes about the people and places she knows... the
shadows, too, of the home to which she will presently return, of
the plans that she is forming or that others have formed for her;
and above all that it is she, with her desires, her sympathies, her
revulsions, her obscure and incessant will (vol. i, pp. 851–2).

Marcel is speaking here of what makes a person fully a person, one
who has a life such as only a creature who speaks a language can

have, a person as opposed to a thing, and as such the particular person he or she is. It is this which makes for the inevitable separateness of human beings from one another, that separateness which in the case of those he loves and needs fuels Marcel's imagination and yearning:

> I knew that I should never possess this young cyclist if I did not possess also what was in her eyes. And it was consequently her whole life that filled me with desire, a sorrowful desire because I felt that it was not to be fulfilled (p. 852).

It is the fact that she has a life of her own, one in which he can at best have only a partial place, that awakens this yearning in him, one he knows to be doomed to turn into anguish. The fact that he finds her 'impregnated with so much that was unknown, so apparently inaccessible', sustains it.

To possess what was in Albertine's eyes means to know every thought of her, everything she has known, experienced, enjoyed, and to become part of it. Hence later when he discovers that 'she existed on so many planes and embodied so many days that had passed' her beauty becomes 'almost heartrending'. Beneath her rose-pink face he feels 'there yawned like a gulf the inexhaustible expanse of the evenings when I had not known Albertine.' So he compares her to 'a stone which encloses the salt of immemorial oceans or the light of a star' (vol. iii, p. 393).

To possess what was in her eyes also means to keep her thoughts, her interests, her will directed to him. Yet to try to do this is like trying to freeze a smile or domesticate a wild beast; and this is an impossibility. For a smile is a smile only when it moves. Freeze it, through a paralysis of the face, so that it no longer varies with the circumstances, and you no longer have a smile. By the same token, domesticate a wild beast, tame a lion, and it will no longer have that about it which keeps you in awe of it.

It is the same with a person. For, as Proust puts it, 'a person does not stand motionless and clear before our eyes with his merits, his defects, his plans, his intentions with regard to ourselves, like a garden at which we gaze through a railing, but is a shadow behind which we can alternately imagine, with equal justification, that there burns the flame of hatred and of love (vol. ii, pp. 64–5). A person too is mobile. He can take us into his confidence, share his hopes and worries with us, take an interest in and respond to our hopes and worries, or he may move away, turn to us the cold face of indifference. He may even try to deceive, cheat or make use of us. This is something you cannot make otherwise without killing the spirit in him or driving him away. You can, of course, trust him, build a relationship in which you put your faith in him. But the fact that you cannot have a cast-iron guarantee while he remains alive, mobile and free, does not make such trust impossible – any more than the fact that the kind of justification which the philosophical sceptic seeks cannot be obtained makes knowledge impossible.

5.3   Proust and Freud on Transference Love

Proust, however, is inclined towards philosophical scepticism with regard to our knowledge of others, and of our knowledge of the beauty of things, indeed of anything that attracts and dazzles us:

> We think we know what things are like and what people think for the simple reason that this doesn't matter to us. But the moment we burn with the desire to know, like the jealous man does, then it is a dizzying kaleidoscope where we no longer distinguish anything.

And again:

> Man is the creature who cannot escape himself, who knows other people only in himself, and when he asserts the contrary, he is lying (vol. ii, p. 459).

Thus Proust has been described by some as a 'subjective idealist'.

It is this scepticism and subjectivism which he combines with his individual experience and his perception as a novelist to think of the characteristics of the love he portrays to be the inevitable features of *any* love in which we crave for contact with the object of our love and desire to savour it and delight in it. Since he holds that such a desire is of the very essence of love itself he believes that in what he has portrayed in his novel he has depicted what belongs to the essence of love. While I reject this contention or pretension I believe that what he presents in his portrayal strikes a powerful chord in us and indeed depicts a form of love which exists in reality.

I have characterized it as 'solipsistic'. It is a love in which the lover is surrounded by his own yearning soul, cannot break through it to touch the beloved and so cannot find any reciprocity. It is thus doomed to remain unrequited; it is sustained by a thirst which it finds unquenchable by virtue of the beloved's separateness – as it takes in this separateness. The anguish which it brings, Marcel tells us, is one he experienced for the first time when his mother had been unable to kiss him goodnight as was her wont to do. The kiss, normally received, brought him peace because it bridged the separateness which he discovered when his mother was unable to give it him: 'that untroubled peace which no mistress, in later years, has ever been able to give me, since one doubts them even at the moment when one believes them, and never can possess their hearts as I used to receive, in a kiss, my mother's heart, whole and entire, without qualm or reservation, without the smallest residue of an intention that was not for me alone' (vol. i, p. 202).

The anguish he experiences when on not receiving his mother's goodnight kiss he comes to recognize the fact that she has a life of her own, intentions that are not for him alone, and in that sense a separate existence, 'migrates' into his later loves and carries with it there the whole state of mind and pattern of attitudes and responses of which it is a part. 'Migrates' is the word Proust uses; Freud calls it *transference*. The transference takes place almost as if by association; it is a form of 'affective recollection' to which Proust gives an important place in his novel. Something in the person destined to be his beloved reminds him of his mother on those evenings when she 'scarcely bade me goodnight, or even did not come up to my room at all, either because she was cross with me or was kept downstairs by guests' (vol. iii, p. 107). The anguish at the realization of her separateness is thus resurrected in the present and gives a yearning aspect to the love which Albertine evokes in him.

As I put in my original paper on Proust (Dilman, 1987, chapter 7): just as it is not the attraction of water that makes a man thirsty for it, but his experience of its lack in him that makes him crave for water, so it is his thirst for what he finds inaccessible, the experience of his own incompleteness, that inspires his love for the woman who triggers off this experience in him, recalls it from his affective memory. She, in turn, does so because her very mode of being gives expression to the separateness of her existence – her untamed liveliness, her unconfinability, her elusiveness in the face of any attempt to pin her down.

This is the basis of her attractiveness for him. Proust describes beautifully the way all this comes into operation on Marcel's first encounter with Albertine in the little 'gang' to which she belonged and destines her to be the object of his yearning love:

> For an instant, as I passed the dark one with the plump cheeks who was wheeling a bicycle, I caught her smiling, sidelong glance, aimed from the centre of that inhuman world which enclosed the life of this little tribe, an inaccessible, unknown world wherein the idea of what I was could certainly never penetrate or find a place. Wholly occupied with what her companions were saying, had she seen me – this young girl in the polo-cap pulled down very low over her forehead – at the moment in which the dark ray emanating from her eyes had fallen on me? If she had seen me, what could I have represented to her? From the depths of what universe did she discern me? It would have been as difficult for me to say as, when certain distinguishing features in a neighbouring planet are made visible thanks to the telescope, it is to conclude therefrom that human beings inhabit it, and that they can see us, and to guess what ideas the sight of us can have aroused in their minds (vol. i, p. 851).

Then, on the next page, follows the few lines I quoted earlier: 'I know that I should never possess this young cyclist if I did not possess also what was in her eyes.' And then: 'But perhaps, also, it was thanks ... to my consciousness that not a single element that I knew or possessed entered into the composition of the nature and actions of these girls, that satiety had been succeeded in me by a thirst – akin to that with which a parched land burns – for a life which my soul, because it had ever until now received one drop of it, would absorb all the more greedily, in long draughts, with a more perfect imbibition' (p. 852).

Thus the yearning which what makes the beloved attractive to the lover *on this basis* evokes in the lover is such that it cannot be satisfied. As Marcel puts it later in the novel when Albertine has become his mistress:

> This anguish ... which for a time had specialised in love and which, when the separation, the division of the passions occurred, had been assigned to love alone, now seemed once more to be extending to them all, to have become indivisible

again as in my childhood, as though all my feelings, which trembled at the thought of my not being able to keep Albertine by my bedside, at once as a mistress, a sister, a daughter, and a mother too, of whose regular good-night kiss I was beginning once more to feel the childish need, had begun to coalesce, to become unified in the premature evening of my life which seemed to be as a winter day (vol. iii, p. 107).

Marcel realizes clearly that now that he is no longer a child he cannot seek or find the appeasement of his anguish and the satisfaction of the craving at the heart of his love in adult life:

But if I felt the same anguish as in my childhood, the different person who caused me to feel it, the difference in the feeling she inspired in me, the very transformation in my character, made it impossible for me to demand its appeasement from Albertine as in the old days from my mother (ibid.).

Indeed, his very craving, the character of his love, turns Albertine away from him – a vicious circle which his love thus feeds. When she finally kisses him good-night, as Marcel puts it, she herself is absent from the kiss she gives him and so it leaves him more anxious as he watches her, with a throbbing heart, make her way to the door.

Clearly the love which Proust thus depicts is a *repetition*, a *transference* of feelings, desires and expectations from the lover's childhood. It is a ghostly visitation from the past and as such the resonance of the echoing chamber of his own soul. It 'pre-exists' the lover's present experiences, it is 'mobile', ready to attach itself to any woman possessing the character needed to resurrect it. It is thus a love, as Proust puts it, not so much for this woman as a love *in* the lover: a state of soul. It is those features which, in their very specific combinations, emphasize her separateness in a way that tantalises the lover, given his particular past experiences, that touch the right chord in him and send him spinning on a predetermined course. This is what Marcel's family's faithful maid recognizes when she says of Albertine: 'That girl will bring you nothing but trouble' (ibid.). That is how the beloved's inevitable separateness, given the right kind of psychological chemistry between lover and beloved, turns into an unbridgeable gulf.

Only by turning round in himself, growing out of his early need to fuse his identity with that of the beloved, can the lover learn to love in a way that does not exclude reciprocity by making absolute demands – such as Marcel recognizes he should not make without being able to free himself from the craving to make them. Only then, with luck, will he be attracted by someone who can reciprocate his feelings. This is growing out of the child's affective orientation which characterizes his love – as illustrated in Marcel's love for Albertine. Freud calls this the resolution of the Oedipus complex.

Thus it is in the immature form of love, common and well known to us, as depicted by Proust, that the craving at the core of such love is unattainable. It is unattainable because, in its inordinate craving for 'symbiotic union' with the loved one which belongs to early childhood, it excludes all respect for the loved one's separate existence. For such respect to be possible the lover has to have reached some affective independence and autonomy in himself, to have severed the affective umbilical chord which still ties him to his mother. But such severance is often partial and admits of degrees.

5.4   Conclusion

I have characterized the kind of union which is the object of the longing at the heart of the love depicted by Proust as 'symbiotic'. It is a union in which the identities of lover and loved one are fused much in the way Aristophanes in Plato's *Symposium* says they were in what he calls our 'original state' before we were split apart. What Plato puts into Aristophanes' mouth is a myth, much in the sense of the myths Socrates expounds at the end of the *Gorgias* and the *Phaedo*. I have suggested that such union is to be found in physical form in the mother's womb where the foetus and the mother form an organic whole – are part of the same organism. It is to be found psychologically, again between mother and child, in the first few months of the baby's life.

The longing to recapture it which remains in the growing child and persists in adulthood, in degrees that vary from individual to individual, is at the core of what Freud called the Oedipus complex. In this longing, Freud argued, the growing boy feels threatened by his father and, indeed, insofar as the father himself has not resolved his Oedipus complex, he *is* the boy's rival.

This union needs to be distinguished from the kind of communion that can be found in adult life. It is the kind of intimate togetherness to be found in friendship when it is pure and in sexual love when it is free from any of the vestiges of immaturity which can, and often does, characterize sexual love in adults. It is rarer than we imagine and in thought it can easily come to seem impossible – conceptually so as we saw in the previous chapter. There I was asking whether the craving which belongs to sexuality as such excludes respect for the person who is its object and whether it can be transformed in sexual love to admit of such respect.

This question will continue to occupy us in the following chapters. In the chapter that follows immediately I turn to what Freud makes of it in the way he related love and sexuality.

6

Freud on Love and Sexuality: a Critique

6.1 Sexual Love

Freud thinks of all forms of love, including, the young child's love – the baby's love for his mother, the slightly older girl's for her father – to be sexual in character, as having its basis in human sexuality. He thinks that this becomes apparent once their surface is scratched. He moves from seeing the child's love as a phenomenon of sexuality to think of all love as essentially sexual in character.

Sexuality, he argues, has two aspects or 'currents', as he calls them: sensual and affectionate. In its sensual aspect sexuality, in the child, goes through certain stages in the child's physical and affective development in accordance with the different parts of his body, 'the erotogenic zones', in which the child finds sensual pleasure. At first 'auto-erotic', later the child seeks to make bodily contact with those who look after him or her, through the stimulation of these zones. Simultaneously, in what Freud calls 'the development of the ego', the child moves towards a fuller recognition of those who care for him as independent beings – as opposed to mere satellites circling around him – and develops ties of affection to them.

As, in puberty, the genitals become the centre around which his sensuality comes to be organized and his affection and his sensuality come to be fused he moves closer towards adult sexual love. When thus 'fused', as Freud describes it, the two 'currents' come to share each other's character: the growing adolescent lover's sexuality is charged with affection, and his affection is sensual: he wants to touch, caress, embrace the loved one. When for one or more of many reasons they remain apart or come to be dissociated, one of the two components of sexual love is repressed. Where sensuality is repressed sexual love becomes lame, as in Dostoyevsky's Prince Myshkin; and where affection is blocked through repression sensuality turns into obsessive lust, again as in Dostoyevsky's Rogozhin.

Their loves for Nastasya Philippovna are thus the antithesis of each other.

In its mature state, Freud points out, the aim of 'genital sex' is copulation which normally combines sensuality and affection and has the beloved as its object. When it is diverted from its aim Freud talks of 'sublimation'. Sexuality is thus transformed, Freud argues, when sublimated, but it is sexuality still and remains so. Thus transformed it is present in other forms of love where it remains unrecognized – in friendship, for instance, and in sympathy.

This is a very rough sketch of Freud's all embracing theory of sex and love. It calls for criticism. Certainly sexuality can take disguised forms of expression and also it can enter into the service of different non-sexual desires and quests in human beings. But from this it is a big step to the conclusion that all human ties are at bottom sexual, that all forms of love and attachments are sexual in character. It is true that various failures and obstacles can turn a person away from sexual pursuits. Such a person can invest the energy he would have invested in sexual pursuits in these other pursuits and interests. He may find some compensation in these for what he has turned away from but still craves for. They may even become a substitute for what in phantasy he still clings to and, indeed, in the affective organization of his life they may occupy the place given to sexuality in the life of a lover. If this is what sublimation is, it does not follow so far that what is described as 'sublimated' partakes of the character of sexuality.

Even if, however, we are willing to allow that it does so, it still does not follow that *all* our interests are of this kind, namely disguised expressions of sexuality. From the fact that sexuality can enter into and hide in almost any area of human life it does not follow that every desire and interest to be found in human life is at bottom sexual in character. Freud does not quite claim this; but he certainly sees the variety of human pursuits and interests as the expression of a very few fundamental instincts with sexuality looming large in the space he accords to it.

As for love, I would say, just as there are expressions of sex which have little to do with love, equally there are forms of love which have little to do with sex. Affection is a form of love. But, in contrast with Freud, I would claim that it does not belong to sexuality as such, although certainly it can be an expression of sexuality. Where, for instance, a person or an animal evokes affection in one so that one naturally wants to hug him or it, in most cases this has nothing to do with sex. Of course sex may enter into a relationship of pure affection and friendship; the affection may then *acquire* a sexual character. But this does not mean that the affection was sexual in character from the start; it may or may not have been so.

As for infantile sexuality Freud's main argument is that the erotogenic pleasures and desires we find in the child's life are to be found in and form part of adult sexuality. It remains true, however, that in the context of adult sexual life they take on an aspect they cannot have in the young child's love. The fact that lovers kiss each other and that their kisses are expressions of sexual love does not make a child's kissing of his mother, for instance, an expression of sexuality. Just as a smile is not just a curling of the lips and can take different expressions in different surroundings, so equally a kiss is not the stimulation of an erotogenic zone of the body. It can be the expression of very different feelings, take on different significances in the surroundings of human life in the case of both adults and children.

It has to be admitted, however, that there is such a thing as regression which is to be found in the sexual life of the adult. This does establish a link between adult sexuality and what Freud draws attention to in the child's life. For here what appears in the context of the adult's sexuality is what is found in his early life as a child. That is what regression is: a going back to what *was* and *still persists*. What thus belongs to childhood and persists in an adult form of sexual love does contribute to its character. This link in turn can throw a new light on *certain* patterns of conduct, interests and preoccupations, to be found in the child's life. It gives some justification for characterizing them as *sexual* – as Freud does. In other words, sexuality is to be found *in certain forms* in childhood and does enter into and characterize some of the child's loves and attachments which we tend to regard as innocent of sexuality. But this does not mean that *all* the child's loves and attachments are, or must be, sexual in character.

While, with this proviso or reservation, Freud's point of view is a legitimate one and his claim for the existence of sexuality in childhood is justified, there may be other points of view. Thus D.H. Lawrence:

Sex … is present from the moment of birth, and in every act or deed of every child. But sex in the real sense of dynamic sexual relationship, this does not exist in a child, and cannot exist until puberty and after. True, children have a sort of sex consciousness. Little boys and little girls may even commit indecencies together. And still it is nothing vital. It is a sort of shadow activity ... It has no profound effect (1977, p. 102).

Lawrence means that it does not, in the child's life, have the possibilities that belong to sexual passion in adult life. Those possibilities that belong to sexual passion in adult life, of course, come from that life. The limits of the child's sexuality which Lawrence has in mind are the limits of the young child's life. If a follower of Freud were to insist that the sex that exists in childhood does have a 'profound effect' in human life, he and Lawrence would be speaking at cross purposes.

From the fact that sex, in one form or other, can be part of a child's love as of course it is at one with love in adult sexual love, one should not draw any general conclusions concerning the sexual character of love in general. Freud did do so. He thought of love as necessarily an expression of sex. It is interesting to note that he uses two different words in this connection: 'libido' and 'eros'. When he speaks of eros he is thinking of the attributes which sex acquires through its identification with love – such attributes as creativity. Hence the way he contrasts it with a 'death instinct', the main expression of which is destructiveness. Thus while his identification of love with sex sometimes limits his understanding of what love can bring to a person's life, at other times it is just this which he means to bring into prominence. But more of this later. At the moment I am concerned with the limitation in his understanding of love – sexual love included.

In *Group Psychology and the Analysis of the Ego* Freud tells us that we call many different things 'love' and that among these things the love between man and woman, 'sexual love', occupies a central position. They differ in accordance with the person's conscious desires and aspirations with regard to what he loves, although each exhibits various degrees of affinity to sexual love: 'All these tendencies are an expression of the same instinctive activities' (see Freud, 1949c, pp. 37–8). This is an instance of Freud's 'essentialism'. He writes further down that 'even in its caprices the usage of language remains true to some kind of reality' (p. 71). It is capricious in that 'it gives the name 'love' to a great many kinds of emotional relationship'. But the application of the name is not really capricious or arbitrary, as it may appear, for it is responsible to 'some kind of reality'. The reality in question is what the diverse forms of love have in common. In their surface, that is in what the subject is conscious of, they appear different; but psycho-analysis finds the same thing – the same phantasies, desires and attitudes – in the subject's unconscious. So Freud claims: 'A psychology which will not or cannot penetrate the depths of what is repressed regards tender emotional ties as being invariably the expression of tendencies which have no sexual aim, even though they are derived from tendencies which have such an aim' (Freud, 1949c, p. 118). By way of substantiation Freud cites two kinds of case. In the first kind, in the course of a purely tender relationship, or one based on esteem and admiration, sexual desires make their appearance: 'It is well known how easily erotic wishes develop out of emotional relations of a friendly character, based upon appreciation and admiration, between a master and a pupil, between a performer and a delighted listener' (p. 119). He mentions 'how easily even an intense religious tie can revert to ardent sexual excitement' (p. 119). But these cases prove nothing about the character of love, friendship, appreciation and admiration. They only show that in *some* cases, for example, a religious tie masks or is the vehicle of sexual feelings, and in others it is transformed and becomes sexualized.

In the second kind of case, two people are brought together by sexual attraction and then, in time, affection grows and cements their relation. Freud speaks here of the sexual tendencies being 'transformed into' a lasting and purely tender tie (p. 119). What is true is that in these cases affection grows within a relationship that is based on sensuality and transforms the character of the sex in the relationship. For with the development of affection the whole affective orientation of the couple towards each other changes and with this what part of themselves they give to each other and so what sex comes to mean to them. It is true that we can distinguish between the sensual and the tender aspects of the relationship; but this does not mean that they are two separate things joined together. We can say here that these two people's sensuality has become a form or an expression of their affection, and also that their affection is a form which their sensual longing for each other has come to take. This is what Freud must mean by the sensual and affectionate currents coming to be 'fused'. But the change in each is more like what happens in a chemical reaction. You can identify the elements that have entered into the fusion, but you cannot say that they have the same character now as before. Thus from the sexual character of the affection in these cases one is not justified in concluding that of necessity affection is a state of sexuality. It is *one* of the states of sexuality, which means that it *can* have a sexual character and that a sexual relationship is one of its homes. But it has other homes and other faces.

This is just as true of love. We call many different things 'love', we speak of 'loving' many different things, and we use the word 'love' in different ways in these different connections – 'I love you,' and 'I'd love to have a holiday in the Bahamas.' Thus a man can love a woman, or a woman can love a man. We often distinguish this by speaking of 'sexual love'. Where a man loves a man we speak of 'homosexual love' and where a woman loves a woman we speak of 'lesbian love'. Then we speak of parental love, of maternal, paternal and filial love. Again a person may care for and love an animal he keeps as a pet. We often speak of other things that a person cares for and looks after as things that he loves – his garden for instance. We speak of friendship as involving love, of love of one's country or 'patriotism', of 'love of one's neighbour' in the religious sense, and of 'the love of God'. We speak of something one enjoys and appreciates as something one loves – a piece of music, a work of art, or the work in which one is engaged. And we also speak of the way one puts oneself out, holds oneself together, and works in caring for something or making it grow as 'a labour of love'. Thus creation is described as a labour of love. (See section 2 below.)

This already takes in a wide area of human endeavour, relationship and affectivity, and covers a great variety of phenomena in which human personality finds expression. The desires and attitudes that belong to love in these different cases, and the qualities of character that flourish as aspects of the love exemplified in them, vary a great deal from case to case. Thus we may speak of affection or fondness, or friendship, loyalty, concern, admiration, appreciation, sympathy and compassion as forms of love. Though they differ from each other – admiration and compassion for instance – they are expressions of tendencies, impulses and orientations which constitute the many faces of love.

There are many such tendencies and impulses, and none of them are necessary to love. Any one or more of them may be in the background or altogether absent; or they may dominate the 'lover's' actions and affectivity, they may be exaggerated and even warped.

Thus in sexual love the desire for contact and communion with the beloved may eclipse the concern for his or her welfare and take on the form of possessiveness out of which may grow jealousy. We may say that in such a case jealousy is an expression of love, of a possessive love, a love which craves to keep the relationship with the beloved completely exclusive. We can easily understand this craving as part of sexual love, and we know that where the lover makes no claim at all to some form of exclusiveness, he has become indifferent to the beloved and stopped loving her. For wanting the other person is part of what we understand by sexual love, and wanting in the sphere of sex does not tolerate sharing when it is passionate. On the other hand, devoid of all regard for the beloved and shorn of the bond of affection it becomes an expression of lust. As Freud points out, it is affection that gives permanence to a sexual relationship. But his understanding of the way affection contributes to such permanence is inadequate: 'Those sexual instincts which are inhibited in their aims have a great functional advantage over those which are uninhibited. Since they are not capable of really complete satisfaction, they are especially adapted to create permanent ties' (pp. 118–19).

The point, however, is not that affection cannot be completely satisfied so that the person in question stays around for further satisfaction. This is a grotesque misrepresentation of the permanence of which human relationships are capable. The point rather is that affection does not seek satisfaction but is orientated towards the individuality of the other person. What gives permanence to the relation is the attachment of affection and the loyalty which belongs to love. Here we have the give and take constitutive of a loving relationship. The lover treasures what he receives from the beloved and is grateful for it. It is this that creates the bond of loyalty. Furthermore his concern for the beloved's well-being and his desire to care for her, to take responsibility for her welfare, which grows out of the gratitude and appreciation, contributes to his loyalty. The permanence of the relationship of love and affection thus has its source in the moral dimension of such love.

Sexual love, of course, is more than affection for the beloved. Affection for another person can be very deep, but it is a calm form of affectivity. Whereas in sexual love as a passion the beloved excites the lover. What excites him are the beloved's attributes seen by him under the aspect of beauty. Here the lover is not fond of the beloved he is held spell-bound by her. She is a magnetic centre to him.

This is not simply a question of desire, although sexual desire comes into it. But its satisfaction merely adds to the fascination he finds in the beloved; it reveals further facets of her personality that increase the wonder he feels for her. Unless, that is, his love is an illusion and the reality of its object disappoints or disillusions him. It is in this that sexual love differs from lust. Lust is inspired by the desirability of the beloved, love by her beauty. That is why love has the possibility of depth; lust does not.

We are talking about *one* form of love which is a phenomenon of sex, and I have said that it can in no way be reduced to desire. At the core of it is the magnetism of beauty. This, in turn, cannot be understood in terms of the idealization of qualities which one finds desirable – as Freud is inclined to do. Hence love as a sexual passion is a phenomenon of civilization. For a person must find something beautiful if he is to be moved by its beauty. This vision, and such reactions as wonder and humility which belong to it, presuppose thoughts and attitudes that bring in a whole culture with its literature and art, its poems and songs of praise, its forms of worship and thanksgiving. Beauty is something we praise, something we like to contemplate, and we find that it is always more than what we can say about it. Hence we often speak of beauty as 'mysterious'. We find that nothing that we can do can quite match up to what it inspires in us. Sexual love which is inspired by beauty partakes of this character.

I used to think that Proust's description of the inaccessibility of Albertine is an expression of Marcel's inability to make contact with things, 'to break out into the world', of his 'sensation' of being 'always enveloped in, surrounded by our own soul'. It certainly is that; but not simply that. It is also an expression of the way in which what we find beautiful holds us by the fact that we cannot touch it (Proust, 1952, Pt II, vol. x, pp. 248–9):

At moments, in Albertine's eyes, in the sudden flush of her cheeks, I felt as it were a gust of warmth pass furtively into regions more inaccessible to me than the sky, in which Albertine's memories unknown to me, lived and moved. Then this beauty which, when I thought of the various years in which I had known Albertine whether upon the beach at Balbec or in Paris, I found that I had but recently discovered in her, and which consisted in the fact that my mistress was developing upon so many planes and embodied so many past days, this beauty became almost heartrending. Then beneath that blushing face I felt yawned like a gulf the inexhaustible expanse of the evenings when I had not known Albertine. I might, if I chose, take Albertine upon my knee, take her head in my hands; I might caress her, pass my hands slowly over her, but, just as if I had been handling a stone which encloses the salt of immemorial oceans or the light of a star, I felt that I was touching no more than the sealed envelope of a person who inwardly reached to infinity.

In what way is the sudden flush of Albertine's cheeks part of the heartrending beauty in her before which Marcel feels helpless? It is such when in Marcel's apprehension it is connected with the memory of days he spent with her and her friends in Balbec, beside the sea, described in an earlier volume (*A l'ombre des jeunes filles en fleurs/Within a Budding Grove*). These are memories of days not only when he had known her but also when her life, mingled with that of the group of young girls with whom he played but to which he was an outsider, offered rich pastures for his imagination. The fact of her having a life necessarily separate from and independent of Marcel's became for him an endless subject of imagination. The terms in which Marcel imagines that life fill him with both longing and wonder, exaltation and jealousy. But the main point to which I want to come is that these terms belong to a language, literature and mode of sensibility which exist independently of Marcel and to which Proust has made a major contribution, although they are at the same time the terms most suited to Marcel Proust's individual psychology. Without them he could neither remember 'so many past days', think of what life would be without her, nor imagine 'the inexhaustible expanse of the evenings' when he had not known Albertine. And without the support of such memory and imagination all the fullness and magic she has for him would dwindle into nothing.

To see a person in his or her fullness, that is as a person with thoughts, feelings and intentions, with a past about which he may have regrets and a future in connection with which he has hopes and anxieties, some of which one knows, others about which one may be curious or apprehensive, all this presupposes the kind of life we live with language, the kind of life which makes it possible for one to think, imagine, take an interest in and show concern for others. Such a life is just as necessary for the other person to have the fullness and humanity of a person. I have discussed this question elsewhere[5] and it is not my intention to elaborate on it now. To see a person in his or her magic, to respond to that magic, to be captivated by it, this has often been attributed to 'the chemistry of the sexes'. While this is not wrong, it fails to mention everything which the workings of that chemistry presupposes.

What would show the existence of such magic in a relationship between lovers? What would show that they are captivated by each other's magic? What would show that their desire for each other is lit up by it and is not just straightforward, ordinary sexual desire? The answer is, surely, the terms in which they think of each other, the significance which each has in the other's life, the way they miss each other, the character of their longing, the despair with which the possibility of a life without the other would fill the soul of each. These terms and this mode of sensibility come from what Rush Rhees has called 'the language of love' (1969, pp. 122–3). And where has this language developed primarily but in literature, in love poetry and songs, novels and drama.

The lover finds his individuality in a life which has produced such literature and can boast of a literary heritage that stretches back into the past. His own life bathes in it, even if he is himself not acquainted with most of this literature. Its forms of sensibility and modes of expression are available to him through the life he shares with others – if not pure then in their adulterated varieties. They are in any case part of the language he speaks. The dependence between what happens in the lives of individual people and the literature which belongs to the language they speak is two-way: the literature portrays incidents in those lives and shows us what men are capable of, it shows us what love is like for different people and in different circumstances, the different forms it can take, its power for good and evil, its glory as well as its power to destroy. But it also constitutes aspects of the character of those lives, contributes to the determination of what men are capable of envisaging and experiencing, through the modes of expression it develops in the language they speak.

Earlier I mentioned the fact that beauty is something that we wonder at and praise. Without these responses what would the recognition of beauty be among men? It would be nothing, there would be nothing corresponding to such recognition. We could not say that beauty played a role in the lives of men. The contemplation of

---

5. See Dilman, 1975, Pt II, especially Chapter 2.

beauty is a further extension of these responses and reactions. We could speak of such reactions as 'natural' to men in the sense that we find them wherever men have formed communities and developed a life they share – I mean such responses as praise, awe, gratitude, dedication. But though natural they could not have existed without the language in which they are given expression. The development of these responses among men *is* the development of the language of praise and worship, the terms in which men express the value of what they praise, exalt it and reflect on it. This language, through the responses that develop in harness with it, is constitutive of the character of its object – its beauty, its goodness, its magic or spell.

I have been thinking about sexual love, which of course itself can take different forms, and I have been concerned with the way it goes beyond what is biological and instinctive in sexuality, although what constitutes it are phenomena of sexuality. I have pointed out that the character of these phenomena lies partly in their various connections with phenomena outside the domain of sexuality. We could say that phenomena which in other contexts of human life do not have a sexual significance – praise, gratitude and dedication for instance – enter into it. These phenomena here assume a sexual significance, become phenomena of sexuality, and also transform the character of the sexuality that is sexual love. Rush Rhees, in developing Wittgenstein's discussion of language, emphasized the interconnections between what Wittgenstein called 'language-games' and tried to understand the sense in which these belong to a language spoken by a people with a particular life and culture (Rhees, 1970). In a somewhat similar way sexuality is not a compartment of human life and links with other aspects of human life. A great deal that enriches it and endows it with the significance it can have in individual lives goes through much of human life. This contribution, also, is a two-way one, for it is equally true that people enter most of the things they do as sexual beings – their sexuality, like their morality, is an important part of their perspective on the world. It plays a part in determining what they can make of things in various connections of human life and what they can bring to their engagement in various practices.

I spoke of the interdependence between the phenomena of sexual love and literature (to which I should add other forms of art, especially music). The latter develops the forms of expression and sensibility which in an important sense constitute the phenomena of love, even though these obviously have a biological aspect. On the other hand, the phenomena exist independently of each individual artist and writer who, through his portrayal of various aspects of them, makes us see these aspects anew.

The point at which I started was to note the variety in the tendencies which 'sexual love' shares with other forms of love. I broke off my presentation of this variety in order to discuss the question about the sense in which these tendencies have a sexual character and the way in which they differ from sexual desires, for instance in the case of lust, where we should not wish to speak of love. I spoke first of affection and then of being captivated by the magic, the beauty of the beloved. Love, I suggested, is a turbulent passion, one that takes possession of a person and becomes the centre of his world, changing his values and affecting his way of making sense of things. Elsewhere (Dilman, 1984, chapter 3) I considered the way in which emotions transform one's awareness of the world – *vide* Sartre – and the dispositions to action that are constitutive of them – *vide* Hampshire. Love, however, is not just one emotion among others, an emotion like any other. Otherwise why should it have been 'the theme of poems and plays and stories more frequently than any other'?

It incorporates many different emotions, tendencies and desires which vary from case to case so that we have many different forms or expressions of love in human life. I mentioned the desire to have and to hold, to touch, to communicate and enter into some form of communion, to contemplate, to take delight in the person loved, to create or beget through the beloved, to give, to care, to protect, to be worthy of love. These desires and dispositions are inspired by the beauty, the magic which the beloved has in the lover's apprehension, the dearness he or she has in the lover's feelings. Love itself is perhaps better described as a mode of sensibility in which what is loved becomes an object of delight. It can be described as an attitude of will exemplified in caring and commitment. It is also a mode of relationship. Interest and admiration are others, although each of these overlaps with love and they all share some of each other's character. Love offers the possibility of intimacy, sincerity and growth. That is why its problems are the problems of human relationship and affect the meaning one can find in life. There are not comparable problems of hate for instance. A person who is unable to love is one who is unable to relate himself to things properly. Love also raises the question of whether one is worthy of what one loves.

6.2   Love and Creativity

What I have said so far naturally leads to two further questions. Both relate to Freud's view that all forms of love, even interest and admiration, are expressions of sexuality. First, what makes him think so and where does he go wrong in thinking this? Second, could it be, in part, because he sees in these diverse phenomena something that links them with what rejuvenates human life that he thinks of them, wrongly, as expressions of sexuality? If so, then behind his sweeping claim there may be something worth investigating.

In *Group Psychology* Freud claims that all ties between people are 'libidinal' (1949c, pp. 44–5). He then considers an objection which John Anderson was to raise in his discussion of Freud's later book *Civilization and its Discontents*: 'The question will at once be raised whether community of interest in itself, without any addition of libido, must not necessarily lead to the toleration of other people and to considerateness for them.' Freud's answer is that 'no lasting limitation of narcissism is effected in this way.' 'This tolerance does not persist longer than the immediate advantage gained from the other people's collaboration … Experience has shown that in cases of collaboration libidinal ties are regularly formed between the fellow-workers which prolong and solidify the relation between them to a point beyond what is merely profitable.' He concludes that 'love alone acts as the civilising factor in the sense that it brings a change from egoism to altruism' (Freud, 1949c, p. 57). In *Civilization and its Discontents* he writes: 'The masses of men must be bound to one another libidinally; necessity alone, the advantages of common work, would not hold them together' (1949f, p. 102).

Anderson criticizes Freud's idea of libido being necessary to the co-operation between men (1940, p. 347): 'Man is *not* confronted with the task of living with his fellows, but is social all along.' Being social, men '*are* held together in common work'. It is not 'the advantages of common work' that hold men together, but 'the common work itself' (Anderson, 1940, p. 345). What I should like to point out here is that love is a mode of relationship, not the only one, but the earliest. It is in the course of the development of love that a child learns to control his immediate impulses, to relate to and co-operate with others, notably his parents. What he thus learns enables him to learn other modes of relationship, such as the joint pursuit of common interests, and it is carried over into them.

This is what Malinowski has in mind when he says that 'common sociability develops by extension of the family bonds' (1955, p. 165). It is true that 'man is not confronted with the task of living with his fellows.' But only because most men are on the whole co-operative, are interested in things and pursue their interests in common activities. Anderson is quite right in thinking that these interests come from outside and presuppose the existence of a social life. To have them is to be part of that life. Without them, if we also include men's values, there would be little on which to co-operate. However, if men are capable of co-operating with each other, capable of learning and of becoming part of the life of a community, this is because of their early experiences in their family. If they do not develop the ability to love and co-operate, then living with their fellows becomes a task and a problem. Freud thinks that these two abilities are intimately interrelated: 'love ... brings a change from egoism to altruism.' By 'altruism' he means interest in other people and concern for their welfare.

These do indeed form part of our conception of love which does not mean that love cannot be selfish, nor that there cannot be co-operation without love. It is well known that men who actually dislike each other often co-operate when it is in their interest to do so. But even when they do not pretend to like each other there is a strain: 'No lasting limitation of narcissism is effected in this way.' However, in the absence of positive dislike for one another men do generally co-operate, and what brings this about is common work, common interest, common values; not interest in each other. Freud recognizes this and speaks of 'identification' as a special kind of relation in contrast with what he calls 'object choice'. He says that here a number of individuals share a common 'ego ideal', i.e. look up to and admire the same person or are inspired by the same values and ideals, and consequently 'identify themselves with one another in their ego' (Freud, 1949c, p. 80). As he puts it: 'A soldier takes his superior ... as his ideal, while he identifies himself with his equals' (1949c, p. 111). In *Civilization and its Discontents* too he contrasts 'sexual love' and 'identification': 'The conflict between civilization and sexuality is caused by the circumstance that sexual love is a relationship between two people, in which a third can only be superfluous or disturbing, whereas civilization is founded on relations between larger groups of persons.' In these larger groups men are tied together by 'powerful identifications' (1949f, pp. 79–80). However, he seems to think of both as 'libidinal ties'.

Compare and contrast with D.H. Lawrence writing on the same question (1977, pp. 109–10):

> Is this new polarity, this new circuit of passion between comrades and coworkers, is this also sexual? ...

> This meeting of many in one great passionate purpose is not sex, and should never be confused with sex. It is a great motion in the opposite direction.... When man loses his deep sense of purposive, creative activity, he feels lost, and is lost. When he makes the sexual consummation the supreme consummation, even in his *secret* soul, he falls into the beginnings of despair ...

> The great collective passion of belief which brings men together, comrades and coworkers ... this is not sex-passion.... Sex holds any *two* people together, but it tends to disintegrate society, unless it is subordinated to the great dominating male passion of collective *purpose*.

Lawrence is saying that sex or what Freud calls 'eros' is not the only 'life force' or 'constructive principle' in human life. There is another principle at work in men's lives which has an important contribution to make to the meaning of their lives. This is what Freud calls 'common ego-ideal'. Lawrence and Freud disagree about its character.

The term Lawrence uses for it, 'collective purpose', covers a range of phenomena. He has in mind friendships inspired by common ideals, comradeships that develop through participation in common activities, the tie between colleagues who belong to the same profession, the regard for each other of people fighting for the same cause. His term 'passion of belief' is more accurate, though by 'purpose' I take him to mean that such passion gives purpose to men's lives in the sense of 'direction' or 'orientation'. There is no implication that the direction in question is that of means to an end. I agree with Lawrence; I see no reason for characterizing such ties as 'sexual' or 'libidinal'. I also agree with his characterization of what is at work here as a 'passion'. What he calls 'passion of belief' is devotion to an ideal, loyalty to a cause, dedication of the self to a value.[6] These are phenomena of love – with an important qualification.

---

6. This is what is meant by a 'belief in' a value or ideal.

People can be brought together by a common enemy; they can be held together by sharing what Erikson calls 'negative identities' – by hating the same things, having contempt for the same values. These are not phenomena of love, although friendship may grow between people who have come together in this way. If this happens, the friendship may transform their hatred. Secondly, whether or not devotion to an ideal is a phenomenon of love depends on the ideal and can be seen in what it is capable of inspiring in men who devote themselves to it. But, by and large, men's devotions to positive ideals have involved some measure of love.

I think that Freud was right in distinguishing between sexual love on the one hand and admiration and identification on the other. He saw both of these beginning to develop in the child's relationships with members of his family. He thought that in these beginnings we have the precursor of the great variety which phenomena of love take in adult life. Critics were right in emphasizing how much that is new comes into adult life from *outside*; how much what a person learns from his participation in the life that goes on around him and from his contact with those sharing it *transforms* the character of what comes from his childhood. On the other hand Freud is right in thinking that the kind of relationships a person can enter into, what he can make of them and what he can learn depend on what he brings to these. The most important part of what he brings to them dates back to his childhood and includes the kind of love of which he is capable. His capacity for contact, co-operation and creativity springs from it.

We have seen that men can co-operate with one another in a limited way out of self-interest. A deeper co-operation takes love and friendship, or a common interest or concern. I suggested that the latter also are phenomena of love or have some affinity to such phenomena. Ian D. Suttie, one of the critics of the central importance which Freud attaches to sexuality, indicates the affinity succinctly. After noting the way the growing child's widening environment replaces the world of which his mother occupies the centre, he continues (Suttie, 1948, p. 16):

A joint interest in *things* has replaced the reciprocal interest in *persons*; friendship has developed out of love. True, the personal love and sympathy is preserved in *friendship*; but this differs from love insofar as it comes about by the *direction of attention upon the same things* (rather than upon each other), or by the pursuit of *the same activities* .... The interest is intensified even if it is not entirely created ... by being *shared*; while the fact of sharing interest deepens the appreciation of the other person's presence even while it deprives it of sensual ... qualities.

Of course love can be selfish, it can introduce strife and conflict between people – strife and conflict which would not be there but for love. For although generosity and concern are expressions of love, it is also true that love can be the source of demands which the lover makes on the beloved, demands for what ideally the beloved is willing to give unsolicited as part of her love. I am thinking of sexual love, but this is equally true of friendship. Thus the lover desires that his love should be returned, and the friend that his friendship should be reciprocated. This is part of sexual love and of friendship, and there is nothing selfish in this desire as such. But when it turns into need the demands that issue from it become expressions of selfishness. This selfishness was in the lover before he fell in love and his love becomes the vehicle of his selfishness. But in doing so it becomes selfish itself; the desire which is an expression of love and belongs to it takes on a selfish character. Given its common occurrence it can be described as one form of love. Thus we sometimes speak of 'selfish love', 'possessive love', 'destructive love', 'dependent love', and so on.

In view of this variety, are we to say that the connection I hinted at between love and the capacity to give and take and to co-operate is purely gratuitous? I do not think so. I said that the phenomena of love are various and can be classified in different ways. One distinction one can make within this variety is this: in some cases we have love which is directed to a particular person on account of who he is. We can describe it as 'selective' or 'personal' because it chooses its object. Thus in maternal love a mother loves her child because the child is her offspring, because she has brought him into the world, nursed and cared for him. In sexual love the lover loves the beloved because of whatever it is in her that inspires this passion in him. If and when this passion is consolidated with affection, common memories and shared experiences will add a new dimension to the particularity of the beloved. It is in some ways the same with friendship. In contrast, compassion or what Christians call 'love of one's neighbour' is not selective in this way – for everyone without exception is one's neighbour in this sense. It is the same with a person's belief in, loyalty and devotion to certain moral

values. The practices which embody these values do not differenti-
ate between one person and another. In these latter cases the values
themselves give us a measure for distinguishing between pure and
impure forms of their love, between genuine compassion and its
corrupt varieties. Hence Simone Weil characterizes compassion as
love of justice.

We can, of course, do the same in the case of those phenomena of
love which are 'selective' in the sense indicated. Thus Simone Weil
on friendship: 'All friendship is impure if even a trace of the wish
to please, or the contrary desire to dominate is found in it' (1959,
p. 157). Similarly for sexual love and affection: 'When the bonds of
affection and necessity between human beings are not supernatu-
rally transformed into friendship, not only is the affection of an
impure and low order, but it is also combined with hatred and
repulsion. That is shown very well in *L'Ecole des Femmes* and in
Phèdre' (Weil, 1959, p. 159). One problem concerns the compatibility
between sexual love (what she calls 'carnal love') and friendship.
Simone Weil is well aware of this problem: 'The essential thing
about love is that it consists in a vital need that one human being
feels for another.... Because of this the problem is to reconcile this
need with the equally imperious need for freedom; this is a problem
that men have wrestled with since time immemorial' (Weil, 1951,
p. 35). When writing about friendship she refers to this 'need for
freedom' as the need to 'respect the distance which the fact of being
two distinct creatures places between them', i.e. between the friends
(Weil, 1959, p. 157). Her problem there is to show how friendship,
which is necessarily 'personal', *can* be 'supernatural' and, therefore,
pure: 'Friendship is a miracle by which a person consents to view
from a certain distance, and without coming any nearer, the very
being who is necessary to him as food' (p. 157). The problem with
sexual love and passion is whether it can view the beloved from a
distance in this way without stopping to be what it is.

My problem now is a different one, namely whether there is an
inherent connection between love and generosity, between love and
creativeness, between love and the capacity to co-operate. This is a
problem in view of the fact that love *itself* can be selfish, destructive
and tyrannical. But to speak of an 'inherent connection' here is not
to claim that love is always generous, that it can never be selfish; it
is not to deny that love can bring out the worst in a man as well as
the best. To deny this would be to deny that love offers problems
and that struggling with these problems is the kind of growth which

love brings into human life. Thus to claim that there is an inherent connection between love and generosity is to claim that a love that is selfish necessarily has certain tensions within it, so that a person who loves selfishly can reconcile himself to it only through self-deception. Again love, sexual love, is captivating; in it the lover falls a prey to the magic of the beloved. Being the way he is his love may take a dependent form. He may resent this and hate the beloved for it. The hatred here does not, of course, belong to the love, so that the conflict we have is not one between different parts of the love in question. However, this dependency could easily come into conflict, given the right circumstances, with the lover's concern for the beloved and his desire to be worthy of her love. He would then see it as something of which he wishes to purge his love. If he describes his love as a 'low' form of love the measure of his condemnation comes from love itself. Here the disposition to care for the beloved which the lover has by virtue of his love will be in conflict with his need for and dependence on the beloved. Where that disposition changes into a 'commitment of will' the lover will view his dependence as a weakness and feel unworthy. Here then we have a form of love which has within it the principle of its development.

I am suggesting that although love for another person can take many different forms and can become a vehicle for the expression of what is good and bad, constructive and destructive in human beings, they are not all on an equal footing. In grasping some of these as forms of love we see them as variants of other forms, variants in which tendencies that are expressions of love *par excellence* are warped or distorted by the idiosyncrasies of both the lover and the beloved. We understand that love can go these ways because we understand what love is and know what human life is like. Thus love could not be jealous and possessive were the beloved not precious to the lover; and one individual becoming precious to another is part of what we understand by love. The jealousy and possessiveness are not necessary to love and come from idiosyncrasies of the people in love, but that they should be precious to each other is necessary, although this can take many different forms. Again, while love can take a selfish form or be exacting in particular cases, generosity is an expression of love, selfishness is not. By generosity I understand the ability to give and share willingly and without any condition.

Love can be harsh and cruel, but cruelty and harshness are the contribution of the idiosyncrasies of the lover and the circumstances of his love. They are the expression which his love takes in these circumstances, but we cannot speak of them as expressions of love as such. Compassion on the other hand is an expression of love. By compassion I understand feeling sorry for those who are hurt, deprived of what they need, and suffering. Its counterpart, where there is no hurt, is sympathy, that is, the ability to enter into another person's concerns, interests and joys. It makes it possible for the other person to share these with one. That is why it is sometimes said that love brings understanding or that it is discerning. But it is also well known that love can be blind and bring illusion. The blindness and the illusion come from other aspects of love, from desire and wishful thinking.

Again, love can be unforgiving; but it takes love both to forgive and to feel grateful. Generosity concerns not only the spirit in which a person gives, but also that in which he receives what he is given. A person who has no love in his heart will see no reason for thanking anyone. He may thank someone out of expediency or politeness, but he will not feel grateful. It takes love not only to feel sorry for those in pain and to forgive those who have wronged one, but also to feel guilty and remorseful for the wrong one has done to others. Thus forgiveness, gratitude, compassion, sympathy, grief, guilt and remorse are all expressions of love, in the sense that they are responses which presuppose love.

This is true also of trust. Love, of course, need not be trusting – hence Marcel's suspicions of Albertine. But where there is no love there can be no trust, only the judgement that a particular person is reliable or honest. For there is a difference between trusting that a machine will not break down and will accomplish a particular task and putting one's faith in another person, trusting that he will not let one down. Such an act of faith involves both judgement and generosity. For in trusting someone not only is one of the opinion that he is trustworthy, but one is willing to put oneself in his hands, to speak and answer for him. This is taking a risk and thus an act of faith in this sense is an act of love. Loyalty is closely connected with it: it is a response to what in the other inspires one's trust. It means that one is prepared to stand by him in adversity, stick one's neck out for him, defend him. Patience, too, which is the suffering of wrong without complaint and without attempting to repay the wrongdoer for it, takes love. It presupposes a loving attitude. So does accepting a person with his shortcomings and weaknesses. For it is easy enough to associate with and like someone who is pleasant, interesting, charming and enjoyable. This involves little giving or putting oneself out. The test of love is whether one can take him with his faults, carry his burdens.

We see that despite its great diversity of forms and faces we can still say that love is a mode of affectivity. Where it goes deep it is also a mode of will which finds its centre outside the self. From that centre the lover derives sustenance, paradoxically, not by what he takes but by what he gives of himself. He is enriched by this giving. What he receives from the other person is not what he takes, it is a gift. If we say that this is what love is like 'in an ideal world', then we should remember the way our application of the concepts of pure geometry and theoretical physics helps us to understand the world in which we live. We can still understand what love is like 'in the real world' best if we can relate instances of it to what it is like when the tendencies and dispositions that belong to it are 'pure and unadulterated'.[7] For we can see the variety of forms these assume in the special circumstances of human life. It would not be too difficult to find a place for what Freud calls 'secondary narcissism' among the many forms of love; but this is not so easy with his 'primary narcissism'. Perhaps it is a taking on, on the part of the young child, of a doting mother's affective attitude towards him – a form of identification with her.

If I am right about the inherent connection between love and generosity, then its creative character flows from this connection. Thus contrast any number of attitudes and emotions such as hatred, resentment and envy with love. These will direct and fix a man's actions and life on certain targets and objectives, as when he nurses a grudge or is bent on revenge, which will prevent anything new entering his life. Generally the response which these will evoke in others will perpetuate these attitudes and add to the staleness of such a life. With love, however it is awakened, we have the possibility of something new entering into and renewing that life. For instance, he may be able to forgive his adversaries, find that he can respond to them in new ways, enter into their ways of thinking in a way he could never do before. This may change his relationship to his adversaries into a moving thing and also broaden his horizons. Or he may give up craving for everything he does not have, seeking to spoil it for others and annexing it to himself. Doing so never

7. Thus I find no incompatibility between this kind of Platonism and Wittgenstein's anti-essentialism. See Dilman, 1980, Chapter 10, section V.

enriched him, never mitigated the sense of deprivation that drove him to it. Now no longer treating things, including other people's qualities and achievements, as what only he must be allowed to enjoy, he has for the first time the opportunity to see them for what they are. Consequently he may not want some of them and be happy to allow those who do to enjoy them. He will, in turn, be able to enjoy the things he has and even to add to them.

This is also true of grief, guilt and remorse. They are sometimes regarded as what arrests the flow of life. If someone grieves or feels remorse this obviously means that he cares about the person he has lost or hurt, feeling bad about being the bearer of the harm he had done him. What arrests his life is not what he feels, but what he has lost or what he has done. If he did not care his life would go on as before; but it would not have been the life we imagined, one in which love and affection for a particular person held an important place. The flow of his life would not have been arrested, but it would have been the flow of a much flatter life. This would be equally true if he were a man who did not care about cheating a stranger, telling a lie, or letting a friend down. If, on the other hand, he did care about these things but was gradually led to neglect them, then remorse, however painful, would be a return to caring for these things. It would arrest the flow of a life that has become stagnant with indifference to these values. At the end of *Crime and Punishment* Dostoyevsky shows very clearly how the arrest by remorse and repentance of his earlier schemes is a thawing out of much that was frozen in Raskolnikov's life and heart. I am suggesting that grieving and mourning for the loss of a loved person *is* something creative, in contrast with not allowing oneself to feel pain. The same is true of remorse and repentance.

On the other side of love we have put indifference, which allows selfishness to grow rampant, and hatred, which is a response to anyone who stands in the way of such selfishness. Hatred, resentment and envy, when we say of a person that he is 'eaten up' with these things, prevent gratuitous contact with the outer world and starve man's spirit. They drive a person to the pursuit of their objectives and narrow his contact to the orbit of their requirement. Of course, love too can drive a person in this way when it is possessive and jealous, and in its obsessive forms it too will come between him and the world's offerings. But what we are dealing with here are needs that stem from feelings of persecution and deprivation of the self, lack of faith in others and the inability to trust them. It is these that shape and twist the love in question, even when they become the vehicle through which love finds expression.

When love is free from such fear and anxiety, when it is purged of the needs of the self, it can be itself and bring generosity into a man's life, and thought for other people. Regard for their good can thus come to have a firm place among the sources that inspire action. It also brings a new kind of responsibility into that life, such that a man feels sympathy and concern for others, feels sorry if he has done them harm, is pained if he lets down his friends. The many aspects of the meaning of the word 'care' in our language reflects what I am trying to bring together. For to care is to look after, to nurse and to nurture. It is also the opposite of indifference in a special way: if I care for something then I shall be concerned for its well-being in such a way that anything that hurts that well-being will hurt me. Consequently I will do my utmost to provide conditions that favour its development, protect it, grieve when it is damaged, attempt to restore it. This is obviously creative if the opposite of creativeness is either destructiveness or so insulating things that nothing will change them. I have suggested that love is creative in that it exposes one's life to contact with what lies outside it so that it remains mobile and growing. It is creative in contrast with attitudes that come from hatred, greed and selfishness. These turn the spirit inwards and keep it circling around the same spot. It is creative in its power to diminish selfishness and mitigate hatred. The fact that a person's love can be selfish or destructive does not show that it does not have this power.

I think that Melanie Klein would agree with much of what I have said about the creative character of love. One of the central tenets of her thought is that creativeness is the prerogative of a life that is built around loving relationships. Its foundations are laid in very early childhood (See Klein, 1960, pp. 6–7). In her discussions of 'envy and gratitude', 'love, guilt and reparation', 'grief and depression', and the child's attempts to avoid feeling these, 'the manic defense', it is clear that she thinks of love as playing a central role in the growth of the child.

What is striking is the change of perspective from Freud to Melanie Klein. Freud considered the child's development largely from the point of view of his struggle for independence from cravings, often encouraged by his mother, which bring him in conflict with his father – a struggle which reaches its climax with the crystallization of the Oedipus complex. Melanie Klein, on the other hand, while not ignoring this, placed greater emphasis on the child's struggle with his own destructiveness and the fears stemming from it – fears both about himself and about those he depends upon and loves. Thus she speaks of 'the constant interaction of love and hate' in the life of the young child. She still speaks of 'love' and 'libido' interchangeably, almost by habit, but it is clear that she takes a wider conception of love than Freud did. This makes for a great difference in their respective treatment of the phenomena of morality.

My main criticism of Freud in this chapter has been concerned with the way he ties up love with sexuality. Failing to recognize that love can have an identity independent of sexuality, he does not appreciate the contribution of love to a relationship when it is one with sexuality, the way it transforms that sexuality. As Guntrip puts it (1949, p. 237): 'Instinct theory interprets personality and its phases of growth by sex. A truly human and personal psychology will interpret sex by the part it plays in the personal life and the process of integration.'

7

D.H. Lawrence: Sexual Love, A Vital Relationship Between Opposites

7.1 Introduction

Proust is a great novelist. His one great novel runs into many volumes. But he is also a thinker; he thinks throughout the volumes of his novel. His reflections, many of them philosophical, are an integral part of the novel. They are not an intrusion. D.H. Lawrence is a novelist of quality, he has perceptions worth considering, but he is not primarily a thinker. He is at his best when he gives himself to the story he writes and lets his perceptions speak for themselves in the story. He has, however, articulated them independently of his stories in essays and even longer works. But their expression is rather nebulous and they lack the discipline which makes a thinker a thinker.

I shall consider them, nevertheless, because he does have something to say which bears on the questions central to this book: about the kind of oneness that sex and love can have in sexual love, about the place of sex in human life, about the kind of separateness there is between human beings not only as individuals but as men and women, that is as members of the opposite sex. As such, he argues, they are attracted to each other, like the two opposite poles of a magnet, but if their attraction is to be renewed they have to retain their polar separateness.

7.2 Sexual Love and the Separateness of the Individual

In the case of what I called human separateness, as embedded in human existence, which often constitutes an obstacle for lovers, I argued there is something which needs accepting, namely the separateness of the beloved *as an individual in her own right* – accepted and, indeed, respected. In one's own case there is something which needs to be preserved, namely, one's integrity as an individual – if one is to be any good to the person one loves. The lovers can then find communion with each other, as opposed to fusion, provided there is integrity on both sides and mutual respect. But this takes emotional maturity.

D.H. Lawrence is speaking of an aspect of this separateness relating, as he sees it, to the polar opposition between the sexes. A person's sex is certainly part of the framework within which each person has to find himself and be an individual. But sex itself, Lawrence claims, in its masculine and feminine character, is impersonal. That is sex as such is instinctive; it transcends the individual. The individual yields to it and partakes of its character. Thus often having said that sexual love is a vital relationship – not the only one but nevertheless a very special one – holding lovers in a sort of union, he writes:

The individual has nothing really to do with love. That is, his individuality hasn't. Out of the deep silence of his individuality runs the stream of desire into the open … squash-blossom of the world. And the stream of desire may meet and mingle with the stream from a woman. But it is never *himself* that meets and mingles with *herself*, any more than two lakes, whose waters meet to make one river, in the distance, meet in themselves.

The two individuals stay apart, for ever and ever. But the two streams of desire … meet and at length mix their strange and alien waters

> ('Love was once a Little Boy' in *Sex, Literature and Censorship*, edited by Harry T. Moore, William Heinemann Ltd, 1955, pp. 94–5).

He says that 'love, as a relationship of unison … must mean, *to some extent*, the sinking of the individuality' (ibid., p. 82). He speaks of woman for centuries being expected to sink her individuality into that of her husband and family, and nowadays the tendency to insist that man should sink his individuality into his job, or his business first of all and only secondarily into his wife and family (ibid.).

There is much that is unclear in what is being said here. To begin with *yielding* to one's desire as an individual, as I put it earlier, is one thing *sinking* one's individuality in one's family or job is another, and *finding* one's individuality in one's job or family is yet another thing. Whether or not these expressions are clear there are certainly distinctions to be drawn. Yielding to one's sexual desire may be an expression of an ability to let go which often betokens a secure personality. I am thinking of cases where this is completely gratuitous and where there is an unsought and unexpected bonus: an enrichment of life. I feel fairly confident that this is what Lawrence has in mind and I shall return to it.

Sinking one's individuality in one's job or family, on the other hand, is allowing oneself to be taken over. This may be an expression of inner emptiness which the person in question seeks to compensate. As such it is a form of evasion – evading the work it takes to grow up and be oneself. By contrast one may speak of finding oneself in one's work or family. This is a form of *giving*. To give oneself to something one has to 'lose oneself' – that part of oneself that is self-seeking: the ego. In thus losing oneself one finds oneself, one becomes an individual. One has to be oneself in this sense in order to be able to consider others, in order to be able to give of oneself to another. Equally, and *mutatis mutandis* it is in giving oneself to someone or something that one finds oneself.

Which is it that Lawrence means when he says, 'Hate is not the opposite of love. The real opposite of love is individuality'? 'We live [he says] in the age of individuality, we call ourselves the servants of love … we [thus] enact a perpetual paradox' (p. 82). He is clearly thinking of the self, in the sense of ego, and of an ethic of self-realization which has sometimes been called a philosophy of individualism. It can very easily be confused with something which can properly be seen as a pre-requisite of love, including a love of the good, namely being an individual so that one is oneself in what one does and so that one's convictions are one's own. Though easily confused they are in reality each other's antithesis.

Even then there is a genuine conflict between the demands of *immature* love and the call to be oneself. This is the problem I discussed in earlier chapters. The lover wishes to sink his individuality in order to find union with the beloved, and the beloved too wishes him to give up his individuality so they could find oneness in their love. But this, sooner or later gives rise to a conflict between the lovers; love between two immature lovers contains the seeds of conflict. If such conflict is to be resolved both lovers have to grow up emotionally, learn to consider and respect each other and be willing to give each other a space in which they can be themselves with their own interests and convictions. Lawrence recognizes this well enough and this is the way he expresses it:

> You can't worship love and individuality in the same breath. Love is a mutual relationship, like a flow between wax and air. If either wax or air insists on getting its own way ... the flame goes out and the unison disappears. At the same time, if one yields itself up to the other entirely, there is a guttering moss. You have to balance love and individuality, and actually sacrifice a portion of each (p. 83).

This may be the case: a compromise. But it is a second best. To be an individual, to be oneself is not to be *for* oneself. To grow out of 'being for oneself' is not to give up one's individuality. A lover may be totally devoted to the person he loves, put her good and welfare first, and respect her need to be herself. This does not mean that he has to be her slave. Having interests outside of her does not mean disloyalty to her; it does not mean that his consideration of her is limited.

Let us imagine that he is working on cancer research (Rush Rhees' example – 'Wittgenstein's Lecture on Ethics: Some Developments in Wittgenstein's View on Ethics' by Rush Rhees, *Philosophical Review*, January 1965, pp. 22–3) and that this makes demands on the time he could otherwise give to her. This is part of the life in which he is himself. He may feel that if he were to give that up he could not be the man he is to her. This need not be selfishness on his part: thinking too much of himself and not enough of her. Another person in his place may be able to give it up and find something that would not conflict with the demands of his love. This depends both on him, on what he is like and where he stands, and also on her. Supposing she had an illness or physical disability that required his constant attention. He may then feel this changes everything and willingly give up his research. It is a sacrifice he makes in his love for her.

Suppose now that this is not the case and the demands she makes on him are the demands of an immature love which sees his work as in competition and rivalry with her. In other words, in her jealousy she is unable to consider him, that in her inner insecurity she can only think of herself – or rather that she thinks more of herself than him. He may understand all this and feel all the more compassion for her on that account. But he may equally clearly see that it would not help her if he were to cede to her demands.

There is no *general* answer to such situations. Each couple has to work out their own answer. In some cases the relationship breaks up; in others the conflict is contained in becoming a way of life in which each party finds some psychological food; in yet others a compromise is reached with which each is able to live. These are all second-best solutions measured by the ideals of a mature love. But in many cases nothing better may be possible.

Lawrence goes further: 'perfect love is an absurdity'. As for 'absolute intimacy' he finds it 'loathsome – especially the married sort'. 'It is a mistake [he says] and ends in disaster' (p. 96). He is thinking of what I called the search for union, which I contrasted with communion in which the lovers accept and respect their separateness. To achieve such communion, I argued, the lovers must grow in maturity – both of them – and their love for one another change in character. This is the ideal which in many cases may be unrealizeable – I would say in most cases. Simone Weil goes as far as to speak of the realization of this ideal as a miracle: 'it is made possible [she says] by the miraculous intervention of the supernatural' (*Waiting on God*, p. 156). Here she is thinking of friendship.

'Friendship [she writes] is a miracle by which a person consents to view from a certain distance, and without coming any nearer, the very being who is necessary to him as food' (p. 157). But she too stresses that it must be on both sides: 'A certain reciprocity is essential in friendship. If all good will is entirely lacking on one of the two sides the other should suppress his own affection, out of respect for the free consent which he should not desire to force' (p. 157).

Lawrence is not thinking of friendship but of sexual love and he does not think of the two as compatible. 'Affinity of mind and personality [he writes] is an excellent basis of friendship between the sexes, but a disastrous basis for marriage' (p. 254). Sexual love, he argues, is based on what he calls 'blood-sympathy' and this has its source in our 'lower self', our 'night-time self', not in our higher, spiritual self (see *Fantasia of the Unconscious*, Ch. 15, Penguin Books, 1977).

I spoke of the separateness of human beings as individuals. Lawrence speaks of the 'polarity of the sexes'; they attract each other because they are 'opposite poles'. As such there is a 'gulf' between the sexes. The gulf is between two different modes of existence which, Lawrence believes, is based on their biology. Culture can, to some extent, eliminate the differences between the modes of existence of men and women, make them more alike, for instance, in the name of the equality of the sexes, but to the detriment of sexual passion. This at any rate is Lawrence's view. The differences which make for the gulf are essential to the attraction between the sexes and to the passion it fuels. In their different modes of existence men and women are alien to each other, it is *as such* that they complement and enrich each other. But it is as such too that their relation *excludes* the kind of intimacy there can be between friends. If, therefore, the lovers, the man and the woman, are to be themselves – himself and herself – in their sexuality, they must stand apart, be 'other' to each other.

> It is a pity of pities [he writes] that women have learned to think like men .... Our education goes on and on, and on and on, making the sexes alike, destroying the original individuality of the blood, to substitute for it this dreary individuality of the ego, the Number One (p. 97).

Here the blood is being contrasted with the ego which Lawrence at times confuses with individuality as such – the identity of a human being as an individual. But normally Lawrence contrasts what he calls 'the blood' with 'the mind' of which he speaks with some contempt. The mind, as Lawrence speaks of it, is that part of us which is 'civilized', 'superficial', and, indeed, 'artificial'. It is the defensive part of us. It is an organ of the ego; used to safeguard and promote its interests.

Here I hear strong echoes from Freud's conception of the division between the ego and the id, where the id is the source of the energy of life, of the vitality of human beings, and the ego having no energy of its own, has to tap the energy of the id if it is to move anything in life – like a rider and his mount, the horse. Thus Lawrence: 'The night-self is the very basis of the dynamic self. The blood-consciousness is the very source and origin of us' (*Fantasia of the Unconscious*, pp. 182–3). If we turn away from it, in what Freud calls 'repression', we become the puppets of 'civilization', 'the grey cold lizards of the vulgar ego' (Lawrence, 1955, p. 83). Thus in Lawrence's story *St Mawr*, Lou Witt, whose marriage to Rico (a flirt and play-boy, destined to become Sir Henry, a pillar of civilization) has become 'more like a friendship ... without sex', is contrasting her husband with the horse St Mawr who is yet to throw him off his back:

> At the middle of his eyes was a central powerlessness that left him anxious. It used to touch her to pity, that central look of power-lessness in him. But now, since she had seen the full, dark, pas-sionate blaze of power and of different life in the eyes of the thwarted horse, the anxious powerlessness of the man drove her mad. Rico was so handsome, and he was so self-controlled, he had a gallant sort of kindness and a real worldly shrewdness. One had to admire him: at least *she* had to.
>
> But after all, and after all, it was a bluff, an attitude. He kept it all working in himself, deliberately. It was an attitude. She read psychologists who said that everything was an attitude. Even the best of everything. But now she realized that, with men and women, everything is an attitude only when something else is lacking. Something is lacking and they are thrown back on their own devices. That black fiery flow in the eyes of the horse was not 'attitude'. It was something much more terrifying and real, the only thing that was real. Gushing from the darkness in menace and question, and blazing out in the splendid body of the horse
>
> (*The Tales of D.H. Lawrence*, William Heinemann Ltd, 1948, pp. 566–7).

'With men and women, everything is an attitude only when something else is lacking.' An attitude is something that is put on by what Lawrence calls the mind. It is put on when something is lacking: what Lawrence calls the life of 'the dynamic self'. That is lacking when we are mere products of civilization, of the culture which comes to own us. But, if I may add to this, we do not have to reject civilization so as to avoid being 'mere products of it'; we can *find* ourselves in the culture which belongs to civilization. Indeed, we can *only* find ourselves there; and then what we acquire becomes something we own, it stops being an 'attitude', something we put on or copy, a role we play. The dynamic self may derive its sustenance from 'the blood'; but the blood in human beings is kneaded with human culture.

Let us return to the point where we started: the conflict between love and individuality as Lawrence sees it. I had argued that human individuality lies at the basis of human separateness but that human separateness does not have to separate lovers or friends. Whether or not it separates them depends, paradoxically, on whether or not is it accepted and respected. In contrast with Lawrence I hold that individuality is not the opposite or enemy of love, and that a person's love is real to the extent that he is *himself* in it – not a mere copy or product. But I agree with Lawrence that in sexual love – as in other forms of love too – we have to give up ourselves: the ego in us. We have to (i) yield before the call of sexual passion and *also* (ii) give ourselves to the consideration of the other. But, as I asked earlier, can we do these two things at the same time? Is there a contradiction at the heart of sexual love? I shall return to Lawrence's answer to this question in the following section. But before I do so, let me emphasize that my conception of what *separates* lovers and Lawrence's conception of it are not the same. In my view what separates lovers is their inability to accept *human separateness*. The obstacle thus is the craving for union which belongs to their immaturity and which is part of their immature love for each other.

For Lawrence the core of the problem lies elsewhere, in the polarity of sexuality and the gulf it creates between the sexes. This polarity is the basis of the sexual attraction that lies at the heart of sexual love and at the same time it is the source of the conflict and the battle between the sexes. So does Lawrence think that communion between the lover and the beloved is possible?

7.3 Polarity of the Sexes: How is Communion Possible in Sexual Love?

As we saw Lawrence thinks that as far as sexuality is concerned there are two modes of being, male and female, masculine and feminine, which men and women possess in various degrees of purity. These are the two polarities of sexuality. To the degree in which individual men and women possess them they are sexually attractive to each other; they attract each other like the North and South poles of a magnet. These polarities are inherent to sex and are independent of the culture to which men and women belong. But while they make men and women attractive to each other, at the same time they make them 'incommensurable' (Lawrence 1955, p. 96). This incommensurability lies at the core of their attractiveness to each other; sexual attraction is the attraction of opposites. 'We are two,' he writes, 'isolated like gems in our unthinkable otherness' (p. 61).

What then are the characteristics of maleness and femaleness in their purity? How does Lawrence think they differ from each other? Very briefly, where maleness is assertive, femaleness is receptive. A woman in her femaleness is earthy, men in their masculinity carry a purpose outside love and the family; they are more receptive to the interests of the wider world – the day-time world as Lawrence sometimes calls it. A woman in her femaleness is more at home in the world of feeling, she is intuitive and generally her talents lie in the artistic direction. A man, by contrast, in his masculinity is a thinker, more inclined to trust reason than intuition, and his creative talents lie in the forms of creativity where the employment of reason is in the fore. A woman in love, in her femaleness, is tender, enticing, enveloping, where a man, in his maleness, is a 'go-getter'. Where the woman is patient a man is prone to be active and interventionist.

It is in these characteristics, Lawrence believes, that men and women are incommensurable. Since they attract and need each other in their 'otherness', this otherness should be kept pure, not diluted or denied (Lawrence, 1977, p. 188). But what sort of communion could there be across this gulf between the opposite sexes? The polar opposition between them is bound to create conflict: how is such conflict to be resolved and harmony to be established? As I understand it Lawrence does not believe that harmony ought to be established:

> The moment you put young Tom in one scale, and young Kate in the other, why, not God Himself has succeeded as yet in striking a nice level balance. Probably doesn't intend to, ever.

> Probably it is one of the things that are nearly possible, yet absolutely impossible. Still, a miss is better than a mile
> (Lawrence, 1955, p. 83).

We have seen that he finds intimacy between the sexes loathsome, especially in marriage. He believes that men and women being incommensurable intimacy would end in disaster.

> It is far more important to keep them distinct than to join them. If they are to join, they will join in the third land where the two streams of desire meet (p. 96).

He thinks that there can be something he calls 'correspondence of blood' or 'conjugation of the blood' between a man and a woman and that this is what is important. It does not exclude conflict, but what it brings is preferable to intimacy. He speaks of the 'duality' of sexual love: it has two phases between which it alternates. What the lovers find in their relationship is not stable; it is constantly changing, in motion:

> The coming together depends on the going apart... the flow depends upon the ebb. ... Because love is strictly a travelling 'it is better to travel than to arrive' (p. 55).

Lawrence says that love has a tide and an ebb:

> It is the melting into pure communion, and it is the friction of sheer sensuality, both. In pure communion I become whole in love. And in pure, fierce passion of sensuality I am burned into essentiality ... I become my single self, inviolable and unique. ... In the fire of extreme sensual love ... I am destroyed and reduced to her essential otherness. ... It is only fire that will purify us into singleness, fuse us from the chaos into our own unique gem-like separateness of being (pp. 59–60).

He calls this 'the wholeness of love'. When love is 'all gentle, the merging into oneness' it is 'half love, what is called sacred love'. I shall return to this in the following section.

Thus Lawrence's view is that sexual love, when it is whole, accommodates conflict: conflict between the individual's need to remain an individual and his love's demand to give himself to the beloved, conflict between the polarity of the sexes, the lovers' need to preserve this polarity, to remain true to their distinct otherness on the one hand, and to 'come together... unite in a oneness of joy and praise... in pure communion'. To remain true to one's sex is, of course, part of the integrity of a person as an individual since a person's sexuality is part of the framework in or background against which he has to find himself, be an individual. Hence there are not two conflicts here, but one with different dimensions to it. For Lawrence thus the constant coming together and separation of the lovers is a distinctive part of sexual love, the affective counterpart of coitus in which physical contact is short-lived and constantly renewed. But the separation is often not achieved without battle.

The lovers have each to learn to accept it out of respect for the other. To do so there must be something else in their life – in the life of each – something into which they separate themselves. Otherwise they would not be able to renew and sustain their love, they would not have something in which to renew themselves and bring something new into their love, give something new to the loved one. Without it the meaning would go out of their lives. And if only *one* had it, this would sour the relationship, it would lead to jealousy on the part of the person who did not have it. *Both* must have it.

In this connection Lawrence says many things which would be characterized as 'sexist', and so characterized with justification. But excise the most extreme parts of it, and the gist of what he says is this. Man cannot live for sex alone and cannot sustain sexual love on the basis of sex on its own. He has to have a life outside in which he is himself so that he can be himself in his love-life – e.g. as a husband. A woman can be herself as a mother and as a wife: there is life enough there for her to be herself – an affective life in which she gives herself to the home she makes and all that she takes care of there. Here Lawrence sees a difference between the sexes which goes beyond culture, a difference rooted in biological, animal life. There may be a grain of truth here, but still much that can be questioned.

He speaks of the need in man for new collective activity, his work, in which he can both find comradeship and exercise his powers of creativity. This 'new circuit of passion between comrades and co-workers', he says, is not sex. He describes it as 'a unison in spirit, in understanding, and a pure commingling in one great work – a mingling of the individual passion in one great *purpose*'. He describes it as 'a grand consummation for men', 'a great motion in the opposite direction' from sex (1977, pp. 108–9). He says, 'when man loses his deep sense of purposive, creative activity, he feels lost, and is lost' (p. 109). Here Tolstoy's depiction of Vronsky in Italy in *Anna Karenina* is a good example of what Lawrence has in mind.

Now it is true that men need to believe in something and need work to be creative in, something to give themselves to, to care for, in order to be themselves and lead a meaningful life. But I would say that this is equally true for women. Work, caring, creativity and contact with the realities in the life which belongs to one's culture can be found in many different contexts. Lawrence was speaking very much out of the class and ethos of his time. It is true that women can exercise their creativity in raising a family. But that is a relatively limited period of life and though within it a woman can find a whole world in which she finds sustenance and growth, she can also be stifled by it. Just as a man can become stifled by his work.

What I take from Lawrence here and regard as true is that neither men nor women can live by sex alone, and need (in the sense in which Simone Weil speaks of 'the needs of the soul') to believe in something, to be creative and (this is something I add, something I got from Simone Weil) contact with reality – not reality with a capital R, but the realities that belong to the life in which one makes one's own life. Confined to a quest for pleasure, sex not only gets detached from love but also degenerates. 'Sex as an end in itself,' writes Lawrence, 'is a disaster: a vice.' He then adds, 'an ideal purpose which has no roots in the deep sea of passionate sex is a greater disaster still' (Lawrence, 1977, p. 187). The latter claim is a concession to Freud. For to say that both must be present in a meaningful life is one thing, to say that an ideal purpose must have its roots in passionate sex is another thing.

7.4 Profane and Spiritual Love: Are they Compatible?

I raised the question earlier whether a person can yield to the call of sexual passion and *also* give himself to a consideration of the other. I considered this question in an earlier chapter: can care and respect for another be reconciled with sexual desire? To put it in Simone Weil's language: can one 'consent to view from a certain distance' the person one desires sexually? In other words, can sexuality and spirituality be reconciled? I want now to consider Lawrence's answer.

As we have seen he holds that in its 'wholeness' sexual love is 'dual': 'it is the melting into pure communion, and it is the friction of sheer sensuality, both'. But not both at the same time.

> Sacred love is selfless, seeking not its own. The lover serves his beloved and seeks perfect communion of oneness with her. But whole love between man and woman is sacred and profane together. Profane love seeks its own. I seek my own in the beloved, I wrestle with her to wrest it from her ... I am in the

beloved also, and she is in me .... Therefore I will gather my own from the beloved, she shall single herself out in utter contradiction from me (1995, p. 59).

Lawrence's view, we have seen, is that sexual love, when it is whole, full blooded, incorporates both by accommodating conflict.

Where there is only desire we have lust, not love. But where there is no desire Lawrence holds that we have only 'half love' (p. 60). And when we are capable only of half-love our life becomes grey: 'if we lose desire out of our life [sexual desire] we become empty vessels' (1955, p. 94). So he urges: 'Be Thyself! Be Desirous!' (p. 100).

We are reminded of Freud's conception of sex as having two 'currents': sensuality and affection. He holds that when sensuality is missing or repressed love is lame. Freud, of course, assumes that all forms of love are in reality sexual in character. We have seen that Lawrence does not agree. There is also, he writes, 'a new circuit of passion between comrades and co-workers' which 'is not sex' (1977, p. 199). He refers to it as 'purpose' and 'belief'. He further disagrees: 'Freud is wrong in attributing a sexual motive to all human activity' (p. 111). Lawrence is wrong about Freud here: he held 'a dualist theory of instincts', even though Freud's dualities were not the same as Lawrence's: sex and purpose.

Still Lawrence agreed with Freud about the importance of sex in human life. Without it we are 'empty vessels'. 'Assert *purposiveness* as the one supreme and pure activity of life, and you drift into barren sterility' (p. 111). What about spirituality which has self-denial at its core? I compared Lawrence's dual conception of whole sexual love as being both sacred and therefore selfless and profane with Freud's conception of sexual love as having two currents: sensuality and affection. Let me make it clear that affection and selfless or sacred love are not the same. Furthermore Freud regards his two currents as capable of 'fusing' together whereas Lawrence sees the two sides of sexual love as capable of co-existence in conflict. As for self-denial on its own, he believes it to be castrating and therefore deadly, as Freud does too. This, as we shall see, is the exact opposite of Kierkegaard's view – and the question 'who is right?' is at least partly a value-question, that is how one answers it depends on where one stands morally as a person.

There is nevertheless a question as to how far self-denial is compatible with the sexual element in sexual love. Lawrence is right,

I think, in seeing them as in conflict when they co-exist in full-blooded sexual love. In extreme cases he sees two possibilities:

> Not all love between man and woman is whole. It may be all gentle, the merging into oneness, like St Francis and St Clare, or Mary of Bethany and Jesus. There may be no separateness discovered, no singleness won, no unique otherness admitted. This is a half-love, what is called sacred love. And this is the love which knows the purest happiness. On the other hand, the love may be all a lovely battle of sensual gratification, the beautiful but deadly counterposing of male against female, as Tristan and Isolde. ... This is the profane love that ends in flamboyant and lacerating tragedy when the two which are so singled out are torn finally apart by death. But if profane love ends in piercing tragedy, nonetheless the sacred love ends in a poignant yearning and exquisite submissive grief. St Francis dies and leaves St Clare to her pure sorrow (1955, p. 60).

He concludes: 'There must be two in one, always two in one – the sweet love of communion and the fierce, proud love of sensual fulfilment; both together in one love' (p. 61). Otherwise we have either a 'half-love' or a 'love unto death'.

But if there is to be one, Lawrence prefers a great passion to the purest happiness of St Francis' love. In *Fantasia of the Unconscious* he writes: 'Death is the only pure, beautiful conclusion of a great passion. Lovers, pure lovers should say "Let it be so"' (1977, p. 194). This is where Lawrence stands. 'Better Anna Karenina and Vronsky [he adds] a thousand times, than Natasha and that porpoise of a Pierre. ... Better Vronsky than Tolstoy himself. Better Vronsky's final statement: "As a soldier I am still some good. As a man I am a ruin" – better than Tolstoy and Tolstoyism and that beastly peasant blouse the old man wore.'

This is in chime with what he says about 'brotherly love':

> However much I may be the microcosm, the exemplar of brotherly love, there is in me this necessity to separate and distinguish myself into gem-like singleness distinct and apart from all the rest, proud as a lion, isolated as a star. This is a necessity within me. And if this necessity is unfulfilled, it becomes stronger and stronger and it becomes dominant.

Then I shall hate the self that I am ... this microcosm that I have become, this epitome of mankind. I shall hate myself with madness the more I persist in adhering to my achieved self of brotherly love ... [And] then I shall hate my neighbour as I hate myself. And then, woe betide my neighbour and me (1955, p. 61).

I take this to be an honest confession of where Lawrence stands as a man, an individual, with his values. As I understand it he is not prepared to go the whole way, to lose himself and to find his soul. He believes that would make him half a man.

There must be brotherly love [he writes], a wholeness of humanity. But there must also be pure, separate individuality, separate and proud as a lion or a hawk. There must be both. In the duality lies fulfilment. Man must act in concert with man, creatively and happily. This is greater happiness. But man must also act separately and distinctly, apart from every other man – moving for himself without reference to his neighbour. These two movements are opposite, yet they do not negate each other. If we understand, then we balance perfectly between the two motions (p. 62).

However, it is not clear whether Lawrence is speaking here of what he calls 'the great unison of mankind in some passionate *purpose*' or of spirituality, of brotherly love in the sense of 'love of one's neighbour', or of the camaraderie between co-workers. I doubt that Lawrence himself is clear about this. But brotherly love and camaraderie are not the same thing; the latter is at best a worldly counterpart of the former.

7.5   Summing Up: Sex, Love and Beyond

I criticized Lawrence as a thinker: his thinking is nebulous, he is not clear about certain distinctions. On the other hand, he is sensitive to some of the same philosophical questions I raised in earlier chapters and he has something to say – something distinctive and interesting. With his concept of the polarity of sexuality he brings something new to our discussion of human separateness and the way love struggles against it.

I had concentrated on our separateness as individuals – that is insofar as we *are* individuals and maintain our individuality.

Lawrence sees our distinctiveness in our sexuality, as male or female, as also separating us, as lovers, in creating a gulf between us. This separateness between or 'incommensurability' of the sexes, he argues, is neither personal nor cultural. It constitutes a gulf between lovers insofar as they remain individuals – maintain their integrity as individuals.

His view is, we have seen, that we cannot overcome this gulf as individuals and should not want to do so: if a man and a woman who love each other as man and woman are to join 'they will join in the third land where the two streams of desire meet.' He calls this 'conjugation of the blood' and contrasts it with 'an affinity of mind and personality'. A man and a woman can be friends, of course, he holds, but not as man and woman.

> Women and men are dynamically different, in everything. … The *apparent* mutual understanding, in companionship, between a man and a woman is always an illusion, and always breaks down in the end (1977, p. 188).

Lawrence holds that when the love between a man and a woman is whole it is *dual*: pure communion and sheer sensuality. In communion lovers yield their individuality, but in sensuality they become their single selves. Hence in their relationship each has to learn 'to balance love [and hence the desire for communion] and individuality, and actually sacrifice a portion of each' (1955, p. 83). But these are in conflict and not reconcilable. Therefore insofar as individuality has to be reclaimed conflict between lovers is inevitable. To try to avoid it is to quell the passion of love. As he puts it:

> Instead of this leprous forbearance which we are taught to practise in our intimate relationships, there should be the most intense open antagonism (pp. 189–90).

Lawrence sees this antagonism as directed to something that cannot be changed. But there is no question for him of making peace with it.

I do not agree with Lawrence in his claim that individuality is the opposite or enemy of love. For a person's love is real to the extent that he is himself in it – not a mere copy or product. What is true is that individuality is an enemy of *immature* love. Still I agree with

Lawrence that a person in love has to *yield* before the call of sexual passion. However, he has to do so as an individual. It is true that he has *also* to be able to give himself to the consideration of the other. Both are a measure of his love. But there is a question as to whether anyone can do both these things at the same time: is there a contradiction at the heart of sexual love? Lawrence's answer is that there is, although the contradictory elements can co-exist in conflict, but a conflict in which the lover and the loved one are renewed and enriched.

Lawrence further argues, rightly, that human beings cannot live for sex alone, and that where sex becomes an end in itself it becomes a vice. Sex on its own cannot sustain sexual love. There is more in life than sex and this wider life enables the lovers to sustain their love. This wider life is essential for the lovers to find themselves, for it is in giving themselves to what they find there that they come to themselves and then, in turn, can give themselves to each other. I have put this in my own words; but I think that it sums up the gist of what Lawrence says here. Sex as an end in itself ends up by becoming a vehicle for and an expression of the ego. It comes to exclude love – the antithesis of the ego – and then the sexual partner becomes a means to the lover's pleasure and the gratification of his ego. Furthermore in the service of pleasure it is perverted and becomes a vice.

There are two separate points here; one about sex as an end in itself and the other one about a sexual love that segregates the lovers from the rest of life. Lawrence puts this in relation to men:

> If the man has no purpose for his days, then the woman alone remains the goal of her mights: the great sex goal. And this goal is no goal, but always cries for the something beyond ... (1977, p. 194).

But I don't see that this observation does not apply equally to women.

In connection with the first point he contrasts that which leads to promiscuity with what makes for 'real marriage', namely what he calls 'correspondence of the blood'.

> Don Juan was only Don Juan because he *had* no real desire. He had broken his own integrity. ... No stream of desire, with a course of its own, flowed from him. He was a marsh in himself. He ... desired no woman, so he ran after every one of them, with

an itch instead of a steady flame. ... It is sex-in-the-head, no real desire, which leads to profligacy or squalid promiscuity.

By sex-in-the-head, I think, he means sexual desire that has its source in psychological need. It is not fed by genuine attraction. Psychological need is always *personal*. By contrast, Lawrence writes, 'love is neither absolute nor personal. ... It is no more than the stream of clear and unmuddied, subtle desire which flows from person to person.' 'This subtle streaming of desire [he adds] is beyond the control of the ego' (1955, p. 94).

Lawrence has many criticisms of post-Freudian, commercially orientated modern culture:

Sex is a thing you don't have [these days] except to be naughty with. Apart from naughtiness, that is, apart from infidelity and fornication, sex doesn't exist. ... Sex is almost non-existent, apart from the counterfeit forms of prostitution and shallow fornication. And marriage is empty, hollow (ibid., pp. 244–5).

Again:

Nowadays a lady's chemise won't save her face. In or out of her chemise doesn't make much difference to the modern woman. She's a finished-off ego, an assertive conscious entity, cut off like a doll from any mystery. And her nudity is about as interesting as a doll's ...

The same with the men. No matter how they pull their shirts off they never arrive at their own nakedness. They have none. They can only be undressed. Naked they cannot be (ibid., p. 102).

By 'naked they cannot be' he means that all there is to them is the ego, the personal, that in which their psychological needs are rooted. Assertion comes from the ego. Lawrence contrasts it with what is generous, spontaneous, gratuitous – what flows like a stream from its source.

One last point, which opens up to some of the later chapters of this book where I turn to spiritual love. Lawrence calls it 'sacred love' and admits it as part of sexual and other forms of love. On its own, however, he sees it as incomplete. He also finds it to be in irreconcilable conflict with profane love – referred to as 'natural loves' later on in this book. We shall see that C.S. Lewis in *The Four Loves* takes the opposite view. It is profane or natural loves that he finds incomplete – 'not enough'. But he does not think that spiritual love is 'in rivalry' with them. It *transforms* them.

This notion of the transformation of our natural loves, indeed of sexual love, is alien to Lawrence. He thinks of them as co-existing in sexual love, when it is whole, in conflict, with the lover in balance between them. He is uncompromising on the sensual element of sexual love: as uncompromising on keeping it pure as Kierkegaard is on keeping the spiritual element pure so that it can cauterize the sensual element.

In this three-sided conflict my own thinking is most at home with C.S. Lewis'. I find a close affinity between his conception of the transformation of our natural loves and the notion of their changing into mature forms of love as the person, the lover, becomes more mature – learns to consider others and to keep his feet on the ground, remaining imaginative without taking refuge in phantasy.

8

Erich Fromm on 'Love as an Art'

8.1 Introduction

Erich Fromm is a thinker and psychoanalytic writer who has both taken something from Freud and criticized him and revised Freud's views of emotional development, of morality and religion, and of man's relation to society. He has rejected Freud's biological orientation and replaced it with what one may call an 'existential' one. He has also criticized recent trends and developments in Western society and focused on the resulting alienation of the individual in such a society. He has argued that the stages of development in the child which Freud distinguished are in reality products of the culture and society in which the child develops. They are sociologically conditioned, not biologically as Freud had claimed.

I have discussed sympathetically but critically his revisions, in his book *Man for Himself*, of Freud's views of morality (Dilman 1997). I argued that his 'humanistic ethics' is a morality of love marred by the stress he puts on 'self-realization' as a value. His discussions of moral conscience and the individual's relation to his morality are an advance on Freud's conception of the place of morality in human life.

The same is equally true of his discussions of love and sex in his book *The Art of Loving*. His choice of the title is somewhat unfortunate as it makes it sound as if love – 'loving' – is something we do deliberately, a practice like 'painting': 'the art of painting'. And though he compares the two, it becomes clear as we read on that this is not what he wants to say.

The greater part of the book is concerned with developing what he calls a 'theory' of love and he discusses different forms of love within its framework. He has many good things to say about these different forms of love. He then discusses what, by contrast, he calls the 'practice' of love. He compares it with the practice of other arts and again has some good things to say when he speaks about the

117

personal qualities which are of specific significance for the ability to love. These, he argues, are qualities to which we come or fail to come in the course of our personal development. They are qualities we attain in our emotional maturity and so he describes the love we become capable of in our attainment of them as 'mature love'. Such love is characterized by these qualities. To come to such qualities takes time and learning – what I would call 'emotional learning' – and discipline. That is what lies behind his conception of love as an art.

8.2   Love and Human Existence

Fromm argues, rightly, that human existence differs radically from animal existence and that such existence is *inherently* problematic. That is his very mode of existence – human existence – poses a problem for man: an existential problem, the problem of human existence, of our inevitable existence as human beings.

What characterizes man's existence is 'the fact that he has emerged from the animal kingdom, from instinctive adaptation' (p. 14). That is, unlike animals, he does not live in the natural world, but in a world shaped by human culture and shot through by myriad forms of significance. The things and situations he meets are in their very identity defined by these forms of significance. In his responses to them he has to use his own individual assessment and judgement. He cannot rely on instincts with which he is endowed by virtue of belonging to any species – the way animals do when they hunt for food, and raise their young. They have to make choices, take decisions, judge things for themselves. They carry the responsibility of their choices and actions, and if and when things go wrong they have only themselves to blame. Even if they have followed someone else's advice, it was up to them whether or not to accept it, up to them to weigh its soundness or wisdom. Fromm expresses this by saying that 'man can only go forward by developing his reason' (p. 14) – that is by relying on his own judgement and resources.

In this he is a separate centre: he has to think and act for himself and bears a responsibility for what he does – unlike animals whose actions are determined by common instinct. As Fromm puts it:

This awareness of himself as a separate entity, the awareness of his own short life span, of the fact that without his will he is born and against his will he dies, that he will die before those whom he loves, or they before him, the awareness of his aloneness and separateness, of his helplessness before the forces of nature and of society, all this makes his separate, disunited existence an unbearable prison (pp. 14–15).

All this has been expressed at great length by such existentialist thinkers as Heidegger and Sartre (see Dilman 1993). They have spoken of the anguish to which our existential situation gives rise. Fromm speaks of 'intense anxiety': 'separateness is the source of intense anxiety' (p. 15).

Thus animals are one with nature, as we, human beings, are not. Likewise, Fromm points out, the foetus is one with the pregnant mother. This is a symbiotic union and is biological in character (p. 22). This symbiotic union continues during infancy, after birth, on a psychological plane. But just as birth severs the umbilical chord, similarly in the course of his growth he is weaned from this psychological symbiosis. It is then that he is put on the path of growth towards individual autonomy and responsibility. It is then that his final transcendence of nature takes place and he has to find himself in his separate existence.

Fromm mentions the Biblical story of Adam and Eve (p. 15) and the myth spun by Aristophanes in Plato's *Symposium* (p. 33) as giving expression to our existential predicament. But what he says about the Biblical story is very brief and hardly enlightening. I have discussed both elsewhere in this same connection (see Dilman, 1993, Ch. 6, sec. 4, and Dilman, 1987, Ch. 7, sec. 1).

Sartre has argued that the responsibility conferred on us by our freedom is a burden which is the source of our existential anguish and that we attempt to evade it in bad faith (see Dilman, 1993, Ch. 8, sec. 5). Fromm likewise argues that the more we emerge from our 'primary bonds' 'the more intense becomes the need to find new ways of escaping separateness' (p. 17). The 'primary bonds' are the oneness with nature which the human race felt in its infancy, the infancy of its cultural development, and the oneness which the human infant feels with his mother before the process of his psychological weaning.

Man – of all ages and cultures – is confronted with the solution of one and the same question; the question of how to overcome separateness, how to achieve union, how to transcend his own individual life and find at-onement.... The question is the same, for it springs from the same ground: the human situation, the conditions of human existence. ... The answer varies ... [but] one discovers that there is only a limited number of answers (p. 16).

He mentions four types of 'solution': (i) an orgiastic solution such as primitive rituals, alcoholism, drugs and sex in which the individual person escapes from his separate identity (pp. 17–18), (ii) the conformity in which he hides from his separateness and dissolves into the herd: 'the union of herd conformity' (pp. 18–21). These are forms of 'escape' or evasion and what Sartre would call 'bad faith'. (iii) 'A third way of attaining union with nature lies in *creative activity*, be that of the artist, or of the artisan. In any kind of creative work the creating person unites himself with his material, which represents the world outside of himself'; 'man unites himself with the world in the process of creation' (pp. 21–22). What Fromm means, in my language, is that the creative artist or artisan puts himself into his work and finds himself in the process of creation. In such work he is concerned with something outside himself and through it makes contact with it. Furthermore, by way of a bonus, he also makes contact with those who appreciate his work – the artist with those who view it, the concert pianist with his audience: he is together with them, he shares what he expresses and what he feels with them; he is not alone.

Commenting on these three, Fromm writes:

The unity achieved in productive work is not interpersonal; the unity achieved in orgiastic fusion is transitory [the sexual act without love never bridges the gap between two human beings, except momentarily – p. 18]; the unity achieved by conformity is only pseudo-unity. Hence they are only partial answers to the problem of existence. The full answer lies in the achievement of interpersonal union, of fusion with another person in *love* (p. 22).

Here I should like to draw attention to Gabriel Marcel's discussion of the way we emerge from our 'original togetherness' with our mother in our very early childhood – 'the stage of community' as he calls it – pass through a 'stage of communication' where in our interaction with others we develop an independent identity and guard it jealously, constantly fighting for independence. 'That passage back to togetherness ... is accomplished in *communion*.' But this is not a regression to the 'original togetherness' from which we emerge. It is as separate individuals that we give ourselves to each other in friendship or love. But where we refuse to surrender to communion, because we do not trust the other not to take advantage of us or because we do not trust ourselves not to regress, we shall 'dwell in a Sartrean universe where the other is purely and simply the other' (see Dilman, 1993, Ch. 8, sec. 3). What Marcel calls 'communion' is what Fromm has in mind when he talks of 'mature love'.

Here Fromm wavers: shall we call it simply love? Is the expression 'mature love' a pleonasm? He writes: 'This desire for interpersonal fusion is the most powerful striving in man. It is the most fundamental passion, it is the force which keeps the human race together, the clan, the family, society' (p. 22). It has been pointed out by many thinkers, among them the philosopher John Anderson, that common work too holds people together and that it has to be distinguished from love and from friendship. I mention this in passing as something that does not occur to Fromm. He goes on: 'Yet, if we call the achievement of interpersonal union "love", we find ourselves in serious difficulty. Fusion can be achieved in different ways... . Should they all be called love? Or should we reserve the word "love" only for a specific kind of union ... ? ... Do we refer to love as the mature answer to the problem of existence, or do we speak of those immature forms of love which may be called *symbiotic union*?' (p. 22). He goes on to say that he resolves to 'call love only the former'.

This, however, will not do – contrast with Balint. Are immature forms of love not love then? Are there not impure, immature forms of love? Kierkegaard, for instance, in *Purity of Heart* talks of impure forms of love of the good. What is impure about them can only be understood with reference to our ideal of purity for love of the good. Similarly for immature forms of love; it is as forms of love that they are immature. Fromm later talks of 'forms of pseudo-love' (p. 72). But pseudo-love is not love; it is false love; it pretends to be love without being love at all – for instance a pop-star fan's love of the pop-star. I shall not dwell on this point any further. Clearly Fromm places different instances of love on a scale of maturity: there are different degrees of maturity and immaturity.

I want to move to a different point of criticism in this connection. We have seen that Fromm speaks of love as an answer or solution to an existential problem: how to overcome separateness, how to achieve union, how to transcend one's own individual life and find oneness. 'The basis of our need to love [he says] lies in the experience of separateness and the resulting need to overcome the anxiety of separateness by the experience of union' (p. 56). It is not clear whether when Fromm speaks of love as a solution to our existential problem he means this in the sense that human beings in their evolution from animal life have developed love – in other words 'love as a product of evolution'. If so, then what he says has its own interest' but no more. If he means it as a psychological answer it will not do; it would constitute what I call 'psychologism' where what is authentic is reduced to inauthentic forms of it.

Love is not sought as a solution to a problem. The question, 'why do human beings love, why is there love among human beings?' comes from confusion. Human beings love, just as they speak and think. This is something to note, to wonder at. We can ask, what makes the existence of love among human beings possible, what this possibility presupposes. That is an interesting question and reflection on it can throw light on what we mean by love. It is a philosophical, conceptual question. As for the question, 'why did Romeo love Juliet?', the answer is 'for no reason' if the love is authentic. Or taken a different way, we can answer: because they lived in close proximity, saw each other, they appealed to one another, etc. – something along these lines. If the answer in an actual instance were something like, 'because he was very lonely; he wanted a remedy to his loneliness', then we would suspect that his love was not genuine, not authentic. The situation would be similar in the case of someone who is good in order to have his fellow men's approval – *pace* Kierkegaard.

What has psychology to contribute to our understanding of love? What has psychology to contribute to our understanding morality and moral behaviour? These questions I believe to be parallel. So I should like to quote two long passages in which I discuss the latter question.

A. … there cannot be a psychological answer to the question 'what makes him good?' or 'why does he love goodness?' For if one thinks – as Freud did – that goodness is something towards which a person's psychology disposes him then one downgrades it …. What makes a person good is the goodness in him or the goodness to which he comes in his development as an individual. What makes him good is what the goodness that finds expression in his life and actions means to him. This is another way of saying that his goodness, when it is genuine, can have no psychological explanation. One may even say that it is the way that love, the concern and compassion he feels for others work in his life. It is this that makes him good – or this is what constitutes his goodness. But then there is no question as to what makes him compassionate or what gives him a loving nature. At most ... we can say *how* he has come to it.

It still remains true, however, that to come to it a man must overcome certain psychological barriers in himself. A convincing portrait of goodness in a person needs to be psychologically convincing. And this is something any great novelist knows. ... A convincing portrait of goodness would have to be in terms of a psychology that leaves the person open to goodness, one that does not stand in the way of goodness engaging him at the deepest level ... . The freedom which his psychology thus allows him does not, of course, explain his goodness. Otherwise it would not be *he* who is good; whatever he is as a result would not be genuine goodness. If he is genuinely good, that goodness must come from *him*, not from his psychology (from my 'Psycho-analysis as Ultimate Explanation in Religion' in *Can Religion be Explained Away?*, ed. D.Z. Phillips, St Martin's Press, 1996).

B. The goodness of a good person and his psychology are at one with one another. His psychology is 'friendly' to goodness, it does not constitute a 'barrier' to it. It is not any psychological need that makes him good; it is not what he gets out of goodness that turns him to it. The contrast I have in mind is between 'friendliness' (as in 'user-friendly') and need.

The evil person gets something out of his evil deeds – pleasure, self-satisfaction, self-aggrandizement, self-protection. His alliance with evil is thus explicable in terms of his psychology. It disposes him towards evil.

It makes sense to ask, 'why is he full of venom and resentment?', but not 'what makes him trusting and friendly, compassionate, loving?' Or rather, if the latter question makes sense, it is to be answered in terms of the person's historical, psychological development which would show that there was no reason why he should not be. The study of goodness by a novelist such as Dostoyevsky undertook in *The Idiot* would have to take a different approach. It would have to depict, not a psychology which disposes the character to goodness, but one which leaves him open or accessible to it. It would have to show him as lacking what are normally barriers to goodness, what his life is like in their absence, and how others treat such a person and look on him. Whether he is successful or not, this is precisely what Dostoyevsky does in *The Idiot* (from my 'Dostoyevsky's Raskolnikov: Psychology and the Soul' – not published yet).

Likewise with love. It is not for any purpose that love serves that a person falls in love, comes to love someone. Love, so to speak, is gratuitous; it is engaged gratuitously. A person comes to love someone gratuitously for all sorts of reasons – though not for a reason, for what he hopes he will get from it. He may meet someone who is a kindred spirit or who strikes a chord in him and he may lose his heart to her. He may have suffered some setback or pain and find sympathy and understanding from someone. The way he responds, opens his heart to her, may lead to love. Or again a long standing friendship may turn to love. There is no one way in which this may happen. And even when someone turns to love in order to find companionship or to fill in some inner void, what he finds may so change him that he stops caring about what he was seeking. He then comes to love the other for herself rather than for what he was hoping to find in love.

We can, of course, say that human existence is such that there is a place for love in it. Such a statement is a prelude to elucidating the character of human existence and the nature of love. But that is not to say that love is an answer to a problem of human existence – an existential problem. Human existence may indeed pose problems for human beings; human life is inherently problematic. Those problems often come to characterize love itself for individuals. But love is not a solution, whatever bonuses it may bring to an individual, and it does not have to be engaged in for the sake of any solution that is being sought. When it is, while it remains so, it will be impure and soiled by such a purpose.

I will now quote part of a paragraph from Chapter 7 'Proust: Human Separateness and the Longing for Union' in my book *Love and Human Separateness*:

In this myth (from the *Symposium*) Aristophanes treats sexual love humorously, but there is a good deal in what he says .... Indeed in

Freud we find a modern, revised version of this myth, namely that in the beginning of each individual's life there is a symbiotic relation between mother and child in which the child does not yet have a separate identity as a person. Acquiring such an identity... involves coming to terms with painful experiences and relinquishing pleasurable illusions, such as that the mother does not have a separate life and that there is no place for anyone else in her affective life. The discovery that this is not so is Freud's famous Oedipus complex. Those who are unable to grow out of this undifferentiated state in their deepest feelings... will, when they are adults, seek to return to it in their sexual life. Love *for them*, as for Aristophanes' human creatures, will be 'the name for the desire and pursuit of the whole' ... (p. 94, italics new).

In other words, in immature love a person seeks a symbiotic union with the beloved. Even then he does not fall in love *in order to* find such a union, but when he falls in love he seeks it: that is the form which his love takes. Love certainly is or contains the desire for union with the loved person – though it differs in character with the kind of union it seeks. It is love that seeks the union, that gives the lover such a desire. The person does not fall in love in order to find union with another.

8.3 'Love as an Art and so a Practice'

I have already commented on the title of the book. In his comparison of love with art what Fromm wants to bring out is that we can learn from the experience of love, and indeed from life itself and from its difficulties, and that what we learn makes a difference to our capacity to love and to what we are capable of in love. What we learn we learn in our emotions and we change with it: we grow, we become more mature. It finds expression in our love, our life, in our responses. If what we learn is to be called knowledge, it does not have an existence separate from what we are in ourselves: it characterizes our mode of being. I have put all this in my own words, in my own way.

Love is not a practice; it is an engagement with another person, the person we love. In such an engagement we can be active or passive. Fromm is well aware of this. He points out that if we say love is an activity we run the risk of being misunderstood. In the sense that running a business is an activity, indeed engaging in a practice, love is not (p. 24). He then refers to Spinoza's distinction between 'active' and 'passive' emotions. 'Envy, jealousy, ambition, any kind of greed [he points out] are passions' – passive emotions (p. 25). To put it in Heideggerian language: the person does not own them, he is owned by them. 'Love (in contrast) is an action, the practice of a human power, which can be practised only in freedom and never as a result of a compulsion' (ibid.). When he says that love is an action, what he means is that the person is active: he gives of himself, he thinks of the loved one, cares for her, takes responsibility for his responses to her, works on the relationship – in the sense that if, for instance, he is hurt he does not sulk, he tries to understand, to forgive, etc. But this is not true of all love; the more mature a person is in his emotions, in himself, the more active he is, in this sense, in his love.

Love, however, can be a form of passivity. A baby's love for his mother is a form of passivity. Does Fromm want to say that the baby does not love his mother? The baby as it grows will soon begin to give something to his mother in the way he smiles when she appears and he is pleased to see her. Later on, in his childhood, his active love will show itself in the little things he does to help his mother and the concern he shows for her. The more the growing child shows thought for the family, puts himself out, takes care for instance of a little brother and sister, the more he will be acting on his own behalf out of love, out of a love that is growing mature – provided he does not do so in order to be good, to please, to gain approval.

It is this distinction that is important: acting in order to gain something, to feel good and acting out of concern for the other. In the former case the person is dependent on those whose approval he needs; in the latter he is not so dependent. In the concern he feels he finds himself and loves as a separate being, as an autonomous one. He is certainly attached to the person he so loves, his mother or his wife. He would miss her in her absence and would give his life for her, but all this comes from him as a separate being. Here Fromm who uses the word 'fusion' where I speak of 'union', speaks of 'fusion with integrity' (p. 24). I prefer to reserve the word 'fusion' for what he calls 'fusion without integrity', for as I understand this word when two things are fused together they do not retain their distinct identities. Of course, what word one chooses to use is merely a matter of terminology and what is important is to make things clear whatever word one uses.

Speaking of 'active' or 'mature' love Fromm highlights four features which characterize it: it is primarily giving, it is caring, it respects the other, and makes contact with the loved person and does not feed on phantasy (pp. 25–32). In connection with the fourth feature Fromm uses the word 'knowledge' and rightly points out that it is not possible to respect someone without knowing him (p. 30). Let me add that it is not possible to care for someone without knowing his needs and understanding his problems, and equally that generosity without knowledge of the other is giving misdirected. It can easily become 'generosity to satisfy oneself' and so false generosity.

The final chapter of his book is called 'The Practice of Love'. He begins by discussing the qualities required in the practice of *any* art. He mentions four such qualities: discipline, which he contrasts with self-indulgence, concentration (what Simone Weil calls 'attention' which is the antithesis self-absorption), patience which is the opposite of wanting quick results and self-gratification, and fourthly supreme concern or, as I would put it, complete dedication or devotion (pp. 90–97).

Then he turns to 'those qualities which are of specific significance for the ability to love' (p. 98). 'The main condition for the achievement of love [he means mature love] is the *overcoming* of one's *narcissism*' (ibid.). Let me also add: one's ego-centricity. This is clear from the four qualities which we have seen he has selected: one has to have turned away from self-indulgence, grown out of being self-absorbed, stopped needing to gratify oneself, and be interested in something outside oneself. He contrasts narcissism with what he, I think wrongly, calls self-love. He means self-respect and being on good terms with oneself. As for narcissism as opposed to ego-centricity, it is an immature love of oneself, wanting to be admired and pampered – indeed narcissistic people generally pamper themselves and those creatures, such as a cat, which they make into extensions of themselves.

As Fromm rightly points out, for such people others and 'the phenomena in the outside world' 'have no reality in themselves, but are experienced only from the viewpoint of their being useful or dangerous to one' (p. 98). Such people are not interested in people and things for themselves, but only as they relate to themselves. They live self-absorbed, as in a dream, and see things outside themselves through the medium of their phantasy.

Secondly, Fromm points out, 'the ability to love [with maturity] depends on one's capacity to emerge from ... the incestuous fixation to mother and clan' (p. 100). This is something we have already considered. He points out that all this takes faith, courage, the ability to take risk, the readiness to accept pain and disappointment (p. 104). The faith in question I take to be faith that there is goodness to be found in 'the outside world'. The courage is the courage it takes to expose oneself in one's vulnerability. The faith again is the trust that one will not be taken advantage of or used. In short to love and to be loved one has to be able to give up one's defences, to trust others and in particular the loved one, and to trust one's own capacity to bear pain and to weather difficulties. As Fromm puts it well: 'To love means to commit oneself without guarantee ... Love is [therefore] an act of faith' (p. 105). In short, in active, mature love, a person is 'fully awake', fully *there* for the beloved, accessible, receptive and attentive to her (p. 106).

There are, indeed, close parallels between the way a lover gives himself to the person he loves and cares for her, and the way an artist or artisan devotes himself to his art in creative work and gives himself to what he is doing. Indeed such devotion is itself a form of love.

8.4   Love and its Different Objects

We have seen that in his so-called 'theory of love' Fromm treats love as 'the answer to the problem of human existence'. He considers how human beings both as human beings and also as individuals have moved towards a conception of 'mature love' – that is both ontogenetically and philogenetically. He devotes a section to 'love between parents and child' – as both Freud and Melanie Klein did too – as the birth and origin of love in the individual. This is then followed by a brief discussion of different kinds of love as shaped in its relation to different objects. Having already commented on the child's love in his or her relation to mother and father as shaped by the different responses and expectations of mother and father he turns, in the next section, to five different loves: (i) Brotherly Love, as he calls it, usually known as 'Love of one's Neighbour', (ii) Motherly Love, (iii) Erotic or Sexual Love, (iv) what he calls 'Self-Love', and (v) Love of God. My comments on what he says here will be brief and selective.

(i) He says that 'brotherly love' is 'the kind of love the Bible speaks of when it says: love thy neighbour as thyself' (p. 44).

He says that it is 'the most fundamental kind of love'. It 'underlies all types of love', and he means mature love, because it is characterized by a 'sense of responsibility, care, respect, knowledge of any human being, the wish to further his life' (ibid.). He means that in genuine concern for others and in true compassion the caring and giving aspect of love is at its peak and its taking or pleasure aspect is at its minimum. As he puts it: 'Only in the love of those who do not serve a purpose, love begins to unfold' (p. 45). Such love he points out 'is characterized by its very lack of exclusiveness' (p. 44).

What he does not seem to appreciate is that even though such love lacks exclusiveness it can still be impure and it can still serve a purpose. For it may make one feel good and it may be sought for that purpose. Furthermore while Fromm is right in thinking that in its pure form, that is uncontaminated by any kind of self-regard, it does not serve a purpose, it is in plain contradiction with his conception of love as 'the answer to the problem of human existence'. For as such it would have to serve a purpose, either individual or evolutionary. I think that for Fromm it is a purpose of the individual, even if the individual is not aware of it.

(ii) Motherly love, Fromm points out, is unconditional – it is the 'unconditional affirmation of the child's life and his needs' (p. 45). It is caring and takes responsibility for the protection of the child's life and for furthering his growth. It gives him a goodness which makes him feel life as worth living (p. 46). It is a love between unequals 'where one needs all the help, and the other gives it'. It is thus considered 'the most sacred of all emotional bonds' (p. 46).

He says that the mother's love for the small infant is easy. 'Most women want children, are happy with the new-born child, and eager in their care for it.... This attitude of love is partly rooted in an instinctive equipment to be found in animals as well as in the human female' (p. 47). This is largely though not wholly true. For babies can be very demanding and some mothers find this extremely taxing.

Having pointed out that the mother's love for the young infant is partly instinctive Fromm goes on to say that it contains also 'specifically human psychological factors'. Not surprisingly – and I mean this as a criticism – he mentions four factors, features or motives which turn out to be features that soil such love: narcissism, domineeringness, possessiveness, and the need for transcendence (p. 47). The mother treats the baby as an extension of herself and loves herself in him, she satisfies her desire for power in the way she imposes her will on him, she tries to fill an emptiness in herself in trying to possess him, and/or she tries to live her life through him in fantasy. Any of these may, of course, be true; but none of them has to be. This is the psychologism I pointed out in Fromm earlier: in seeking a psychological explanation over and above the gratuitous, instinctive character of the mother's love and caring attention for her baby he degrades it.

Fromm goes on to point out that the real test for the mother's love comes when the child begins to grow up and to seek an independent life:

> The child must grow. It must emerge from mother's womb, from mother's breast; it must eventually become a completely separate being. The very essence of motherly love is to care for the child's growth, and that means to want the child's separation from herself. Here lies the basic difference to erotic love. In erotic love, two people who were separate become one. In motherly love, two people who were one become separate. The mother must not only tolerate, she must wish and support the child's separateness. It is only at this stage that motherly love becomes such a difficult task that it requires unselfishness, the ability to give everything and to want nothing but the happiness of the loved one. It is also at this stage that many mothers fail in their task of motherly love (pp. 47–8).

It is true, as we have seen in chapter 4 above, that sexual, erotic love cannot be a love that wants nothing for itself; hence its conflicting aspects. This does not mean however, as I have also pointed out, that it is or has to be a selfish love. It is also true that in motherly love, ideally, two people who were one become separate. But although, by contrast, in erotic love two people who were separate become one, ideally they retain their separate identity.

(iii) 'Erotic love (Fromm writes) is the craving for complete fusion, for union with one other person. It is by its very nature exclusive and not universal; it is also perhaps the most deceptive form of love there is' (p. 48). I have already commented on the craving for union at the heart of sexual love.

Very briefly the deceptiveness which Fromm speaks of is that often people who fall in love think they love one another but fail to do so. He describes this well (see p. 49).

He also comments on the relation between sex and love. Sexual desire, he points out, is not mere physical appetite; it too aims at fusion with another. 'But it can be simulated by the anxiety of aloneness, by the wish to conquer or be conquered, by vanity, by the wish to hurt and even to destroy [as in rape], as much as it can be stimulated by love' (p. 49). That is it can serve different needs and desires in human life. These desires then find fulfilment through sexuality. As Fromm puts it: 'sexual desire can easily blend with and be stimulated by any strong emotion, of which love is only one'(p. 50). This is one of the main reasons why people are so easily deceived by sexual attraction: they think they are really in love when what has been stirred in them is something different. But again, let me point out, that something else may be mixed up or 'blended' with love. Human beings are often a mixture, their motives are often mixed, and their feelings are often soiled in different ways.

(iv) When Fromm writes about 'self-love' he is referring to something other than 'narcissism'. He quotes Meister Eckhart: 'If you love yourself you love everybody else as you do yourself' One could put by its side the Christian precept: 'Love thy neighbour as thyself'. As I understand it what Meister Eckhart is saying is that if you are on good terms with yourself you will also be on good terms with others. If you lack self-respect your relations with others will be tinged with servility and with the hatred you will feel for others for the position in which your servility puts them with regard to you. It is true that respect is a component of love; but self-respect is not the same thing as self-love. Equally, one can describe being on good terms with oneself as having a friendly disposition to oneself, or as being on friendly terms with oneself. Friendship, of course, is a form of love. But to say that one is on friendly terms with oneself simply means that one is on good terms with oneself; it is meant to exclude self-hatred and self-contempt.

As for 'love your neighbour as yourself', it means treat him as you would like to be treated yourself; be just to him, remember that he is as vulnerable to suffering as you are yourself, show compassion to him as you would like *others* to show you compassion when you are in a similar plight. Give him your consideration as you would like *others* to give you consideration.

I have underlined 'others'. Indeed to love your neighbour you have to forget yourself. The injunction is that one should think of others as one wishes *others* to think of one, and not as one thinks of oneself. When one is on good or friendly terms with oneself one doesn't think of oneself. Indeed one thinks of oneself, one cannot stop doing so, when one is *not* on good or friendly terms with oneself.

Fromm points out that for Freud self-love is the same as narcissism and that the more narcissistic a person is the less is he capable of loving others (p. 52). Freud is absolutely right on this and, indeed, Fromm himself agrees with Freud on this point as we have already noted: 'the main condition for the achievement of love is the *overcoming* [or growing out] of one's *narcissism*' (p. 98).

(v) Writing on the love of God, Fromm says:

> It has been stated above that the basis for our need to love lies in the experience of separateness and the resulting need to overcome the anxiety of separateness by the experience of union. The religious form of love, that which is called the love of God, is *psychologically speaking*, not different. It springs from the need to overcome separateness and to achieve union. In fact, the love of God has as many different qualities and aspects as the love of man has – and to a large extent we find the same differences (pp. 56–7, *italics mine*).

I have italicized 'psychologically speaking'. My earlier point about 'psychologism' stands here too. Psychologically speaking a psychologist can only give a degraded or immature account of the love of God. Within the limits of my knowledge the only psychologist who has largely, though not entirely, succeeded to escape such psychologism in his account a spiritual love of God is Rycroft (see my paper 'Psycho-analysis as Ultimate Explanation of Religion' in *Can Religion be Explained Away?*, ed. D.Z. Phillips, St Martin's Press, 1996).

Fromm, like Freud, arranges different forms of religious worship and their gods in an ascending order. He thinks of them as stages in the development of human culture and its religions. Yet he conceives them in psychological terms and thinks of the ascending order in which he arranges them as an order of maturity. Very roughly his account goes as follows. In its development 'the human race' has emerged from nature, from mother, from the bonds of blood and soil. 'In the beginning of human history man, though thrown out of the original unity with nature, still clings to these primary bonds' (p. 57). He feels secure in doing so. 'He still feels identified with the world of animals and trees.' He transforms the animals into totems and worships them. This is the totemic stage of religion. At a later stage he 'transforms the product of his own hand into a god.' He now worships idols – idolatry. These idols represent man's own powers and skills idealized and projected into them. Then 'at a still later stage man gives his gods the forms of human beings.' This is the anthropomorphic stage of man's religions. These gods are at first mother figures; later they develop into father figures. The father figure is further transformed from a despotical chief into a loving father (p. 60).

Then finally, 'following the maturing ideal of monotheism in its further consequences … [we see that] God becomes what he potentially is in monotheistic theology, the nameless One … referring to the unity underlying the phenomenal universe, the ground of all existence; God becomes truth, love, justice' (pp. 61–2). As he puts it:

> In his development God ceases to be a person, a man, a father; he becomes the symbol of the principle of unity behind the manifoldness of phenomena, of the vision of the flower which will grow from the spiritual seed within man.

So finally God, having passed through polytheism and its totemic idolatrous stages, and such stages as we find exemplified in early Greece with many human gods, in its monotheistic stage takes on different attributes of the father, as in Judaism followed by Christianity, until finally he stops being any kind of object at all and becomes a symbol. It is then emancipated from theology – theology, presumably, being a description of the attributes of God.

Fromm adds that 'in all theistic systems, even a non-theological, mystical one, there is the assumption of the reality of the spiritual realm, as one transcending man … In a non-theistic system [such as in Buddhism and Taoism], there exists no spiritual realm outside of man or transcending him' (p. 63). He continues:

> The realm of love, reason and justice exists as a reality only because, and inasmuch as, man has been able to develop these powers in himself throughout the process of his evolution. In this view there is no meaning to life, except the meaning man himself gives to it, man is utterly alone expect inasmuch as he helps another (p. 63).

I have several criticisms which I shall express very briefly. First, religions are products of culture and their conceptions, including their conception of God or the gods, have to be understood in the terms of the cultures to which they belong. They cannot be understood psychologically. Totemic religions, for instance, are not immature. The worship of animals as totems are the objects of worship of a people close to animals and in the lives of which animals have a special significance. That should be the starting point of any attempt to understand such a religion.

Similarly for the religion of early Greeks. If one is inclined to dismiss it as yet in an early stage of development then I would suggest one reads the *Iliad* and Simone Weil's essay on it in which she puts it along the few great epics the world has produced, alongside the *Bible*.

The different religions mentioned by Fromm are the products of cultures that have developed in different regions of the world at different times. They do not stand in any historical order.

It is true that within the same religion believers differ in the conception of the God they worship. Here one could speak of some conceptions as deeper in spirituality than others, as showing a more mature spirituality than the others. Here – and this is my view, a view that I should like to think more about and subject to criticism – I think there is a link, indeed I suspect a coincidence, between spiritual maturity and psychological or emotional maturity. And, once more, any attempt to give a psychological account of the spiritual – the spiritually mature: of what constitutes a spiritual ideal – can only result in its downgrading.

Secondly, as I have argued elsewhere (Dilman, 1996) to say that religions are cultural products, that they come into being and develop within cultures, is not to say that human religions are manmade and that God is a human creation.

Thirdly, I think that Fromm is right in thinking that at the height of its spiritual sense, or as understood by those of a deep spirituality, the Christian God is not an object. But that does not mean that when the Christian God is described as a person and various characteristics are attributed to him what is said is false or belongs to a lower understanding of God spiritually speaking. The question is what is meant by saying that 'God is a person' or that 'He loves us' or that 'Jesus Christ is the Son of God'. Fromm's understanding of such claims seems to me to be limited. When, in this connection, he says that 'the logical consequence of monotheistic thought is the negation of all "theology"' (p. 63) he identifies theology with metaphysics. I have discussed this question in my paper 'Psycho-Analysis as Ultimate Explanation of Religion' and also in Chapter 7, 'Wisdom II: Metaphysical and Religious Transcendence' in Dilman 1981, so I will not elaborate on it.

Finally, when Fromm writes that 'in a non-theistic system, there exists no spiritual realm outside of man or transcending him' (p. 63) this may well by true. He obviously approves of this and thinks of 'the assumption of the reality of the spiritual realm, as one transcending man' as belonging to a lower conception of spirituality. Here he is labouring under the same misunderstanding of 'religious transcendence' and 'theology'. To put it very succinctly: of course our conception of reality, of different realities, including spiritual reality, or 'a realm of the spiritual' as Fromm put it, belongs to and is internal to our language, and that in turn, our language, is part of the world we live in – we speak it and hear it spoken in that world. And yet in that language a distinction is made between 'this world' and 'another world, a world of spirituality, which goes beyond the material world, which we shall enter only by detaching ourselves from the material world and dying to ourselves'. There is absolutely no contradiction between assenting to such a claim and holding that the relation between our language and the realities that we confront in our life is internal.

It is only if we think of this relation as external that the idea of realm beyond the only world we know by means of our senses would strike one as nonsensical. That would be a metaphysical conception of that other world, as opposed to a religious conception of it. For 'other', 'beyond', 'transcendent' would be interpreted or understood independently of the religious language and context in which these words are used – as Fromm does with the word 'person' used to characterize God in Christian theology.

8.5 Fromm's Criticisms and Revisions of Freud

His first criticism is directed to Freud's conception of love as the sublimation of the sexual instinct. He argues that in human life the sexual instinct is transformed and has many manifestations, it serves and is blended with other desires and needs. Thus, as he puts it, 'the sexual desire is one manifestation of the need for love and union' (p. 35). Indeed, he rejects Freud's biological conception of sex and of the development of the individual's sexuality from childhood to adulthood and replaces it with an existential one – that is as taking place in the context of human life and not independently of it and as conditioned by variations in human culture. As Fromm puts it:

> love, hate, ambition, jealousy were explained by Freud as so many outcomes of various forms of the sexual instinct. He did not see that the basic reality lies in the totality of human existence, first of all in the human situation common to all men, and secondly in the practice of life determined by the specific structure of society (pp. 78–9).

As a result of the way he conceived of sexuality, Fromm points out, Freud thought that human happiness is co-extensive with sexual gratification, that 'the full and uninhibited satisfaction of all instinctual desires would create mental health and happiness' (p. 79). But, Fromm points out, a life entirely devoted to sex is lopsided. It excludes much of what men find happiness in: relationships of give and take, friendship, interests outside themselves, common work, etc. Indeed, so devoting oneself to sex and pursuing sexual satisfaction is a symptom of something having gone wrong in one's life. Here I should like to quote a few words from a letter by Simone Weil to a young student:

> The life which is truly real is not one that consists in experiencing sensations, but in activity. [she is referring to 'sexual experimentation']…Those who live for sensations are parasites…compared with those who labour and create…and I would add too that those who do not run after sensations are rewarded in the end by much that is more alive…than anything the sensation seekers experience…. My conclusion…is not that one should shun love [here she is referring to those who seek love in sex], but that one should not go out of one's way to try and find it, and especially so when you are very young (1951, pp. 34–5).

Freud, we saw earlier, thought of tenderness, which is a manifestation of affection, as part of the sexual instinct: its affectionate current. Fromm rejects this view: 'tenderness…is the direct outcome of brotherly love' (p. 50). But for Freud 'love was basically a sexual phenomenon…[and] the experience of brotherly love…an outcome of sexual desire' (p. 77). Fromm, we have seen, rejects this.

With reference to his thoughts on 'transference' Fromm points out that 'for Freud love is in itself an irrational phenomenon [Fromm means a form of passivity in Spinoza's sense, something that the person does not own]. The difference between irrational love and love as an expression of the mature personality does not exist for him. ... Transference love is essentially not different from the 'normal' phenomenon of love. Falling in love always verges on the abnormal, is always accompanied by blindness to reality, compulsiveness, and is a transference from love objects of childhood' (pp. 77–8). Here, in parenthesis, let us remind ourselves how close Proust's conception of love is to this view of Freud as summed up by Fromm. Fromm rejects this: 'Love ... as the crowning achievement of maturity, was, to Freud, no subject matter for investigations, since it had no real existence' (p. 78). It is, of course, the subject matter of Fromm's book under discussion.

Fromm, we have noted, thinks of Freud's stages of the development of the libido as the development of the individual and in existential terms. He describes a mature individual as 'productive'. It is worth noting that there is a certain parallel between Simone Weil's conception of 'activity' and what is 'truly real' in life (*vide* her letter quoted above) and Fromm's conception of a 'productive' life. In such a life a person finds plenitude in developing interests in things outside him and gives himself to these in work. This he argues comes with the maturity of the individual and has little to do with what Freud calls 'genitality'. He redescribes Freud's immature stages of development in terms of such adjectives as 'hoarding', 'exploitative', 'marketing' – adjectives which characterize his affective orientation (see *Man for Himself*). Here the person lives a life of passivity and parasitism on others – to use Simone Weil's terms – instead of contributing to the lives of those to whom he is related.

Lastly, we have seen, Fromm rejects Freud's conception of God as an infantile protection. He adds however, I think rightly, that for many believers the idea of God as a helping father is a childish illusion. However, as I pointed out, it does not have to be so. I said, 'I think rightly', but I am afraid Fromm wrongly thinks that it has to be so. For as I pointed out he arranges these different conceptions on an ascending order, which he wrongly takes to be historical, and then identifies it with the affective development of individual believers.

I have criticized Fromm's positive views concerning the religious love of God and I will not add to what I said.

9

C.S. Lewis in Four Loves: Our Natural Loves

9.1 Introduction

C.S. Lewis' little book *The Four Loves* is a discussion of four loves which he has arranged in an ascending order: affection, friendship, eros or erotic love, and charity. I said 'ascending order', but he does not mean to belittle any of them in any sense. Indeed he writes about them simply and refreshingly and with an open mind. He brings his own personal experience to bear on what he says, enriched by his love and knowledge of literature. His reflections are often philosophical but they are not tied up to any preconceptions, and he has no axe to grind – although, of course, he writes as a Christian.[8]

He talks of the first three loves as 'natural loves' while charity is of a different order. He would probably agree with Simone Weil that it is an implicit love of God. Simone Weil uses the word 'supernatural' in this connection, as does Lewis too. He talks of the 'transmutation' of the natural element in our love: 'Only those into which Love Himself has entered will ascend to Love Himself'. I shall return to what he says, but it forces on us the comparison of what Plato puts into the mouth of Diotima in the *Symposium*.

If there is any thesis in the book it is this: 'love is not enough.' Lewis quotes the title of a poem by William Morris: *Love is Enough*. He then mentions someone who has reviewed it briefly in the words, 'It isn't.' He writes:

> Such has been the burden of this book. The natural loves are not self-sufficient. Something else, at first vaguely described as 'decency and common sense', but later revealed as goodness, and finally as the whole Christian life in one particular relation, must

8. I shall in a later chapter contrast him with Kierkegaard.

come to the help of the mere feeling if the feeling is to be kept sweet. To say this is not to belittle the natural loves but to indicate where their real glory lies (p. 107).

C.S. Lewis is also concerned to distinguish between the different aspects of love in their variety and in their different mix or combinations and in the 'dangers inherent' in different forms of love and their 'perversions' – for instance the perversion of friendship into a 'mutual admiration society'. This is of course closely connected with the burden of the book, namely that the natural loves are not self-sufficient. As he puts it in connection with friendship: 'like the other natural loves [it] is unable to save itself. It must invoke the divine protection if it hopes to remain sweet' (p. 82). That protection may be the grace of God, but to invoke it calls for inner work which Plato calls 'purification of the soul' in the *Phaedo*. Lewis expresses this clearly in connection with erotic love and marriage:

He (Eros), like a godparent, makes the vows; it is we who must keep them. It is we who must labour to bring our daily life into even closer accordance with what the glimpses have revealed [when, in falling in love, Eros, in one high bound has overleaped the massive wall of our selfhood]. We must do the works of Eros when Eros is not present. [For between the best possible lovers this high condition is intermittent; the old self soon turns out to be not so dead as he pretended.] ... And all good Christian lovers know that this programme, modest as it sounds, will not be carried except by humility, charity and divine grace (pp. 105–6).

9.2 Beginning at the Beginning with our Natural Propensities

At the end of Chapter 1, the Introduction to his book, Lewis writes:

The highest does not stand without the lowest. A plant must have roots below as well as sunlight above and roots must be grubby. Much of the grubbiness is clean dirt if only you will leave it in the garden and not keep on sprinkling it over the library table (p. 14).

Indeed he begins his discussions of love 'at the bottom', as he puts it, 'with mere likings' and with our enjoying the things we like and our finding pleasure in them.

He distinguishes between two kinds of pleasure. We find pleasure in drinking water when we are thirsty. We drink it because we are thirsty and it gives us pleasure because it quenches our thirst. That is our pleasure here presupposes our need for water and has its source in our need. When my thirst is quenched I no longer want to drink water and would find no pleasure in drinking it. This is an instance of what Lewis calls 'need-pleasure'. By contrast, the pleasure I find in smelling a rose is not dependent on any need in me. I enjoy its smell because *it* is sweet and not because *I* want anything. And if I want to smell it again that is because I have enjoyed its smell. This is an instance of what Lewis calls a 'pleasure of appreciation'.

Although Lewis does not point this out, let me draw attention to the fact that in both examples our desire for what we like and enjoy is 'generalized' (see J.L. Stocks 'Desire and Affection', *Morality and Purpose*, ed. D.Z. Phillips, Routledge, 1969) and what we like or enjoy is not the particular glass of water or rose. Another cool glass of water, another sweet smelling rose would do just as well. This is inevitable in the case of need-pleasures, but not so where the pleasures of appreciation are concerned – for instance where one finds pleasure in contemplating a work of art, a painting.

Lewis, of course, points this out in connection with the transition from sensual, or perhaps better, sensuous pleasures to aesthetic ones. He points out that there is no sharp line between these two: 'there is a seamless continuity' between them, and indeed they can interpenetrate one another – thus the pleasure one finds in listening to a piece of music (p. 20). He points out that beauty comes into what appreciative pleasure foreshadows (p. 19), and with it we have 'a shadow or dawn of, or an invitation to, disinterestedness' (p. 20). Here one is again reminded of what in the *Symposium* Plato calls 'initiation to beauty'.

In the Introductory chapter Lewis distinguishes between what he calls 'need-love' and 'gift-love' (p. 7). He points out that need-love need not be 'mere selfishness' (p. 8), or greedy (p. 13), and that in any case need is a necessary part of love (p. 8). Divine Love is Gift-love' (p. 7). Man's love of God, on the other hand, is need-love: we go to God as a beggar and in humility.

Having argued that 'need-love' is really love (pp. 8–9), he goes on:

> Thus one Need-love, the greatest of all, either coincides with or at least makes a main ingredient in man's highest, healthiest, and most realistic spiritual condition. A very strange corollary follows. Man approaches God most nearly when he is in one sense least like God (p. 9).

'This paradox staggered me [he says] when I first ran into it; it also wrecked all my previous attempts to write about love' (p. 9). I will not go into his attempt at resolving this paradox because I am not sure about its premise that divine love is gift-love – pure and simple. Is not God supposed to have come in the form of Christ to beg man's love – as Simone Weil puts it? And did He not retire from the world and make Himself invisible so that men can love Him, and not something else? But perhaps, one can argue on Lewis' side, this is the highest form of gift-love – for in sending His son on earth, in making Himself invisible to man, he was *giving* man the opportunity to love Him.

Anyway the important point is that need-love is really love, that it does not have to be an impure or corrupt form of love, and that it is a necessary aspect of love. Need, as Lewis points out, is an inherent part of human existence – these are my words. This is how he puts it: 'We are born helpless. As soon as we are fully conscious we discover loneliness. We need others physically, emotionally, intellectually; we need them if we are to know anything, even ourselves' (p. 7). To deny this is arrogant self-deception and emotionally debilitating. It makes us hard-hearted and incapable of loving; it deprives us of love's knowledge and shrinks our world to the size of our self. To acknowledge our neediness, on the other hand, is humility and it opens us to the human world in its richness. Its other face is greed or greediness. Neediness thus has two faces – like dependency: 'mature dependency' (a phrase coined by the psycho-analyst Fairbairn) and, to coin a phrase myself, 'parasitic dependency'.

To return to Lewis's 'beginnings' in his discussion of love, he points out that need-pleasures foreshadow need-love, and that the pleasures of appreciation lead him to discover that his classification, in the Introductory chapter, of loves into those of need and those of gift was deficient, and that 'there is a third element in love, no less important than these' (p. 20). He writes:

> Need-love cries to God from our poverty; Gift-love longs to serve, or even to suffer for, God; Appreciative love says: 'We give thanks to thee for thy great glory.' Need-love says of a woman 'I cannot live without her'; Gift-love longs to give her happiness, comfort, protection – if possible, wealth; Appreciative love gazes and holds its breath and is silent, rejoices that such a wonder should exist even if not for him, will not be wholly dejected by losing her, would rather have it so than never to have seen her at all (p. 21).

He adds: 'In actual life, thank God, the three elements of love mix and succeed one another, moment by moment.' And further: 'Perhaps none of them except Need-love ever exists alone, in "chemical" purity, for more than a few seconds. And perhaps that is because nothing about us except our neediness is, in this life, permanent' (ibid.).

It is through the appreciation of beauty in things that those things in which we find pleasure are particularized for us, that those objects become individuals for which there can be no substitute for us in the feelings and desires they evoke in us – the desire to look at, to contemplate, to have contact with, indeed to give and take. It is thus that we pass from mere liking and enjoying to love. Thus I do not merely like and enjoy, for instance, the slow movement of the first of Beethoven's Razumikhin quartets, I *love* it.

Having thus moved to the terrain of our loves Lewis, towards the end of this second chapter of his book, discusses two loves directed to non-human objects, namely 'the love of nature' (pp. 21–5) and 'the love of one's country' (pp. 25–32), and leaves a third one for the next chapter on affection, 'our love for animals'. He has some very good things to say about the first two to which I do not feel I have anything to add. I shall be very brief and selective. About the first he says that this is not a love of particular objects of nature or natural scenes but rather of nature in her 'moods of time and season' (p. 22). About his next point I am not sure; it is that 'nature does not teach' – if you take her as a teacher 'she will teach you exactly the lessons you had already decided to learn' (pp. 22–4).

In connection with the love of one's country he distinguishes its innocent and its demoniac forms. 'Demoniac patriotism will make it easier for its subjects to act wickedly; healthy patriotism will make it harder' (p. 26). Its innocent form, he points out, has many ingredients: love of home, of the place we grew up, love of old acquaintances, of familiar sights, sounds and smells, of foods, customs. These are things to which we are attached and would miss if they were destroyed. 'Patriotism of this kind is not in the least aggressive. It asks only to be let alone. It becomes militant only to protect what it loves' (p. 27).

The second, he points out, is a particular attitude to one's country's past and its traditions. Here what Socrates says in the *Crito* when his friends want to arrange to take him abroad to save his life comes to mind. There he expresses his debt and gratitude to Athens and its customs and traditions for all that he has received from them. Indeed he brings out how much he owes his very being to Athens. Clearly there is a close affinity between such love and the loyalty and gratitude Socrates expresses and the love of one's parents.

With regard to the second ingredient – 'a particular attitude to our country's past' – Lewis writes:

This past is felt both to impose an obligation and to hold out an assurance; we must not fall below the standards our fathers set us, and because we are their sons there is good hope we shall not.

This feeling has not quite such good credentials as the sheer love of home. The actual history of every country is full of shabby and even shameful doings. ... Hence a patriotism based on our glorious past is fair game for the debunker (p. 28).

Lewis adds, however, that 'it is possible to be strengthened by the image of the past without being either deceived or puffed up' (ibid.).

'No man,' (he quotes) said one of the Greeks, 'loves his city because it is great, but because it is his.'[9] He adds: 'A man who really loves his country will love her in her ruin and degeneration .... She will be to him 'a poor thing but mine own'. He may think her good

9. Clearly 'his' here does not imply that he thinks of it as an extension of *himself*, but rather that he recognizes it as the land where he has found his very being.

and great, when she is not, because he loves her; the delusion is up to a point pardonable' (p. 30).

9.3   Affection

Undoubtedly affection is a form of love. It often exists on its own; but equally often it is an ingredient of other loves (pp. 35–6). As Lewis points out, affection grows between friends and characterize their friendship, and in married couples for instance, affection becomes 'the homespun clothing' of their love for one another:

> There is indeed a peculiar charm, both in friendship and Eros, about those movements when Appreciative Love lies, as it were, curled up asleep, and the mere ease and ordinariness of the relationship (free as solitude, yet neither is alone) wraps us round. No need to talk. No need to make love. No needs at all except perhaps to stir the fire (p. 36).

Of all loves, he points out, affection is 'the humblest and most widely diffused' (p. 33), it 'gives itself no airs' (p. 35), and is also 'the broadest' (p. 38). We can feel affection for a very great many things: for all sorts of people, for animals as pets, for places. We also find it in animals – amongst themselves, a cat and its kittens, and between animals and men – a dog who puts his head on his master's knee while his master strokes it, or licks his master's face. Lewis who points out these things adds that he does not 'on that account give it – affection – a lower value' (p. 33).

It is also, he points out, 'the least discriminatory' of loves (p. 34). One can feel affection for the ugly, the stupid, even the exasperating: 'there is no apparent fitness between those whom it unites' (p. 34). Usually it grows steadily and imperceptibly – as opposed to erotic love for instance. 'To become aware of it is to become aware that it has already been going on for some time' (ibid.). We feel it, he points out, for people and things familiar to us: 'the use of "old" or *vieux* as a term of affection is significant' (pp. 34–5). It is also 'attracted', I think, by vulnerability, even gaucheness sometimes, by innocence, and by goodness. Lewis sees this somewhat differently: it is 'not primarily an Appreciative love … yet … it can in the end make appreciations possible which, but for it, might never have existed' (p. 37). I suppose he thinks it is too humble to be a response to goodness.

He points out a parallel and yet, at the same time, a difference between affection and compassion, or 'charity' as he prefers to call it – love for one's neighbour:

> Affection … gives itself no airs; charity, said St Paul, is not puffed up. Affection can love the unattractive: God and His saints love the unlovable. Affection "does not expect too much", turns a blind eye to faults, revives easily after quarrels; just so charity suffers long and is kind and forgives. Affection opens our eyes to goodness we could not have seen, or should not have appreciated without it (p. 38).

Here he raises the question which I pointed out goes all through the book, directed to our 'natural loves': 'Is love (of this sort) really enough? Are the "domestic affections", when in their best and fullest development, the same thing as the Christian life?' 'He says, No, they are not: as with our other natural loves it has to be 'transmuted' by the supernatural – by our love of God (p. 125).

> Affection produces happiness if – and only if – … something more, and other, than Affection is added … "common sense" … "give and take" … justice … "decency" …. This means goodness; patience, self-denial, humility, and the continual intervention of a far higher sort of love than Affection, in itself, can ever be (p. 53).

He is speaking in terms of the different forms of love – their contributions and limitations. But it is obviously the person who loves in these ways; the contributions and limitations in question are those of the person – *his* capacities and limitations. The development of these capacities, transcendence of these limitations, is of course the growth of the person. This involves the growth of judgement, the capacity to exercise tact, understanding, tolerance, restraint in accordance with judgement. It is such exercise that Lewis has in mind when in this connection – like Erich Fromm – he speaks of 'the *art* of love'. In the previous chapter we saw that Fromm's articulation of what is in question is clumsy and at various points misleading. Lewis avoid abstraction and throughout the book gives many examples which make the point of speaking of an *art* of love clear. He is very good, for instance, when he speaks about affection and its courtesy (pp. 43–4).

At the end of the passage I have just quoted he adds: 'If we try to live by Affection alone, Affection will "go bad on us" '. Thus throughout the book Lewis is concerned with the contributions of the kinds of love he distinguishes, and also with their limitations and perversions. In accordance with the distinction he made in the Introductory chapters between need-love and gift-love he points out that affection has both these aspects (p. 40). At the beginning of the chapter he gives the word which the early Greeks used for it: '*storge*', and he says that his Greek Lexicon defines it as 'affection, especially of parents to offspring', but also he adds of 'offspring to parents' (p. 33). With reference to a mother's love and affection for her offspring he says that it presents him with a paradox: 'It is a Need-love but what it needs is to give. It is a Gift-love but it needs to be needed' (pp. 33–4).

There is, of course, nothing selfish in the need to give as such so long as it is part of the love in question. It perverts the love when it is the need of the ego. But the paradox persists; the need to give is a need to be needed. For the mother needs her child to need her so that she can give to him: take care of him. But to take care of him is largely promoting his growth and enabling him to become independent – enabling him to look after himself, have a separate life in which he will care for others, a wife and his own children. Thus in her gift-love she has to be able, in time and in stages, to renounce the need to be needed implicit in its need to give.

Lewis puts this as: 'it – maternal love as a gift-love – must work towards its own abdication' (p. 50). This is partly true, partly false. True, the mother 'must aim at making herself superfluous' in the sense that as her child becomes an adult he will not need her. But it is not true – as I am sure Lewis knows – that maternal love will thus stop being a gift-love. On the contrary, it will continue to be a gift-love at a deeper level. The mother will renounce a certain form of giving, treating her child as a child and caring for him as such. But she will continue to care for him, to show concern if and when things go wrong for him, to put herself out and help him on such occasions. Here again she will have to exercise tact and discretion. Doing that – 'the art of loving' – is itself part of the giving character of her love.

I have already quoted Lewis's words: 'if we try to live by affection alone, affection will "go bad on us" '. He points out the perversions of affection in both of its aspects. As need-love it is liable to jealousy: 'every kind of love, almost every kind of association, is liable to it' (p. 45). Lewis gives a number of examples. He then points out that 'affection as gift-love has its perversions too' (p. 48). Here too he gives a number of examples. Among these he gives the example of a university lecturer, Dr Quartz, who gives himself totally to his students as a teacher but later, when they have learned from his teaching, cannot bear their independent opinions and criticisms (pp. 50–1). He also mentions how our 'need to be needed' can take the form of pampering an animal. He ends his discussion with a warning: 'Those who say "The more I see of men the better I like dogs" – those who find in animals a *relief* from the demands of human companionship – will be well advised to examine their real reasons' (p. 52).

Before finishing his chapter by pointing out that the possibility of such 'perversions' are inherent in the very character of affection, as of other natural loves, he warns us against calling such perversions 'neurotic'. He writes:

> Medicine labours to restore 'natural' structure or 'normal' function. But greed, egoism, self-deception and self-pity are not unnatural or abnormal in the same sense as astigmatism or a floating kidney. For who, in Heaven's name, would describe as natural or normal the man from whom these failings were wholly absent? (p. 53)

Of course, these are features which belong to our natural loves by virtue of their being 'natural'. That is why they 'need' (in the sense of 'need' in which Simone Weil speaks of 'the needs of the soul' – *L'Enracinement: The Need for Roots*) to be 'transmuted' by the intervention of something 'supernatural' – something that goes against the grain of all that comes naturally to man. Lewis says that these things that threaten to pervert our natural loves belong to the 'fallenness' of man; 'their occurrence is not a disease', yielding to them is 'sin' (p. 53).

I have no quarrel with C.S. Lewis on this point. I differ from him in holding that 'neurosis' is not a medical term, neuroses are not diseases, they are affective conditions which stand in a two-way relation to our spiritual condition (see Dilman, 1988, Chapters 2–4). That is why throughout this book I make a close connection between individual development towards affective, psychological maturity and the purification of the soul from all contamination by the self in the sense of 'the ego'.

9.4 Friendship

Here Lewis begins by saying that 'to the Ancients, Friendship seemed the happiest and most fully human of all loves; the crown of life and the school of virtue', but that 'the modern world, in comparison, ignores it' (p. 55). He then makes some suggestions as to why it has been ignored so. (i) It is 'the least *natural* of loves'. Eros is connected with begetting children, affection with rearing them. In contrast friendship has no 'survival value'. (ii) He blames Romanticism, the 'return to nature' and the 'exaltation of sentiment'. Friendship, in contrast with eros, is calm and 'freely chosen' (p. 56). (iii) 'It is a relation between men at their highest level and individuality. It withdraws men from collective "togetherness" as surely as solitude itself could do; and more dangerously, for it withdraws them by two's and three's' (p. 57). 'Because it is selective and an affair of the few' it offends 'democratic sentiment' (ibid.).

In this way Lewis is on the road to characterizing friendship as a distinctive form of love: it is the least natural or biological, the least instinctive, gregarious, and necessary form of love – not necessary for human survival. He also rejects the idea that it is 'really' sexual in character, a form of disguised homosexuality (pp. 57–8).

He contrasts friendship with eros. In sexual love lovers are tied together by their attraction for and interest in each other; indeed they are 'absorbed in each other' (p. 58). They thus stand face to face and look into each other's eyes (pp. 65, 67). Friends, on the other hand, are 'absorbed in a common interest' (p. 58), 'their eyes look ahead' (p. 67). Sexual love is exclusive, it is shared by the two lovers and will not admit a third person to partake of it. In this sense it is inherently jealous – has the potentiality of jealousy written into it (p. 58). 'True friendship – in contrast – is the least jealous of loves' (p. 59). This is not to say that friendship cannot be jealous and possessive. It is the least jealous of loves in the sense that a common interest can join several people together in friendship. There is, of course, a limit, as Lewis points out, to the number of people who can thus constitute a circle of friends.

Given this difference the mutual trust that belongs to all loves is betrayed differently in the two loves. Sexual love being exclusively between two lovers 'seeks privacy' (p. 62) and intimacy. Its trust is, therefore, betrayed when one of the parties to it does not respect this privacy and intimacy, shares it with someone else, or makes public what is 'innermost' to it. Breaking friendship's trust is failing to respect its special tie: failing to respond to the special things a friend can ask or expect of one, such as helping him out of a difficult situation, putting the friendship before one's self-interest.

Lewis points out, further, that friendship 'ignores not only our physical bodies but that whole embodiment which consists of our family, job, past and connections.... It is an affair of disentangled, or stripped, minds. Eros will have naked bodies; Friendship naked personalities' (p. 67).

Sexual love, as Proust has shown so well, is inquisitive: Friendship, by contrast, is uninquisitive:

> You become a man's Friend without knowing or caring whether he is married or single or how he earns his living. ... In a circle of true Friends each man is simply what he is: stands for nothing but himself.... Of course you will get to know about most of these in the end. But casually ... bit by bit (p. 66).

One will, of course, come to know one's friend – not in the sense of how he is connected, what he does, etc. – in the pursuit of the interest one shares with him. One will do so not, as Lewis puts it, 'by staring in his eyes as if he were your mistress' but by reading with him, listening to music together, arguing with him, enjoying walking in the countryside with him.

He contrasts it with mere companionship: 'friends will still be doing something together, but something more inward, less widely shared and less easily defined; still hunters, but of some immaterial quarry' (p. 63).

Having noted that friendship does not have 'survival value', Lewis points out that it has 'civilisation value' (p. 65). Learning to survive is one thing, it has practical value. But it does not make us better people; indeed it may make us very much worse – viz. surviving in commerce and business, in cut-throat circumstances. Here the good and the scrupulous go under. But in friendship we learn to give, we learn loyalty, we learn respect. That is why, as Lewis points out, the Ancients regarded it as 'the school of virtue'. 'Life – natural life – has no better gift to give' – than friendship (p. 68).

> This love, free from instinct, free from all duties but those which love has freely assumed, almost wholly free from jealousy, and free without qualification from the need to be needed, is eminently spiritual (p. 72).

This makes it sound as if friendship is corruptible only as a spiritual form of love – by vanity and arrogance for instance. I said that friendship can be jealous and possessive. I cannot believe that Lewis would deny this. Perhaps he would say that it is so when it is mixed with sexuality. He certainly points out that where two people are of different sexes their friendship 'will very easily pass into erotic love' and 'conversely, erotic love may lead to friendship between the lovers' (p. 63). He says that where friendship passes into sexual love jealousy will easily make its appearance (pp. 63–4). He points out that where there is such a transition the two loves often 'co-exist' (p. 64).

Writing about the corruptibility of friendship Lewis says that 'because it is spiritual [it] therefore faces a subtler enemy' (p. 82).

> Friendship (as the ancients saw) can be a school of virtue; but also (as they did not see) a school of vice. ... It makes good men better and bad men worse. ... This love, like the other natural loves, has its congenital liability to a particular disease (p. 75).

The source from which its corruptibility emanates is at the same time its highest point; 'it is a relation between men at their highest level of individuality'. As such 'it withdraws men from collective "togetherness"' (p. 57). Lewis refers to this later as 'the element of succession'; it is liable to make friends, in their friendship, 'deaf to the voices of the outer world' (pp. 75–6) – that is outside the world of their friendship, the world they share in their friendship. This, in turn, can become a breeding ground of pride, vanity and arrogance. Lewis articulates the way the circle of friends turns into a *coterie*, a 'mutual admiration society', in which snobbish pride flourishes, and the way those who belong to it start disdaining and ignoring those who are on the outside of the charmed circle. 'Indeed, the friendship [now] may be "about" almost nothing except the fact that it excludes' (p. 80).

> The danger of such pride – the pride of Friendship – is indeed almost inseparable from Friendly love. Friendship must exclude. From the innocent and necessary act of excluding to the spirit of exclusiveness is an easy step; and thence to the degrading pleasure of exclusiveness. ... The common vision which first brought us together may fade quite away. We shall be ... a little

self-elected (and therefore absurd) aristocracy, basking in the moonshine of our collective self-approval (p. 80).

'Just because this is the most spiritual of loves the danger which besets it is spiritual too' and so 'needs to be triply protected by humility' (p. 81).

Lewis concludes:

> Friendship is not a reward for a discrimination and good taste in finding one another out. It is the instrument by which God reveals to each the beauties of all the others. They are no greater than the beauties of a thousand other men; by Friendship God opens our eyes to them (p. 83).

9.5   Eros or Sexual Love

Here Lewis begins with love and sex: 'sexuality may operate without Eros or as part of Eros' (p. 85). Sexual desire, without Eros, wants sensual gratification. The man or woman is a means; he or she is used or treated as a vehicle of pleasure. He or she is replaceable; a different man or woman could serve the same purpose and so would do just as well. Lewis writes: 'we say of a lustful man prowling the streets that he "wants a woman". Strictly speaking...he wants a pleasure for which a woman happens to be the necessary piece of apparatus' (pp. 87–8). But we use the word 'lust' both in this sense of sexual appetite, and also in the sense of sexual passion aroused by a particular woman and so directed specifically to her – David's lust for Bathsheba. It is purely carnal. Eros or sexual love is directed to a particular woman – in the case of a man – as a person. The whole person is encompassed by it and it has therefore a moral dimension. As I said before the lover gives or loses his heart to the beloved for her to keep and risks having it broken.

The lover finds pleasure in contact with the beloved and seeks proximity with her; he is attracted by her magnetism and beauty. As Lewis puts it: 'Eros thus wonderfully transforms what is *par excellence* a Need-pleasure into the most Appreciative of all pleasures' (p. 88). That is it transforms the character of the sexuality which animates it. But the magnetism it finds in the beloved is such that the lover seeks fusion with her. Lewis says that the lovers sometimes express this by saying they want to 'eat' one another (p. 88) – in other words to make each other part of themselves, to become one, to 'achieve total interpenetration instead of mere embrace' (pp. 88–9).

'One of the first things Eros does is to obliterate the distinction between giving and receiving' (p. 89). The lover receives pleasure in giving it and gives pleasure to the beloved in receiving it from her.

It is often thought, Lewis writes, 'that the spiritual danger of Eros arises almost entirely from its carnal element' (p. 89). The idea is that surrender to the senses is soul-destroying. Lewis believes that this is a mistake which comes from taking Venus, the carnal element of eros, too seriously. This leads him to write at some length about the body (pp. 93–8): 'we are composite creatures ... akin on one side to the angels, on the other to tom-cats' (p. 93). Needless to say this is not Cartesian dualism. He then mentions three different views of the body, of the carnal in us: the body as a tomb of the soul, the body as something glorious, and St Francis' view of the body as 'Brother Ass'. Lewis writes: 'All three may be – I am sure – defensible; but give me St Francis for my money' (p. 93).

He finds the former a gloomy view and takes it to involve hatred of the body. This is an oversimplistic view of what such a conception of the body comes to.[10] Lewis equally thinks that the pagan conception of the body as something to be revered goes too far in the opposite direction. 'Ass,' he says, 'is exquisitely right because no one in his senses can either revere or hate a donkey. It is a useful, sturdy, lazy, obstinate, patient, lovable and infuriating beast; deserving now the stick and now a carrot; both pathetically and absurdly beautiful. So the body. There's no living with it till we recognize that one of its functions in our lives is to play the part of buffoon' (pp. 93–4). He goes on: 'Eros ... may at moments cause us to take it with total seriousness. The error consists in concluding that Eros should always do so and permanently abolish the joke .... There is indeed at certain moments a high poetry in the flesh itself; but also, by your leave, an irreducible element of obstinate and ludicrous un-poetry' (p. 94). He is thinking of what is portrayed in slap-stick comedies about Eros: the valet chasing the chambermaid.

He contrasts Eros with Friendship, the most personal of loves. He points out that Eros is partly impersonal: 'in the act of love we are

10. I have discussed this in my book on the *Gorgias* (Dilman 1979), and the *Phaedo* (Dilman 1992).

not merely ourselves; we are also representatives' (p. 95) – he means of our sex, of something we have in common with others, of something in which we are alike. I find interesting what he says about nakedness in this context. In moral contexts the image of nakedness is meant to highlight what we are really like behind our social position, other people's opinions of us, our prestige, etc. ... Thus the image of nakedness in Plato's *Gorgias*. In the context of sex, however, Lewis points out, nakedness reveals the impersonal in us which belongs to our sex: 'by nudity the lovers cease to be solely John and Mary; the universal He and She are emphasized' (p. 96).

When Lewis turns from the carnal element in sexual love to Eros as a whole he emphasizes its 'total commitment', its 'reckless disregard of happiness', its 'transcendence of self-regard' (p. 99). He also points out that 'speaking with that very grandeur and displaying that very transcendence of self' Eros 'may urge to evil as well to good'. He says that 'nothing is shallower than the belief that a love which leads to sin is always qualitatively lower ... than one which leads to faithful, fruitful and Christian marriage.' Thus, if I may add, in *Anna Karenina* Tolstoy contrasts the love of Anna and Vronsky with that between Kitty and Levin; but he never suggests that the former is a shallow love. It is not so by any means.

I now return to Lewis's point that 'the real spiritual danger in Eros as a whole lies ... elsewhere' – not in its carnal element (p. 90). It lies in making Eros into a god, in giving it unconditional obedience when it speaks most like a god: 'Eros, honoured without reservation and obeyed unconditionally, becomes a demon' (p. 101).

Divinely indifferent to our selfishness, he is also demonically rebellious to every claim of God or Man that would oppose him (pp. 101–2).

He then quotes two lines from a poem:

People in love cannot be moved by kindness,
And opposition makes them feel like martyrs.

So the real danger, as with other loves, is the one that has its source in something endemic to the natural love in question itself; in this case to Eros: 'of all loves, Eros is, at its height, most god-like; therefore most prone to demand our worship.... The real danger ... [is] that the lovers will idolise Eros himself' (p. 102).

Lewis finally points out the 'insufficiency' of Eros. I quote:

He (Eros) is notoriously the most mortal of our loves. The world rings with complaints of his fickleness. What is baffling is the combination of this fickleness with the protestations of permanency. To be in love is both to intend and to promise lifelong fidelity.

The event of falling in love is of such a nature that we are right to reject as intolerable the idea that it should be transitory. In one high bound it has overleaped the massive wall of our selfhood; it has made appetite itself altruistic, tossed personal happiness aside as a triviality and planted the interests of another in the centre of our being. Spontaneously and without effort we have fulfilled the law (towards one person) by loving our neighbour as ourselves. It is...a foretaste of what we must become to all if Love Himself rules in us without a rival. It is even (well used) a preparation for that.[11] Simply to relapse from it...is a sort of *disredemption*. [But] Eros is driven to promise what Eros of himself cannot perform (pp. 104–5).

He (Eros), like a godparent, makes the vows; it is we who must keep them (pp. 105–6).

(I quoted the last part of this passage in full earlier in the introductory section of this chapter.)

11. See Plato's *Symposium*: Diotima's speech.

10

C.S. Lewis in Four Loves: Charity and the Christian Love of God

10.1 Natural Loves and the Supernatural

So far I have discussed what C.S. Lewis writes about the natural loves. Why 'natural' and in what sense? Sometimes he talks of them as our 'earthly' loves – earthly as opposed to 'heavenly' or 'eternal'. The contrast is a religious one and belongs to Christianity.

What is natural is what belongs to our nature as human beings. We have seen that he speaks of human beings as 'composite creatures'. We have a physical existence, that is we need food, water, air, are subject to pain and diseases, have appetites in the satisfaction of which we find pleasure. As human beings, rooted in such a physical existence and living with other human beings, within the form of life we have developed, we are subject to the conflicts which belong to the different types of relationships we develop amongst ourselves. Thus we are subject to ambitions, rivalries, anger, resentment, jealousies, all sorts of desires which would not be possible but for the kind of life we have developed and the human world in which we live and interact with one another. This constitutes our earthly life and the different things I have mentioned are natural to us within that life. In all of it, and within certain limits, we think of ourselves, not necessarily selfishly, but in the sense that when pressed or threatened we protect ourselves. What I am inclined to call 'the instinct of survival' in its broadest sense sets limits to what we do for each other, limits that vary from person to person in accordance with their character – their greed, their anxieties, and their self-protective defences.

Within the kind of life I have indicated human beings, of course, love one another, go to each other's help, respond to one another's needs, and show generosity towards each other. But all the good and generosity which thus finds expression in us, varying in degree from person to person, bears the stamp of the life I have indicated. It is the goodness and love of creatures who have been formed in and belong to such a life – earthly life.

Here one may ask: what other kind of life can there be? The answer is: a life conditioned by a transcendence of the limits, the barriers that are endemic to our earthly life, a life in which what we can achieve, manage to do, goes against the grain of everything *natural* to us in our earthly life. What the very few of us thus achieve, or at any rate move towards, and what thus finds expression in their ordinary lives, has been characterized as having a spiritual, 'other worldly' character. It is the fact that human beings have, within the logical space of their earthly life, such a capacity or potentiality that makes them 'composite creatures' to use Lewis' expression. Plato is thinking of the same thing when he says that we are made of body and soul – 'body' in the sense of 'flesh' as this term is used in Christianity (see Dilman, 1992, Chapter 5).

So it is by the *transcendence* of the limits which characterize our earthly life, limits which belong to what is *natural* to human beings in that life, that human beings can gain access to what is spiritual. Lewis, a deeply Christian writer, agrees with Plato that it takes labour to do so and that such labour consists in purifying the soul from the 'body' in the wide sense which has the self at its centre in the way I have indicated:

> Natural loves can hope for eternity only insofar as they have allowed themselves to be taken into the eternity of charity; have at least allowed the process to begin here on earth, before the night comes when no man can work. And the process will always involve a kind of death (p. 125).

The kind of death is death of the self – not the cessation of our earthly engagements but their purification. The self has to die in those engagements so that, though they continue, they are transformed in their character. As a Christian Lewis says that it is God who comes to us in our love for him, a love implicit in charity, who transforms those engagements.

But let me begin at the beginning, where Lewis begins his chapter on Charity. There he raises the question of the 'rivalry' between our natural or earthly loves and the love of God. He is particularly concerned to redress a misunderstanding hidden in the idea of their 'rivalry'. The idea is that we have to turn away from our everyday engagements in order to find the love of God – a kind of asceticism. He mentions a passage from St Augustine's *Confessions* to illustrate it, though he points out that this passage is not typical of Augustine's Christianity – it is 'a hangover from the high-minded Pagan philosophies in which he grew up' (p. 111). The context of the passage is Augustine's desolation at the death of his friend Nebridius. This is the gist of what he says as Lewis puts it:

> This is what comes of giving one's heart to anything but God. All human beings pass away. Do not let your happiness depend on something you may lose. If love is to be a blessing, not a misery, it must be for the only Beloved who will never pass away (p. 110).

Lewis points out that the prudential character of such a precept is not compatible with any kind of love, let alone the love of God. In any case how else can one's love of God find expression but in one's earthly life – in one's engagements there? How else can one love God but in one's love for His creatures? Tolstoy has shown us in his story of Martin Avdeitch how Christ came to the old cobbler in the form of the poor and downtrodden. There is a similar story about St Nicholas. On his way to keep an appointment with God he stopped to help a peasant whose carriage was stuck in the snow. He would have perished if his carriage were not freed. Thus delayed St Nicholas thought he had missed his appointment; but it was God who had appeared to him in the form of the peasant. That was his appointment with God and he kept it without knowing it. If he had thought that God was in that peasant he would have stopped on that account in which case God would not have been in that peasant. To put the dot on the i, it is in the spirit of one's engagements that one finds God, that one loves Him – and finding Him and loving Him is one and the same thing.

To return to the passage from St Augustine, Lewis points out that there is no insurance in love against heartache. Not even in one's love of God. It did not protect Christ on the Cross when he thought he had been forsaken by God. 'There is no safe investment' – that is giving of oneself. 'To love at all is to be vulnerable. Love anything, and your heart will certainly be wrung and possibly be broken.' But to lock it up is to put it in 'the coffin of your selfishness'. There it will become 'unbreakable, impenetrable, irredeemable' and that is 'damnation' (pp. 111–12). 'I believe (Lewis says) that the most lawless and inordinate loves are less contrary to God's will than a self-invited and self-protective lovelessness' (p. 112). He concludes:

> We shall draw nearer to God, not by trying to avoid the suffer-ings inherent in all loves, but by accepting them and offering them to Him; throwing away all defensive armour. If our hearts need to be broken, and if He chooses this as the way in which they should break, so be it (p. 112).

Still, he points out, our natural loves can be inordinate, which does not mean 'too much'. What is in question is who one puts or serves first. One's natural loves would be inordinate, as Lewis means this, if one allows them to eclipse one's love of God, if – as he put it in earlier chapters – one makes any of them, say Eros, into a god. One cannot love one's parents, one's wife, or one's friend too much; it is *the way* that one loves them that is of concern. 'Our Lord [he says] says nothing about guarding against earthly loves for fear we might be hurt' (p. 113). He then quotes some words from *Luke*: 'If any man come to me and hate not his father and mother and wife ... and his own life also, he cannot be my disciple' (XIV, 26). He explains that 'hate' here should not be understood as we normally understand it; in that sense a man who hates father, mother and wife, and thus one full of hate, could not love God. No, what is meant is that one who is to follow Christ must not give pride of place to any of his earthly loves.

So, Lewis emphasizes, our earthly loves are not rivals to our love of God, and God does not enjoin us to reject our earthly loves. To think so would be a serious misunderstanding. What someone com-mitted to Christianity is enjoined to do is *to order* his loves (p. 114). He quotes two lines from a Cavalier poet:

> I could not love thee, dear, so much.
> Loved I not honour more.

These are words addressed to his mistress. What he is saying is that if he did not love honour 'more', i.e., put it first, love it with *all* his heart, he would not be the man he is. In that case he could not love his mistress the way he does; for then he would not honour her the way he does and so his love for her would be an inferior love. She, on her part, understands this and so finds no rivalry between his love for her and his love for honour, she feels no jealousy for his love of honour and for the way he gives pride of place to it. There is thus a parallel between the relation in which sexual love stands to love of honour in chivalry and the relation in which our earthly loves stand to the love of God in Christianity.

10.2 The Christian Love of God

> The humblest of us, in a State of Grace, can have ... some 'tasting' of Love Himself; but man, even at his highest sanctity and intelligence, has no direct 'knowledge about' the ultimate Being – only analogies (C.S. Lewis, p. 115).

'We cannot see light (he says in a way reminiscent of Plato in the *Republic*), though by light we can see things' (ibid.). The light of God, the framework of our religious beliefs, puts things in a certain light for us, make us see them in certain aspects under which we would not see them but for those beliefs. Consequently they transform our feelings towards them, the way we apprehend them affectively. For instance we see other men as creatures of God, as ourselves, and in our feelings take them as 'fellow creatures', 'our brothers'. We take what we enjoy as 'gifts of God' and so feel thankful; we see our misfortunes as 'the will of God' and so accept them without resentment and without looking for an explanation: 'Why has this befallen me?'

'God is love' (p. 116). In other words God is not an object. He dwells in the believer's love, his love of another human being, when that love is absolutely pure. Thus the believer knows Him *there*; even, I would say, the non-believer can be said – by the believer – to know Him there. I add 'by the believer', since only he speaks this language and not the non-believer. He is known there, but never directly or openly. For He is hidden. This is a second reason why He cannot be known directly. If He were not hidden, he would not be there, in our love for another human being. One can say that God is necessarily hidden – the way He was hidden in the Russian peasant whom St Nicholas rescued.

Simone Weil says that God created the universe by retiring from it out of love so as to force human love to become supernatural. Christ remained faithful to God in his love while he believed he had been abandoned, that is in the void, without the consoling belief that God was with him. 'What a gulf of love on both sides' she says while reflecting on the crucifixion. God's 'absence' in His creation, the way He has abandoned human life to the mercy of chance and necessity, she argues, is something positive. The natural necessities that encroach on human lives are at once a veil of God which screens Him from us, and also a mirror (Weil, 1968, p. 194). They mirror God's absence from this world, His way of not inter-fering with it out of love. In His way of hiding Himself He loves us. Natural necessity is thus at the same time a gateway to God. It makes it possible for human beings to love Him without any thought of return. If He did not hide Himself from us thus, if He were not absent from His creation, our love of Him could not be supernatural. In that case what we love would not be Him.

There is something of the same thought, expressed in the much gentler style of Lewis, in the following passage:

> The real work must be, of all our works, the most secret. Even as far as possible secret from ourselves. Our right hand must not know what our left is doing.

He then gives an example we find equally in Simone Weil and dis-cussed by Peter Winch in his inaugural lecture 'Moral Integrity' (Winch, 1972, p. 181).

> We have not got far enough if we play a game of cards with the children 'merely' to amuse them or to show that they are for-given. If this is the best we can do we are right to do it. But it would be better if a deeper, less conscious, Charity threw us into a frame of mind in which a little fun with the children was the thing we should at the moment like best (p. 123).

Only then, when we are totally absorbed, do we give ourselves wholeheartedly, do we forget ourselves. Thus to take an extreme case, if we give money to a beggar for God's sake, we shall have been recompensed. We will have had our reward in this world, our giving would have been worldly; and if our giving were for the sake of such reward it would be corrupt. In either case God would not have been present in our giving, our charity would be a 'natural love'. For this to be otherwise God must be hidden in it from us.

The passage I am quoting continues:

> We are, however, much helped in this necessary work by that very feature of our experience at which we most repine. ... In

everyone, and of course in ourselves, there is that which requires forbearance, tolerance, forgiveness. The necessity of practising these virtues first sets us, forces us, upon the attempt to turn ... our love into Charity.[12] These frets and rubs [e.g. one's children – being infuriating, even odious, one's husband being lazy, extravagant, one's wife being subject to moods, one's father being close-fisted] are beneficial. It may even be that where there are fewest of them the conversion of natural love is most difficult. When they are plentiful the necessity of rising above it is obvious p. 124).

This is the meaning, Lewis points out, of the saying that it is hard for 'the rich' to enter the Kingdom of Heaven.

10.3 Charity or Compassion: Love of One's Neighbour

As a Christian Lewis speaks of our natural loves as God's gift to us. This goes with his earlier remark that in saying of each that 'it is not enough' he does not mean to belittle them. To say this is 'to indicate where their real glory lies' (p. 107). For their real glory lies in what, with God's grace, they promise to grow into.

When God planted the garden of our nature and caused the flowering, fruiting loves to grow there, He set our will to 'dress' them. Compared with them [i.e. without them] it [the garden of our nature] is dry and cold. And unless His grace comes down, like the rain and the sunshine, we shall use this tool ['decency and common sense'] to little purpose. But its laborious – and largely negative services – are indispensable (p. 108).

'But in addition to these natural loves [he writes] God can bestow a far better gift ... two gifts': (i) a share of His own Gift-love towards others, namely charity and (ii) a Gift-love towards God Himself (p. 117). Our natural loves, he had pointed out, have a giving, caring aspect: they are in part 'gift loves'. Here, under (i), he is speaking of godly or supernatural gift-love; what he calls 'charity'. This is

---

12. C.S. Lewis uses the word 'charity' as the name of a supernatural love – unlike the way I used it just above.

a love that is 'wholly disinterested' and is not put off by the repulsiveness, physical or moral, of those towards whom it is directed.

> Natural Gift-love is always directed to objects which the lover finds in some way intrinsically lovable. ... Divine Gift-love in the man enables him to love what is not naturally lovable; lepers, criminals, enemies, morons, the sulky, the superior and the sneering (p. 117).

There is a parallel to this in Simone Weil's notion of a natural equilibrium and the way it distinguishes a 'social' morality from one permeated by supernatural goodness. In times of stability and with social arrangements that ensure people more or less similar powers men respect each other, observe rules of justice, co-operate with each other, punish those who have transgressed such rules of law. But where the circumstances change in a person's or group's 'favour' a new equilibrium is reached. The same person who previously respected others now starts taking advantage of them. It takes a supernatural love which establishes supernatural justice in the heart for a person to desist: to desist commanding wherever he has the power to do so.

Where we have such power we *naturally* are inclined to expand, to impose our will on others. There is in the soul, she says, something like a phagocyte; it causes it to expand and fill in all the space which the circumstances allow it. It takes supernatural love to bear this void – thus Christ's fidelity to God when he was not sustained by the belief that God was with him: 'Why hast thou forsaken me?' All desire for reward, compensation, consolation which mars so much of our moral life and actions, she points out, has at its root this natural tendency of the soul to expand, its inability to bear the void created in our souls by what comes out of us, by what we give, so that we expect a return, or by the hurt and humiliation we receive, so that we desire to return it. This is the desire for equilibrium which belongs to the part of our soul which makes part of the nature we share with other human beings.

Equally, and in these terms, to love the lovable is easy, for the lovable attract our love. The pleasure we find in doing so constitutes a return of what we give, of what goes out of us. The equilibrium remains, no void is created in our soul. But it is otherwise when it comes to loving the unlovable. That is why charity which consists in doing so is supernatural; it goes against the grain of our nature, of our natural loves.

We saw that Lewis says that besides our natural loves God has given us the possibility of charity and a Gift-love towards God Himself. We have seen that Lewis claims that our love of God is to a large extent, but not wholly, a Need-love. Here we may ask: how can a need-love be directed to God? how can it have the purity required for it to be so directed? I shall return to this. But there is a problem about its giving character too, it involves a paradox: 'how can one give to God anything which is not already his; and if it is already His, what have you given?' (p. 117).

Lewis points out that since we can keep what God has given to us, keep it from God, we can also give it to Him. We can freely offer it back to Him. We can say, 'Thy will be done', give up our own will and accept His. We can, furthermore, return what He has given us in helping the poor and downtrodden, in loving them. When we do so, we have seen, it is God in them that we love – as Tolstoy expressed it in his story of the cobbler Martin Avdeitch. 'And this (says Lewis) is Gift-love to God whether we know it or not' (p. 118). He continues:

> Love Himself can work in those who know nothing of Him. [He means those who know nothing of Christianity.] The sheep in the parable had no idea either of the God hidden in the prisoner whom they visited or of the God hidden in themselves when they made the visit. (I take the whole parable to be about the judgement of the heathen ...) (ibid.).

God thus, Lewis has pointed out, gives us two Gift-loves. He now adds that He also gives us two Need-loves: a supernatural Need-love of Himself and a supernatural Need-love of another. He points out that the first of these is 'a love which does not dream of disinterestedness'.

> God turns our need of Him into a Need-love of Him. What is stranger still is that He creates in us a more than natural receptivity of Charity from our fellow men. Need is so near to greed and we are so greedy already that it seems a strange grace (p. 118).

I should like to comment that there are two different senses in which we, as human beings, may be said to need God, and the need, in each of the two different senses, makes us dependent on God in two different ways. The first is indeed close to greed, the second is not. The first pertains to the individual in his particular character – e.g. he needs coaxing in order to come out of his shell, he has a need for praise and approval. The second pertains to human beings as such and may be attributed to an individual who feels no such need. It is in some ways akin to the sense in which an engine, any engine, may be said to need oil. Thus Simone Weil speaks of 'the needs of the soul' – liberty, roots, etc. This sense of need involves certain value judgements. What is in question is what the soul must have in order to survive or, even, flourish. But the criteria of what counts as the soul's survival, or what counts as its growth or flourishing, are not morally neutral – in contrast with the criteria of what counts as an engine to be in good working order.

Now if a religious believer, a Christian, says that man needs God, he is incomplete without God, that is with his back turned to God in his denial of Him a man would go to the dogs, or even is in Hell, it is the second sense of 'need' that is in question. The dependence which such a need gives man is something to be acknowledged and accepted in humility and not fought. Of course this very statement is one that can only be made from within Christianity, from within the framework of its beliefs. By contrast, when Freud says that Christian believers need God in the way that children need the support, approval and guidance of their father, but that as grown ups they ought to take responsibility for their lives and throw away their crutches, he is saying something mixed. He misunderstands the sense in which in the best of Christian theology God is said to be 'our Father who lives in Heaven', though he understands only too well how it is taken by some – probably a fair number of – Christian believers. He responds to them with a value judgement: grow up, throw away your crutches.

Here, in this second example, the need attributed to believers is a psychological need, not a spiritual one as in the first case. And the dependence which has its source in such a need is an 'immature' form of dependence. It is one in which the individual tries to evade responsibility for his life. It is a serious mistake to think that in saying 'Thy will be done', in putting his trust in God, in accepting His will, the believer is inevitably evading responsibility for his life and actions. If the believer speaks from genuine conviction, if he has made his beliefs his own, if he is behind what he says, there would be nothing childish in the way he puts his trust in God. We have already seen the way in which Christianity is a *spiritual* religion and is meant to lift up the believer to the supernatural, to throw away the crutches, which we *naturally* need, of reward, compensation and consolation.

Now having said this, let me ask, in what sense of need does C.S. Lewis claim our love of God and our charity contain an element of need-love? On the first page of his Introduction to the book, Chapter 1, he writes: 'We are born helpless. As soon as we are fully conscious we discover loneliness. We *need* others physically, emotionally, intellectually; we *need* them if we are to know anything, even ourselves' (p. 7, italics mine). Here clearly he is commenting on human existence as such, and the needs he highlights are 'existential' needs, not psychological ones. He points out that while Divine Love is *par excellence* gift-love it does contain an element of need-love – for though God lacks nothing, he needs our need-love (ibid.). He needs it out of love – gift-love. For our need-love for Him is a good, and turning away from that need on our part is missing the opportunity of gaining access to a spiritual love. If I may put it paradoxically: God's need-love for his creatures is a gift-love.

As for our love of God, Lewis points out that a man who comes before his Creator and says, 'I'm no beggar. I love you disinterestedly' would show a detachment and arrogance which is not compatible with a love of God (p. 9). One can only love God in humility, and the need that characterizes a human being's love of God is an expression of such humility, it is a recognition of his incompleteness without God. Such recognition is an essential part of a creature's love of God, and I take it that it is precisely that which makes it a need-love. Lewis points out that 'those expressions of unworthiness which Christian practice puts into the believer's mouth' are not expressions of servility, forms of grovelling (p. 119).

They are an expression in the believer of his recognition of the distance between God and himself and as such a form of appreciation – what Lewis calls appreciation-love. In contrast, he points out, 'no sooner do we believe that God loves us than there is an impulse to believe that He does so, not because He is Love, but because we are intrinsically lovable' (p. 119). This is the pride which turns a person away from God. Lewis points out that it is very tenacious: 'Beaten out of this, we next offer our own humility to God's admiration .... Or, if not that, our clear-sighted and humble recognition that we still lack humility. Thus, depth beneath depth, and subtlety within subtlety, there remains some lingering idea of our own, our very own, attractiveness' (p. 119). He adds that 'it is... almost impossible to realize for long, that we are mirrors whose brightness, if we are bright, is wholly derived from the sun that shines upon us' (pp. 119–20).

This need then being a person's recognition of his 'neediness' as a creature has nothing to do with greed. Lewis describes it as 'the innocent need that is inherent in [our] creaturely condition' (p. 120).

In the case of charity the giving has to be free of any thought of oneself and of all forms of condescension. There is also a way of receiving this, of accepting one's need for help, one that is free of pride, in which the person receiving help and compassion responds with gratitude. Genuine charity does not demean or humiliate and it is directed to a person as a creature of God, our neighbour, whatever he may be like.

10.4   The Transmutation of our Natural Loves

The kind of love with which a believer loves his God and the kind of God he loves and, therefore, believes in are internally related. One cannot love a supernatural God, in the sense that both C.S. Lewis and Simone Weil use this term 'supernatural', with a natural love. But we have seen that a supernatural God can transform a person's natural love for God by His Grace through the eradication of the self-regard it contains. The purification of such natural love from the self-regard which contaminates it involves inner work or labour in which the person engages. Simone Weil describes the division of labour (though she does not use such an expression) between such work and God's grace by saying that the work consists in turning the soul to God and keeping its gaze in the direction of God. When the soul can keep its gaze fixed in that direction – she speaks of it as *'attente de Dieu'*, waiting on God – God comes to the person, traversing an infinite distance to do so. It is the spiritual contact, thus, which is made possible by attention on the part of the person and the emptying of his soul of all self-regarding desires and sentiments, on the one hand, and what emanates from the goodness that he finds in what then comes into focus, that transforms him in his soul and the loves that are there – the natural loves. But time and hence waiting, patience, and sustaining the not wanting anything for oneself, is a necessary part of the process of such transformation. Hurrying and haste and the wish for quick results belong to greed and the self.

As Lewis puts it: 'God turns our need of Him into a Need-love of him' (p. 118). It also transforms our natural need-love for one another into 'charity' and equally 'our natural receptivity of Charity from our fellow men' (ibid.). Charity, we have seen, is a love that loves the unlovable, a love therefore that loves us irrespective of what we are like, a love that is not interested in our cleverness, beauty, generosity, fairness, usefulness. That is not the love we naturally want at all. The indifference of such love to the self in us – the ego – is (Lewis points out) 'a terrible shock' (p. 120).

Lewis gives the example of an infirm husband who has to depend on his wife's inexhaustible loving care. 'In such a case [he says] to receive is harder and perhaps more blessed than to give' (p. 121). He points out that everyone who has a good family is at times the recipient of charity.

> Thus God admitted to the human heart, transforms not only Gift-love but Need-love; not only our Need-love of Him, but our Need-love of one another (pp. 121–2).

In some extreme cases a natural love may have to be totally renounced: 'A high and terrible vocation, like Abraham's, may constrain a man to turn his back on his own people and his father's house. Eros, directed to a forbidden object, may have to be renounced' (p. 122). But in most cases our natural loves become modes of charity. Thus the wife who looks after an infirm husband, a son who cares for an old and difficult mother and tolerates her cantankerousness. In an earlier chapter I mentioned the example of T.S. Eliot who cared for his wife after she had lost her mind.

> The natural loves are [thus] called to become perfect Charity and also perfect natural loves (ibid.).

Lewis makes a parallel with God's incarnation in Christ: charity enters into our natural loves so that they take on the character of charity as God becomes man. He points out that 'nothing is either too trivial or too animal to be thus transformed: a game, a joke, a drink together, idle chat, a walk, the act of Venus – all these can be modes in which we forgive or accept forgiveness, in which we console or are reconciled .... Thus in our very instincts appetites and recreations, Love has prepared for Himself "a body" ' (p. 122).

Lewis points out that this takes work and that it is easy to 'take a wrong turn' (p. 123). But, he says, the trials and difficulties that stand in our way are *necessary*. Simone Weil speaks of them as ladders to the supernatural. They are necessary because where life is easy, where our natural tendencies meet no obstacle, we remain on the plane of the natural; we are not forced to, we have no motive to change direction, no reason to examine our life. This, says Simone Weil, applies not merely to the 'frets and rubs' that Lewis mentions, but even more so to the evil in the world and affliction. I shall quote two very short passages from *La Pesanteur et la Grâce – Gravity and Grace* – the translation is mine:

> When one loves God through evil as such, it is really God that one loves ...

> As mystery [i.e. its secrecy from itself] forces the virtue of faith to become supernatural, similarly evil forces our love to become supernatural – to take on the character of charity (Chapter on Evil).

> The extreme greatness of Christianity comes from the fact that it does not look for a supernatural remedy for suffering but a supernatural usage of it (Chapter on Affliction).

C.S. Lewis, having made a parallel between such transformation and the incarnation of God in Christ, speaks of the transformation of natural loves as 'the resurrection of our greater body' (p. 124). The 'greater body' is 'the general fabric of our earthly life with its affections and relationships'. It is the life in which we engage as 'composite beings' – as 'embodied beings'. Spiritual life is, of course, our life as 'embodied beings'. 'Embodied' is in a sense a pleonasm since there is no intelligible alternative to it, as Lewis indicates at the very end of the book when he comments on death and the Christian belief in Heaven. I shall quote two sentences I quoted before:

> Natural loves can hope for eternity only insofar as they have allowed themselves to be taken into the eternity of charity; have at least allowed the process to begin here on earth, before

the night comes when man can work. And the process will always involve a kind of death (p. 125).

Lewis makes it clear that he does not speak of 'eternity' as endless duration, nor does he mean 'another place' by Heaven. He contrasts 'to meet in the eternal world' with meeting a school friend later on in life as an adult. 'Neither of you (he writes) now plays conkers. You no longer want to swop your help with his French exercise for his help with your arithmetic. In Heaven, I suspect, a love that had never embodied Love Himself would be equally irrelevant. For Nature has passed away. All that is not eternal is eternally out of date' (p. 125). In other words, when our earthly love is over meeting as we understand it, for instance in 'we met at the station' or in 'we met after an interval of a great many years and there was still a meeting of minds between us', no longer makes any sense: and what other sense of 'meeting' is there?

Lewis then adds that 'reunion with the loved dead is not the goal of the Christian life' – as it is widely thought (p. 126). We must not 'pin our comfort on the hope – perhaps even with the aid of *séance* and necromancy – of some day, this time forever, enjoying the earthly beloved again ... It is hard not to imagine that such an endless prolongation of earthly happiness would be completely satisfying' (p. 126). He points out, like Simone Weil, that Christianity, as a spiritual religion, is not a religion of consolation: 'the moment we attempt to use our faith in the other world for this purpose, that faith weakens' (ibid.).

Earlier, in connection with what he calls 'our Need-love of God', he spoke of ' joy in total dependence: we become "jolly beggars" ' (p. 120). He is not denying that the Christian faith offers hope and comfort – but not earthly hope and comfort:

There is no good applying to Heaven for earthly comfort. Heaven can give heavenly comfort; no other kind (p. 126).

He then adds:

And earth cannot give earthly comforts either. There is no earthly comfort in the long run (p. 127).

Why does he say this? Partly, I think, because the comforts we find in things of this world for its pains is temporary – e.g., drowning one's sorrows in work, sex or alcohol, looking for compensations for our insecurities in success or material goods, seeking revenge for wrongs done to us. But they are not only temporary but, from the perspective of Christianity, they are also harmful, they deprive us of the motive for and opportunity of finding 'heavenly comfort'. They separate us from God: 'our heart has no rest till it comes to Thee' (St Augustine). 'Down here [Lewis writes] it is all loss and renunciation. The very purpose of the bereavement...may have been to force this upon us. We are then compelled to try to believe, what we cannot yet feel [in our bereavement] that God is our true Beloved' (p. 127).

When he says, 'down here it is all loss and renunciation' the contrast is with what it is like in Heaven. And we shall find Heaven 'when [as he puts it] we see the face of God' – he means here in the mirror of our earthly life and in the things that surround it and form part of its environment. 'In Heaven there will be no anguish and no duty of turning away from our earthly beloveds. First, because we shall have turned already; from the portraits to the Original...from the creatures He made lovable to Love Himself. But secondly, because we shall find them all in Him. By loving Him more than them we shall love them more than we now do' (p. 127).

10.5   Some Concluding Remarks

One can attribute a love of God to a heathen, but one cannot speak of a love of God at all except from within a religious perspective – the perspective of a religion. C.S. Lewis speaks and writes as a Christian. I am interested to shed light on the concepts he uses and the connections he makes by means of them. I do so as a philosopher, not as a Christian. In any case I am not one. I try to understand, to enter into his perspective, to understand the meaning of what he says, to borrow his eyes and appreciate what comes to view from the perspective of the concepts he uses. I do no more than this in previous chapters when discussing what psychoanalysts have to say about love.

Where do I stand myself? First of all in my belief that there is something important in what each wants to say about love and, secondly, that these do not stand as far apart from each other as we may think at first. As I see it there is *some* affinity – I stress the word 'some' – between the psycho-analytic concept of maturity, as it applies to the individual and to his loves, and the religious concept of purity of soul, as it is used to characterize an individual's life and his relations with others. To repeat, my concern in this book is with different forms of love, the way they stand to each other and each to the person's character, affective maturity, and spirituality. The dimensions of the different loves are the possibilities within them as determined by what part of himself the lover is able to put into them.

C.S. Lewis's little book is packed with insight and has helped me to articulate some of the things I have myself wanted to bring out. In the next chapter I move on to Kierkegaard.

11

Kierkegaard on the Christian Injunction to Love One's Neighbour

11.1 Preliminaries

In his book *Works of Love* Kierkegaard is concerned primarily with Christian or spiritual love, what I have earlier referred to as 'supernatural love' – after Simone Weil and C.S. Lewis. He writes as a Christian and has a lot to say about what commitment to its perspective means for the individual: how the genuinely committed individual is seen from the point of view of the world and how he fares in the hands of what Plato called 'the great beast'. The distinction he makes between Christian love and human or pagan love and the way he contrasts them presupposes the perspective of Christianity. He also discusses their relation and asks whether they are at all compatible – a question on which, as we have seen, C.S. Lewis had something important to say. Indeed Kierkegaard's book divides in two: a detailed analysis of the Christian precept 'You Shall Love Your Neighbour' and a discussion of what he calls 'the works of love'. In these two contexts he has a great deal to say about Christian or spiritual love, as directed to other human beings and as directed to God. In the present chapter and the following one I shall discuss what he says about love under these two headings.

He begins with what he calls 'love's hidden life'. He compares love's life, that is the way the individual lives it when his love is genuinely spiritual, to the life of a plant: 'the love of a plant is hidden: the fruit is the manifestation'. He wrongly puts this side by side with: 'the life of thought is hidden; the utterance of speech is the manifestation' (p. 26). True, in both cases the relation in question is internal. But the idea that thought is hidden is a philosophical confusion into which many philosophers have fallen (see Dilman 1987, Chapter 4). Love's life, however, is hidden, in the sense Kierkegaard means this, in that it appears in the fruits of its works and not in its blossoms. Rilke puts this beautifully in his sixth Duino Elegy:

> Fig tree, how long it's been full meaning for me,
> the way you almost entirely omit to flower
> and into the early-resolute fruit
> uncelebratedly thrust your purest secret.
> Like the tube of a fountain, your bent bough drives the sap
> downwards and up; and it leaps from its sleep, scarce
> > waking,
> into the joy of its sweetest achievement. Look,
> like Jupiter into the swan.
>
> > ... But we, we linger,
> alas, we glory in flowering; already revealed
> we reach the retarded core of our ultimate fruit.

He then contrasts the 'we' with the 'few' in whom the 'pressure of action' enables them to resist 'the temptation to flower'. Rilke refers to them as 'heroes, perhaps, and those marked for early removal'. But they must be anonymous heroes, like Simone Weil's Breton seaman who simply said: 'it had to be done' or 'someone had to do it, I happened to be there'. It did not occur to him to think of himself as a hero. He is an unsung hero.

As Kierkegaard puts it: 'no poet, if he understands himself, would think of celebrating it [spiritual love] in song' (p. 26). And again: 'Only in self-renunciation can a man effectually praise love. No poet can do it. The poet can sing of erotic love and friendship, and the ability to do this is a rare gift, but *the poet* cannot praise love [spiritual love]' (p. 335). 'To praise self-renunciation's love and then to want to be the lover is certainly a lack of self-renunciation' (p. 342).

Kierkegaard speaks of 'the inwardness of self-renunciation' (p. 133). In other words, it is not something for anyone to see. It is not anybody's concern. Kierkegaard would say that it is something strictly between the person in question and God. Certainly it must not be something from which he can derive any benefit. This inwardness which characterizes the love in question is precisely what makes it spiritual love – spiritual as opposed to impulsive – Kierkegaard sometimes uses the word 'spontaneous' – merely a matter of the emotions as opposed to involving commitment.

> Love, to be sure, proceeds from the heart, but let us not in our haste about this forget the eternal truth that love forms the heart. Every man experiences the transient excitement of an inconstant heart, but to have a heart in this natural sense is infinitely different from forming a heart in the eternal sense (p. 30).

'Forms the heart': he means that one can learn from love. A person can so change affectively in himself as to grow in wisdom. The transient excitement of an inconstant heart are the impulsive responses that come from the heart; they are responses of the moment, responses to what transpires at the time without any thought to the past or the future. For the person to make such connections, to see and take 'the moment' within the circumstances in which it transpires, he needs to have settled sentiments, a certain unity of self, a togetherness within himself, which enables him to have a basis from which to judge. I was going to say a '*constant* basis', but that would be a pleonasm, since anything which is to provide such a basis has to have some constancy. Such inner togetherness or unity can only come from *believing* in or caring for certain things, giving one's heart to them – and that is the very opposite of thinking of oneself. It is only in the *giving* of one's heart that one's heart is formed. Giving way to one's impulses and inclinations of the moment is not giving one's heart to anything.

Kierkegaard contrasts Christian love with what he calls 'human' or 'pagan' love. In this context 'human' and 'pagan' come to the same thing for, as he argues convincingly, in what makes us 'human', or 'fallen' as C.S. Lewis puts it, in what we find natural, we are pagan – and that, Kierkegaard argues, applies to a great deal of Christianity. Christianity, he argues, may have come into existence eighteen centuries ago – now nineteen – and the change it made possible for people is thus eighteen – or nineteen – hundred years old. But 'it is not so very long ago since both you, reader, and I were pagans, were pagans – that is, if we have become Christians at all' (p. 42). For each person has to turn away from paganism in himself, as an individual, and give himself to Christianity. But that means becoming the target of the scorn of the world and even its persecution. For the reward of being Christian, not merely in appearance, but in reality, in the commitment of inwardness, 'putting it most mildly, is ingratitude from the world' (p. 187). 'The opposition of the world stands in an *essential* relationship to the inwardness of Christianity' (ibid.).

Kierkegaard is thinking of the costliness of being good in the Christian sense, of how often it brings the true believer in conflict with those who want to advance themselves in the world, are prepared to lie for it, to others and also to themselves. He is thinking of the way goodness is scorned for its refusal to avail itself of strength and use it, envied for its inner calm and integrity, hated for its refusal to abide by the rules of the world's practices, and persecuted for standing in the way of its compromises with evil. To be a Christian is to give up a very great deal of what much within and outside us incline and tempt us to want, to do so without expecting any reward for it but rather its opposite. Kierkegaard would say that it is remarkable that anybody should really want to be a Christian, wanting it with his eyes open, that is knowing what he is letting himself in for. It is only Christian love which makes this possible, that which works in one who opens his heart to it and who himself works to keep it open in the face of danger and temptation.

The works of love are the ways in which love works in one who keeps his heart open to it by making it pure and who learns from the experience of its demands. Its works, in the sense of its achievements, are the things it enables such a person to do, the remarkable things it enables him to do. These are gifts – seen from the Christian perspective – which he receives; but he has to labour, to put himself out, in order to receive them. That is he has actively himself to participate, to respond, to give himself to its demands. To do so he has to renounce himself, give up expecting and thinking in terms of rewards for himself. The gifts of love are not rewards; they are not anything that those who receive them can feel pleased for or from which they can derive any gratification. They are gifts in the sense that they are what the person in question receives from love. Being a lover he is at one with the love to which he gives himself, and as such he considers what he receives from love a blessing, a good, and in that sense a gift. He takes no credit for it.

It is these three things that make it a gift: it is something love gives him, anything that comes from love is a good for the lover – the 'true' lover as Kierkegaard calls him – and it is not something for which he takes credit, not something he considers he has earned, something which he has as it were bought with the sweat of his brow or merited. All these three aspects are written into our concept of a gift, although from what Kierkegaard calls the perspective of the world what is in question would not be considered a good and so would not be seen as a gift.

Kierkegaard expresses this contrast in stark terms: the busy people of this world 'sow and reap and sow and reap again', they 'gather stores full of what they reaped and rest upon their earnings – while alas he who in truth wills the good in the same span of time still does not see the frailest fruit of his labour and becomes the object of mockery like one who does not know how to sow'. Christianity then, Kierkegaard points out, 'procures vision through its parable of earthly life as the time of sowing and eternity the time of reaping' (p. 232). But eternity is not a time to come, a time in the future. If it were, the promise of what one will reap would be the reward for which one works and sows, and would make sense from the point of view of the world. Gain would be the motive and would let in the self through the back door and would destroy the spiritual character of the love whose gift becomes a reward in some very distant time to come. 'Earthly life as the time of sowing' – in other words in the course of one's life one should not concern oneself about what one will reap from one's good deeds, what they will produce for one. One's good deeds should be gratuitous; they should issue from one's loving concern for those to whom they are directed.

Human beings are capable of great feats when they want something badly enough. There is nothing remarkable in that. What is remarkable is when they can remain loyal to the demands of love 'in the void', as Simone Weil puts it, that is in the absence of any payment or reward, of any expectation that they will be loved in return, and even in the full recognition of the risk of being abandoned or persecuted for it. She distinguishes between something a person does because he wants to do it and something he does because he has to, like the Breton seaman – what she calls 'purpose' and 'necessity' (see my discussion in Dilman, 1979, Chapter 9). Kierkegaard makes the same distinction in terms of the Kantian expressions: 'inclination' and 'duty' – love as an inclination and love as a duty – and he puts prudence on the side of inclination. But while what he wants to say may be clear, it needs to be pointed out that like 'passion', both 'inclination' and 'prudence' cover a variety of things and that they do not all fall on the same side of this distinction.

11.2 'You Shall Love your Neighbour as Yourself'

Kierkegaard discusses this precept word for word and considers certain conceptual difficulties it is likely to raise for one who is trying to understand it, and through those considerations he sheds light on its meaning.

A. His first question is: why as yourself? All through the book he considers self-love as the very opposite of the love he is concerned with, namely Christian love or love of one's neighbour. 'One can perform works of love in an unloving, yes, even in a self-loving way, and when this is so, the works of love are nevertheless not the work of love' (p. 30). 'True love (he writes) is self-renunciation's love' (p. 339). Self-love, by contrast, as he uses the term, is a love that has not been purified by self-renunciation, one that is contaminated by self-regard and self-seeking. But in that case what is 'as yourself' doing in the command to love one's neighbour? As Kierkegaard puts it: 'is it possible for anyone to misunderstand this, as if it were the intention of Christianity to proclaim self-love as a prescriptive right?' 'On the contrary (he says), it is its purpose to wrest self-love away from us human beings' (p. 34).

Perhaps this phrase 'as yourself' seeks to teach each person who takes the precept to be addressed to him that in order to love others they should have a 'proper-self-love' or 'self-respect'. But what is the proper way to love oneself? 'Christianity presupposes that men love themselves' (p. 35). No doubt. This however is precisely what stands in the way of loving one's neighbours. 'Should it not be possible to love a person *more than oneself*?' (ibid.).

Perhaps one can love another human being in loving oneself. Kierkegaard claims that this is true of erotic love and friendship when the beloved and the friend are not at the same time loved as a neighbour. But, he points out, one cannot love God in loving oneself; insofar as one loves oneself one cannot love God – the God of Christianity. 'There is only one whom a man can with the truth of the eternal love above himself – that is God. Therefore it is not said: "Thou shalt love the Lord thy God as thyself"' (p. 36).

So in the case of other men this phrase 'as yourself' may have some work to do. 'If you can perceive what is best for him [the other] better than himself, you shall not be excused because the harmful thing was his own desire, what he himself asked for' (ibid.). In other words, sometimes, as the saying goes, you have to be cruel to be kind. That is you have to give God unconditional obedience; but with another human being you have to exercise your own judgement. This is what it is to act responsibly.

In an earlier chapter I considered Lady Macbeth's love for her husband. In her love for him she helped him to realize his dream, just because it was his dream, his will, as she surmised, and she loved him. That is she treated him as if he were God. This, I argued, made her love for him *flawed*. It is otherwise with a Christian's love for his God who would consider God's will to be his command – absolutely and unquestioningly.

This, however, does not get us very far in understanding the sense of 'as yourself' in the Christian precept to love one's neighbour. Do not do onto others what you do not want others to do to you. As I see it *this* is all that 'as yourself' could mean in this context. Certainly 'more than yourself' would not be a substitute. For what is in question is not a matter of quantity – of 'more or less' – but of putting others before oneself. This cannot be expressed in the words 'as yourself'.

As for loving oneself 'in the right way' or 'in the proper way', if this means 'you shall love yourself in the same way that you love your neighbour – that is without distinction', then this is either going round in circles or it says that you should not distinguish yourself from others and so put yourself first. If the latter is what is intended then to express this with the words 'as yourself' seems to me to be perverse. But as I argued in the previous chapter, 'to love oneself properly' usually means 'to be on good terms with oneself', and this is not 'love of oneself' or 'self-love'. This, however, has very little to do with what the Christian precept to love one's neighbour commands. It does not say 'be on good terms with him', but 'love him; put him before yourself'. It would be equally perverse to express this with the words, 'Love your neighbour as yourself'.

So, as far as I understand it, the precept certainly tells you not to put yourself before your neighbour. As Kierkegaard insists, I think rightly, the love it commands is *sacrificial* love. Hence all that 'as yourself' means is, as I said, 'do not do onto others what you do not want others to do to you'; and perhaps also 'respect him as you respect yourself – or should'; 'so love him as to allow him his self-respect, as you would wish others to allow you yours in the way they love you'.

It is nevertheless an expression which in this context can be misleading; it may obscure the sacrificial character of the love commanded.

B. Next, Kierkegaard considers the 'shall' – love as a duty. How can love be commanded? How can it be a duty? Indeed, is it not true that some people contrast love with duty – for instance Ernest Jones in 'Love and Morality' (*The International Journal of Psycho-Analysis*, Jan 1937). They think of something done out of duty as something one forces oneself to do, in which case Kierkegaard would agree it is something not done with the right moral attitude, not lovingly. When one performs 'works of love in an unloving … way' then 'the works of love are … not the work of love' (p. 30). We find a classical example of this in the case of Mrs Soleness in Ibsen's play 'The Master Builder'. As Professor Winch puts it of her: 'If she had occasionally forgotten her "duty" and let herself go, this might have cleared the air and opened the way for some genuine human relationships' (Winch, 1972, p. 180).

Rightly Winch puts 'duty' here in inverted commas; it is Mrs Soleness's word: 'It is only my duty.' It is nevertheless true that many people talk of their duty in this way: 'He visited her only out of duty; he would rather have had a night out with the boys.' Where this is the case we could add: 'If he really loved and cared for her, he would have wanted to go to see her.' That is he would have done so whole-heartedly, 'lovingly', his heart would be in it – as in Simone Weil's example, mentioned by Winch in this context, of the father who plays with his child not 'out of a sense of duty' but because he likes to, because he finds pleasure in doing so.

When Kierkegaard speaks of duty he does not mean it in this way; he is thinking of a duty which contains the person's whole soul – what a person considers his duty with his whole heart and soul and who, therefore, performs it 'lovingly', giving himself to it. So I return to the question: How can love be a duty in this sense? How can love be commanded?

Obviously it is for the individual to rise up to the call. To do so he has to see sense in Christianity and in its call for him to love his neighbour. What Christianity calls him to do is to commit himself, to give himself to the care of whoever is in need, whoever is afflicted. If it seems odd it is because we think of the order 'fall in love with this person', and obviously this is not something one can do to order. Two people, a man and a woman, meet and if the circumstances and the psychological chemistry between them are right they fall in love. This is something that *happens* to them: they are taken by storm. But for this to be converted to love they have to come to care for each other; each must find in the other something for which he is willing to commit himself to, to stand by, to devote himself to the other. This 'something' may vary from person to person and go to determine the character of his love. In the case of Christian love this something may be the other's humanity – the fact that he is a human being or a living creature seen from the perspective of Christianity.

Such a person will hear the call in its full significance, he will hear it as a duty or necessity, as something to which there is no 'take it or leave it', and he will respond to it positively, willingly. This is the kind of love that 'forms the heart', brings it together, evaluates inclinations, discarding some and incorporating others to the will. But it takes time and labour on the part of the individual for this transformation to take place. It is thus a transformation in which the individual participates, but it is a fruit of the love he comes to bear for others. I have put it in my own way and without distinction between Christian love and other forms of deep love.

Kierkegaard too distinguishes between 'falling in love' and the kind of love which he characterizes as a duty. The former is a matter of 'inclination' – what I called 'psychological chemistry', something to which the individual yields, a form of 'passivity' in the sense that Spinoza means this. The latter is something which the lover puts himself into in response to something that calls him. He puts himself out and works for it, and he is changed in the process. It is a form of activity in Spinoza's sense – an activity of the person in his emotions. The former is a form of self-indulgence; the latter is a form of self-renunciation. The lover renounces himself for what he loves, in his concern for the beloved he forgets himself. The concern and interest that enters into his life with love eclipses the needs and cravings of the self in him. In his 'forgetfulness' of this self and the way he 'neglects' those cravings, they diminish in time. They atrophy in being under-nourished.

Kierkegaard makes a radical distinction between Christian love, love of one's neighbour, and other forms of love, 'human love' as he calls them, erotic love and friendship, however deep, though he admits that one can love a friend or a husband or wife as first a neighbour. When this is the case, he says, there is a third party involved in the relationship, namely God who is Love. We have met this way of talking in C.S. Lewis, and I shall return to this question of the distinction between human and Christian love and of their compatibility in the following section.

Kierkegaard contrasts Christian love, which he often characterizes as 'real love', with erotic love and friendship which he equally often characterizes as 'self-love', in black and white terms. The earthly loves are forms of self-indulgence, according to Kierkegaard, in that in them the lover seeks, indulges or feeds himself, and when he can no longer find nourishment, he turns his back on the beloved, stops loving her. His caring for her had strings attached to it; when the strings are broken he no longer cares for the beloved and seeks new pastures to feed on. Hence such love is prone to jealousy, vulnerable to change, dependent on the beloved, and lacks endurance. Whereas, by contrast, Kierkegaard argues, Christian love or love of one's neighbour is unconditional, and in that sense independent of what the neighbour is like and therefore 'eternally secure'.

It is not the loved one's lovability that holds such love, but the love that is taken as a duty, in the sense I have tried to explain, that makes the neighbour 'lovable' or, should I say, worthy of love, however unlovable he may be from a non-Christian perspective – however cantankerous, nasty, ugly, morally repulsive he may be. One does not have to like one's neighbour to love him. But then, someone may point out, one does not have to like one's brother to love him either with the most human and flawed of all loves – 'blood is thicker than water' as it is said. I would reply, for Kierkegaard, that the difference wherein such love is flawed is that it makes a distinction between one's brother and others in contrast with Christian love where everyone is one's neighbour without any distinction. Indeed in putting one's brother before others one runs the danger of putting first what is 'one's own' and in doing so in nurturing what is surely a form of self-love.

Before turning, thirdly, with Kierkegaard, to 'one's neighbour', I want to comment on Kierkegaard's claim that while erotic love cannot itself ensure its endurance, Christian love is 'eternally secure' (pp. 45–7). His reason for holding this is that while erotic love is dependent on the temporal so that if the beloved changes the love that she inspires in the lover also changes so that he may stop loving her – indeed his love may turn into hate. In contrast, he writes, 'when love has undergone the transformation of the eternal by being made duty, it has won continuity, and then it follows of itself that it survives' (p. 47).

Truth and falsehood are intermixed in this reasoning. It is perfectly true that Christian love is secure in being unconditional and

directed to the neighbour, that is to everyone as an individual without distinction: he is to be 'loved' whatever he is like and however
he changes. This is what the Christian believer and, therefore, lover
is committed to. All right, this is what Christian love is; its unchange-
ability follows *logically* from its definition. What Christianity gives
us is a 'geometry of love' which the believer makes his own.
Having done so his love is secure so long as he is sustained by his
faith, and hence so long as he can remain loyal to it. But this sustenance and his reciprocal loyalty is *in time* – necessarily so. So it cannot be secure against change. That is nothing can guarantee that *he*
will not change and so lose the love he has that is secure against
change. That is nothing can guarantee it except his faith.

Put it like this. In his faith he may have gained access to the eternal, but his faith – his being in possession of that faith – is in time
and it is therefore not immune from change, destruction and loss.
Only God's love is forever secure – and it takes the Christian perspective to *say* this and so to believe it. For God is not in time and
so cannot change. Human beings, on the other hand, live in time,
even when some of them may have gained access to the eternal. So
everything about them – not withstanding the claim about the
immortality of their soul – is subject to change. They live in a world
of contingency and so their life is subject to chance. This is by no
means something that Christianity denies; on the contrary the faith
which a Christian finds gives him a way of coping with chance by
accepting *whatever* comes his way as the will of God. It teaches him
not to question the contingent when it does not suit him by
renouncing himself so that whether what happens does or does not
suit him is a matter of indifference to him.

Kierkegaard constantly stresses how much Christianity 'wants to
turn you [the believer] away from the external; but without taking
you out of the world' (p. 354). 'Christianly understood one has ultimately and essentially to do with God in everything, although one
nevertheless must remain in the world and in the relationships of
earthly life allotted to him' (p. 348). 'Christianity ... teaches that
everyone shall *lift himself above* earthly distinctions. ... [But it] lets
all the distinctions of earthly existence stand' (p. 83). 'Christianity is
no fairly tale ... These [distinctions] must continue and must continue to tempt every man who enters into the world, for by being a
Christian he does not become free from distinctions, but by winning the victory over the temptation of distinctions he becomes a
Christian' (p. 81). The point that Kierkegaard constantly emphasises

is that what Christianity says about the eternal is meant to apply to what is *actual* in this world.

In a sense this is reminiscent of what Wittgenstein says about mathematics and 'civil life'. Without its application in civil life mathematics is no more than a wall-paper pattern. Likewise when a believer loses his 'foothold in actuality' (p. 161) he loses touch with the God of Christianity, his God becomes something 'airy'. His God becomes a God of escape. 'Delusion [writes Kierkegaard] is always floating, for that reason it sometimes appears quite light and spiritual, because it is so airy' (p. 161). Thus the God who lives in heaven is to be sought here, down below, and not in heaven. But what Christianity reveals to the believer *there* is not something earthly – such as a social message for instance. This is something that Simone Weil expresses very clearly again and again:

> The Gospel contains a conception of human life, not a theology.
>
> If out of doors at night I light an electric torch it is not by looking at the bulb that I judge its power but by seeing how many objects it lights up.
>
> The brightness of a source of light is appreciated by the illumination it projects upon non-luminous objects.
>
> The value of a religious or, more generally, spiritual way of life is appreciated by the amount of illumination thrown upon the things of this world.
>
> Earthly things are the criterion of spiritual things.
>
> This is what generally we don't want to recognize because we are frightened of a criterion.
>
> The virtue of anything is manifested outside of the thing.
>
> If on the pretext that only spiritual things have a value one refuses to take as criterion the illumination projected on earthly things, one risks having nothing for one's treasure.
>
> Spiritual things alone have a value, but only earthly things have an observable existence. Consequently the value of the former can only be appreciated as illumination projected on the latter.
>
> ... if a man gives bread to a beggar in a certain way or speaks in a certain way about a defeated army, I know that his thought has been outside this world and sat with Christ alongside the Father who is in Heaven.

If a man describes to me at the same time two opposite sides of a mountain, I know that his position is higher than the summit.

It is impossible to understand and love at the same time both the victors and the vanquished, as the *Iliad* does, except from the place, outside the world, where God's Wisdom dwells (*La Connaissance Surnaturelle*, Gallimard, 1950, pp. 98–9).

Thus, she says, 'the faith of a judge does not appear in his attitude in the church, but in his attitude in the court' (ibid., p. 97) – that is in the way he passes a sentence on criminals. 'It is not from the way that a man speaks of God, but from the way he speaks about earthly matters that one can better discern if his soul has passed through the fire of love for God' (p. 96).

On this point Kierkegaard and Simone Weil are in complete agreement. Kierkegaard quotes from the Bible:

If anyone says 'I love God' and hates his brother he is a liar; for he who does not love his brother whom he has seen cannot love God whom he has not seen (I *John* 4: 20).

He comments further down that when a man rejects those he sees and loves the unseen, 'God is changed to an unreal something, a fancy' (p. 158).

C. I now turn to the question: who is my neighbour? Kierkegaard mentions Jesus' answer to the lawyer who asked him this question – an answer which took the form of telling the lawyer the story of the good Samaritan (*Luke*, Ch. 10, verses 30–5). Kierkegaard says that the question was a form of evasion, a personal evasion, and that in his way of answering the lawyer Jesus addressed the evasion. He was not concerned to remove any theoretical ignorance – such as 'What is gold?', 'How do I recognize it?'. Hence, Kierkegaard says, the questioner was 'hypocritical' and Jesus' answer 'imprisoned' him, that is it did not allow him to get away with his evasion.

The question 'What is gold?' is an impersonal question. The answer may take the form: 'Anything which has such and such characteristics.' *Anyone* who knows what the answer tells him will be able to recognize gold. The lawyer was trying to evade his responsibility and was hypocritical in pretending that what is in question is of the kind we have in the case of someone asking

'What is gold?'. 'Gold is any metal that is shiny, etc.' 'But how do I know it is not fool's gold?' One can go on with asking further similar questions. The lawyer, Kierkegaard says, also wanted to 'justify' himself: 'well given such difficulties I cannot be blamed for not recognizing my neighbour immediately.'

Jesus told him of the priest and the Levite who passed the wounded man without going to his help and the Samaritan who stopped to help him. He turned the question back on the lawyer: who do *you* think was a neighbour to the wounded man? That is he assumed that the lawyer *could* answer it even though he pretended he could not in order to evade the responsibility this would confer on him. Furthermore to be so forced to answer it *himself* was taking the first step towards the 'knowledge' or 'recognition' he evaded, thus in the process deceiving himself. When in his answer to Jesus the lawyer replied that it was the Samaritan who had been neighbour to the wounded man he was forced to recognize that it is in being neighbour to a man in need that one recognizes one's neighbour. That is the recognition in question is internal to one's mode of being, it lies in what I call 'the personal dimension'.

In other words what the lawyer was evading was a certain way of being – being a neighbour – resisting a personal commitment. What put him off was the cost involved. When Jesus said, 'go and do likewise' he was inviting him to turn his back on his worldliness, reminding him of a duty, enjoining him to make it his own, without in any sense enticing him. For the lawyer to heed Jesus of his own will *is* for him to recognize his neighbour.

Kierkegaard puts this by saying that 'by recognizing your duty you easily discover who your neighbour is' (p. 38). Recognizing one's duty is itself not something impersonal; it is oneself experiencing its call and responding by committing oneself.

> 'He towards whom I have a duty is my neighbour, and when I fulfil my duty I prove that I am a neighbour. Christ does not speak about recognizing one's neighbour but about being a neighbour oneself, about proving oneself to be a neighbour, something the Samaritan showed by his compassion' (ibid.).

He adds a little further down: 'Choosing a lover, finding a friend, yes, that is a long, hard job, but one's neighbour is easy to recognize, easy to find if only one is willing to recognize one's duty' (p. 39).

There is of course no choice in the latter case since love of one's neighbour is not a 'preferential love' and 'everyone is one's neighbour' (p. 58). Think for instance of choosing a wife or a husband, that is someone with whom one intends to spend the rest of one's life. There are various considerations, depending on one's culture and circumstances, that may be relevant. Furthermore one can make a mistake. But with the neighbour, the object of one's compassion, one has no choice. We could even say that it is the neighbour who chooses one – in the sense that it is he, in his need for help, who calls on one's compassion, makes one a neighbour. And here, what is more, one cannot be mistaken or deceived, except by oneself – that is where one's response is phoney, one's compassion is contaminated by self-love.

Supposing the object of one's compassion is someone who pretends to be in need and he takes one for a ride. True, one has been taken for a ride, but one has not been deceived in one's heart. I think Kierkegaard would say that only where one is deflected from one's duty, enticed away from it, is one deceived in one's heart. As Kierkegaard puts it: 'Erotic love is determined by the object; friendship is determined by the object; only love for one's neighbour is determined by love' (p. 77). So erotic love would be deceived by the object if the object pretended to be other than he or she is. Since love for one's neighbour is not determined by its object, and every human being is one's neighbour, no matter what he is like, whatever state he may be in, one cannot be deceived by one's neighbour in one's love for him. One can only be deceived by oneself in the kind of love one gives. If one's love is contaminated by self-love, if one's compassion is not pure, if one is not 'pure at heart', then one is deceived in one's self, and *ipso facto* one does not recognize one's neighbour in the person one gives it to.

'One's neighbour (Kierkegaard says) is one's equal' (p. 72). In other words when the other is seen as a neighbour he is not seen as in any sense lower in status from one; he is not regarded in condescension because in his need for help he has become independent or weak. Here Simone Weil contrasts relationships of power and relationships of love when love is pure. To admire or appropriate power is to feed the self and so is the opposite of self-renunciation. Simone Weil has a great deal to say on this subject. She would agree with Kierkegaard that 'to love in condescension is self-love' and that there cannot be true or pure compassion in the absence of humility. We find this emphasis equally in Plato.

In short then one finds and can only find one's neighbour in self-renunciation. One's neighbour is the antithesis of the self – the self in the sense of 'one's ego', the part of the self which says 'I', as Simone Weil puts it. One's neighbour is the one – anyone – one loves as one's neighbour. It is in one's love for him, when it is pure, that the other becomes one's neighbour. It is one's love that makes him a neighbour to one.

D. Finally Kierkegaard takes up the 'you' of the command to love one's neighbour. Why 'you'? Why not 'one'? There are two points here rolled into one. The first is that the command is addressed to each person *as an individual*. Each person must make the duty to love his neighbour *his own*. This is the only way in which a person can know his duty. As I put it earlier this is not an impersonal matter. Where a person obeys the call to duty addressed to him he is on his own; no one and nothing can make him do it. Where something external makes him do it, where he is enticed or forced to do it, what he does will not count as his having risen to the call, done his duty. What he does has to come from *him* – and that excludes coming from 'the self' in the sense of his 'ego'. For that means doing it for the sake of something he wants for himself and not out of compassion for his neighbour.

I said 'it must come from him'. For this to be the case he must be *himself*, and that means 'authentic', 'an individual'. He must be behind what he does, not do it mindlessly, because he is told to do it, or because others do so. That is what he does must not be something copied. Nor must it be something he is forced to do, something he does out of fear; nor yet something he does for what he will gain out of doing so. Indeed more than this, he must not gain from doing so, even when he does not seek any gain. For such gain will undo the sacrifice, counteract the self-renunciation. As Simone Weil puts it (I quote from memory): God will not thank him, for he will have received his reward in this world.

Thus as it turns out – and this is important for my argument in this book – to be pure at heart he must be himself. A person who is in the service of himself, in the sense of his ego, cannot be himself. To be oneself one has to serve something other than oneself, but one must not serve it mindlessly, nor in a servile way. One must be oneself in what one serves. The relation is a two-way one: one finds oneself in the service of something other than oneself, provided that one is oneself in serving it. There is no vicious circle here; one moves towards being oneself in steps and each step involves inner work.

As Kierkegaard would put it one finds one's neighbour and *ipso facto* one's duty to love him *in one's inwardness*, or as I put it, in the dimension of the personal. This is what Christianity is concerned with. It is not concerned to reform society, as some Christians have believed, to change the world. It is concerned to transform each individual in his soul. If it were otherwise Christianity would be a religion of manipulation, using individuals as *a means* to an end. Obviously the more individuals are transformed in their souls the better a place would this world be *relatively* from the point of view of Christianity.

I say 'relatively' since there is no possibility of achieving for the world what might be achieved for the single individual. For the single individual has to love in *this* world, find inwardness in the face of temptation, goodness in facing evil. Each individual has to find inwardness and goodness, rise up to the duty of loving his neighbour in the surroundings of a life lived in this world. As Simone Weil would put it: this world is a necessary gateway to goodness and eternity. What is a gateway has at the same time got to be a barrier. If I may use an analogy myself: if the car is to move forward the road has to offer some friction.

The second point, although it should be clear now that it is really a statement of the first point in a new form, is that the injunction to love your neighbour is addressed to *you* and not to the 'I' in you, to your ego. This is how Kierkegaard puts it:

> It is characteristic of childhood to say: *Me want – me – me*. It is characteristic of youth to say, '*I* – and *I* – and *I*'. The mark of maturity and the dedication to the eternal is to will to understand that this *I* has no significance if it does not become the *you*, the *thou*, to whom the eternal incessantly speaks and says: '*You shall, you* shall, *you* shall.' It is youthful to want to be the only I in the whole world. Maturity is to understand this *you* as addressed to oneself, even though it were not said to a single other person. *You* shall; *you* shall love your neighbour (p. 98).

That is what *other* people say or do is not your concern; you must do what *you* are enjoined to do irrespective of what others say or do, because it is *your* duty. The Christian command speaks to you and you must hear it as addressed to you. To hear it as such you must be yourself – that is detached from the crowd, detached from your ego. You cannot be yourself, *you*, without such detachment from the 'I' in you and the 'crowd' outside you. The crowd is what Simone Weil calls the 'we' and she finds it spiritually much more dangerous than the 'I'. But, if I may put it so, the 'we' is the collective 'I'.

11.3 Christian Love in Relation to Erotic Love and Friendship

I want to take up now a question I raised earlier: how are erotic love and friendship related to Christian love? Or, another way of putting the question I have in mind: do erotic love and friendship have to be pagan or secular forms of love? What does Kierkegaard have to say about this?

We have seen C.S. Lewis's view on this. These loves are 'not enough' in themselves, but the natural element in them can be 'transmuted': 'Natural loves can hope for eternity only insofar as they have allowed themselves to be taken into the eternity of Charity ... . The process will always involve a kind of death' (Lewis, 1960, p. 125). The death in question is the death of the self or ego – what Plato calls 'the purification of the soul' and Kierkegaard 'self-renunciation'. I shall quote a few lines from C.S. Lewis:

> All natural loves can be inordinate. *Inordinate* does not mean 'insufficiently cautious'. Nor does it mean 'too big'. ... It is probably impossible to love any human being simply 'too much'. We may love him too much *in proportion* to our love for God; but it is the smallness of our love for God, not the greatness of our love for the man, that constitutes the inordinacy. ... The real question is, which ... do you serve, or choose, or put first? (pp. 112–13).

His view is that love of one's neighbour, supernatural love, involves love of God. Love of God is implicit in it; or, as Simone Weil puts it, love of one's neighbour is an implicit love of God. Obviously erotic love is a natural love. But love of God is not a rival to it; there is no rivalry between them. Indeed our natural loves 'cannot even remain themselves and do what they promise to do without God's help'. We have seen that he compares the

way God comes into them with the way Honour comes into chivalrous love:

> I could not love thee, dear, so much
> Loved I not honour more.

'He does not need ... to set his face against her, because he and she
acknowledge the same law' (p. 14). Similarly when God is loved,
He does not 'come between' the lover and the beloved, He transforms their love.

I ask again: when such transformation takes place does not erotic
love maintain its erotic character? What does Kierkegaard think?
There are passages in the early part of his book where Kierkegaard
speaks of erotic love and friendship in demeaning ways – in contrast with C.S. Lewis who speaks of their 'corruptions'. In other
words C.S. Lewis thinks that these forms of natural love are 'not
enough' in themselves and they are vulnerable to corruption,
whereas Kierkegaard suggests that they are invariably corrupt –
corrupt in themselves. He speaks of them as forms of 'self-love' and
'self-indulgence'. 'Passionate preference is self-love' (p. 65). It is
not clear to me that he does not identify 'erotic love' with 'lust'.
Paganism, he says, thought of erotic love and friendship not as self-
love but as genuine loves (pp. 65–6), implying that Christianity
thinks of them as not being genuine loves. Again: 'Erotic love and
friendship are related to passion, but all passion, whether it attacks
or defends itself, fights in one manner only: either – or: "Either
I exist and am the highest or I do not exist at all – either all or
nothing." ... To talk thus is a double betrayal' (p. 59).

This last passage begins with the question: 'are erotic love
and friendship the highest love or must this love be dethroned?'
Kierkegaard is not saying anything different from C.S. Lewis in
saying that it is *not* the highest love and must be dethroned – in
other words it must not be made into a god and worshipped. That
would lead to corruption. But to suggest that *all* passion is on the
side of the self, seeks the promotion of the ego, is to fail to distinguish between different passions and to taint love and friendship
by associating them with passion viewed in this monolithic way.
Here one is reminded of the Kantian dichotomy between reason
and inclination.

I repeat, it is one thing to think of our natural loves as in themselves 'not enough', as vulnerable to corruption; another thing to

think of them as inherently corrupt. Insofar as Kierkegaard suggests the latter he is making the same mistake about natural loves as D.H. Lawrence makes about Christian love, that is love involving a love of God. For D.H. Lawrence praised pagan love and thought of a Christian love of God as emasculating – as Nietzsche did too. Kierkegaard likewise at times seems to suggest that erotic love and friendship are corrupt in themselves.

However, otherwise, much of what he says about our natural loves in alliance with a love of God is on the whole similar to what C.S. Lewis says. He says, clearly, that you must not cease to love 'those for whom you have a preference'. For they too, for instance your wife, are your neighbour. You must love her; but as your neighbour (p. 73). 'In erotic love and friendship preserve love to your neighbour' (p. 74).

> We are first to love our neighbour. For impulse and inclination this is truly a strange, chilling upside-downness.... The wife shall first and foremost be your neighbour; the fact that she is your wife is then a narrower definition of your special relationship to each other (p. 141).

He goes on further down on the next page:

> To be sure, one's wife is to be loved differently from the friend and the friend differently from the neighbour, but this is not an essential difference, for the fundamental equality lies in the category *neighbour*. The category *neighbour* is just like the category *human being*. Every one of us is a human being and at the same time the heterogeneous individual which he is by particularity; but being a human being is the fundamental qualification. ... Thus Christianity has nothing against a man loving his wife in a special way, but he must never love her in such a special way that she is an exception to being a neighbour (p. 142).

So far in these two passages what Kierkegaard says is almost, I am inclined to say, 'common sense', by which I mean it is said from a moral perspective, no doubt belonging to a Christian culture, but about which there is nothing extreme or recondite. 'The wife shall first and foremost be your neighbour.' In other words she is to be respected as a human being. Her sexual attraction must not be allowed to turn her into a sexual object, that is a vehicle of the husband's pleasure. She must not be treated as a chattel. She must not be cast off if she loses her attraction or if someone else comes along who has greater attraction for the husband. And if in old age she becomes a burden, on account of ill health or dementia, she must be looked after with love. The husband's love must be considerate, faithful, tender and compassionate and must remain so even when it is not returned or appreciated or when it cannot be returned and can no longer be appreciated.

That is what I would call a *deep* love for a person to whom one has given one's heart, a sexual love which has developed into a companionship in which the sexual relationship has been integrated. It is still a sexual love, a love between people of the opposite sex, not simply a friendship, though nevertheless one which involves or incorporates friendship. When Kierkegaard says that 'for impulse and inclination this is truly a strange, chilling upside-downness' he is in part speaking like a Kantian philosopher. What is true is that human beings are subject to temptations that test their loyalty and restraint – restraint out of respect and consideration. There is nothing topsy-turvy about believing that one must resist such temptations.

'To be sure, one's wife is to be loved differently ... from the neighbour.' Obviously. It is a radically more intimate relationship and involves special obligations: a wife has a special claim on her husband's care and attention; and *vice versa*. But the husband's claims on his wife, for instance, should never be allowed to override the wife's claims on the husband as a neighbour, as a human being. In any case these claims are not in conflict with his loving her as a wife. 'But he must never love her in such a special way that she is an exception to being a neighbour' – perhaps spoil and pamper her without any regard to the harm this does to her, or so love her without considering her needs.

'Love (writes Kierkegaard) is a matter of conscience and thus is not a matter of impulse and inclination' (p. 143). But this is true of the love of any mature person when it goes deep. It is not something specific to Christian love as such. Kierkegaard develops this by presenting Christian love as a relationship which involves a third, a middle term, namely God. In other words the claim that God makes on, say, a husband's love for his wife is to be put before her claims on his love. This characterizes his love for his wife. Indeed this is what makes such love a matter of conscience in a special way. It is a matter of the purity of such love, of its radical selflessness. The purity in question, whether it is directed to a stranger or to one's wife or mother, presupposes God, as the third party, *hidden* in the love in question.

Kierkegaard makes the distinction between a purely 'human' love, e.g., between a husband and wife, and one in which God is present as follows:

> The purely human conception of love can never go further than mutuality [reciprocity]: that the lover is the beloved and the beloved is the lover. Christianity teaches that such a love has not yet found its proper object: God. The love-relationship is a triangular relationship of the lover, the beloved and love – but love is God. Therefore to love another person means to help him to love God and to be loved means to be helped (p. 124).

And further down:

> In order to remove the humiliation and mortification [when love is not requited, or on the other side where the one in need is attended to], the lover interpolates something higher between the unloving one and himself[13] and thereby gets himself out of the way. When there is no third in the relationship between man and man, every such relationship becomes unsound, either too ardent or embittered. The third, which thinkers would call the idea [e.g. Plato] is the true, the good, or more accurately, the God-relationship; this third is a cooling factor in certain phases of a relationship and in others a soothing agent. In truth, the lover is too loving to take a posture over against the vanquished and himself be the victor who revels in the victory – while the other is the vanquished; it is simply unloving to want to be master of another person in this way. With the help of the third, which the lover gets placed between them, both are humbled: for the lover humbles himself before the good, whose needy servant he is ...; and the vanquished one humbles himself not before the lover but before the good. But when both are humbled in a relationship, there is no humiliation for either one of them alone (p. 313).

13. Here Kierkegaard has the first case in mind.

What Kierkegaard articulates in terms of Christian concepts is the difference which the lover's commitment to or love of goodness makes to his love of another human being. Such whole-hearted commitment or pure-love is attained through the purification of the lover's soul. It is something that shows or finds expression in his life; it is not something that occupies the forefront of his thoughts. So what is in question is the way a certain change in his life and so in himself, a change in which the centre of gravity of his affective responses and considerations shifts away from the self to the other, seen in his need and vulnerability and respected as a fellow creature, affects the character of his love – of his love for whoever it is he loves, his friend, his wife, etc. It enables him to love those towards whom he may otherwise be naturally indifferent.

The third, by whatever name it is called, is goodness, the totality of certain spiritual values. Without any commitment to such values a person remains dissipated, without any unity in himself, without a centre from which he acts, one which gives consistency to his actions and life. Without it his relationships remain predatory and manipulatory, devoid of any loyalty and commitment to the other. This, as I understand it, is something about which both spiritual religions and serious psycho-analysis have something to say.

A person who lacks 'inwardness' is a shallow person and his loves are bound to be shallow. And a person who lives his love as in a dream, one who is unable to allow the beloved an independent or separate existence, or one who cannot tolerate waiting and is forever impatient is immature – much in the sense that psycho-analysis speaks of it. Kierkegaard has much to say on all three: lack of belief, lack of inwardness, lack of maturity.

> To believe nothing is right on the border where believing evil begins; the good is the object of faith, and therefore one who believes nothing begins to believe evil (p. 220).

In other words, if you believe nothing, then nothing restrains you. You are thrown on yourself.

When Kierkegaard speaks of 'spontaneity, impulse and inclination' he means licence, lack of restraint. In this connection he speaks of 'the free heart'. He says that such a heart 'has no concern; heedlessly it plunges itself into the delights of attachments' (pp. 148–9).

He contrasts it with a heart 'bound to God'. The person who loves or is committed to goodness has inner coherence or unity of self.

> Worldliness and busyness are inseparable ideas … To be busy means, divided and scattered … to occupy oneself with all the manifold things in which it is practically impossible for a man to be whole (p. 105).

Kierkegaard points out that 'to be busy' is to evade 'occupying one-self with the eternal', whether by intent or not. It is to turn away from the spiritual dimension of life, to lose whatever inwardness one may have.

Thus when Tolstoy's Father Sergius, after the incident with Makóvkina, the beautiful divorcee, who failed to seduce him, became famous and his fame spread ever more and more widely, his life began to change and to be claimed by 'the world' in Kierkegaard's sense. He became more and more 'busy', again in Kierkegaard's sense, responding to the demands made on him by the people who came to him for his blessing and the sick they brought to him so he could cure them. From that time on, as Tolstoy puts it, 'Sergius felt his own inner life wasting away and being replaced by external life. It was as if he had been turned inside out' (OUP, 1960, p. 331). 'The more he gave himself to such a life the more he felt that what was internal became external, and that the fount of living water within him dried up, and that what he did now was done more and more for men and less and less for God' (ibid., p. 332).

At the same time the unity of his life was shattered much in the way that Kierkegaard has in mind. He was now in the service of men and, therefore, of the self in him which expanded as they praised him. His life lost the centre it had in his whole-souled ser-vice of God implicit in his relationship to the actualities that formed its surroundings. Thus as Kierkegaard puts it: 'to be busy means to be divided and scattered', and in contrast, 'Christian love, which is the fulfilling of the law, is whole and collected' (p. 105).

Finally, Kierkegaard connects *maturity* with the dedication to the eternal (p. 98), with patience and restraint (p. 208), and with living in the actual world instead of escaping into fantasy and wishful thinking, where things are thought to be achieved without work, immediately and easily. Thus immature love is the love of a person who cannot go beyond falling in love: he wants to be fed, gratified, to be the centre of the beloved's attention, and gives for what he expects to receive. It is a jealous, possessive love which ultimately cannot survive the beloved's indifference. I say 'ultimately' because as long as the person can continue to get something from the relationship in fantasy – something that suits him, given his particular psychology – he will keep it going by feeding it on lies and unrealistic hopes. Where a person's love of God is thus immature it is not God that he loves or, to put it differently, he has no love for the Christian God – indeed he has no conception of Him.

By way of conclusion let me return to the question with which I began this section: Are erotic love and friendship – our 'natural', 'human loves' – *intrinsically* pagan according to Kierkegaard? When they are 'transmuted' by the love of God do they lose their character as 'sexual love' and 'friendship'? According to D.H. Lawrence, we saw in an earlier chapter, sexual love is intrinsically and unashamedly, pagan: sexual love and Christianity are not compatible – Christianity emasculates such love. Does Kierkegaard think of erotic love as compatible with Christianity?

Let me first say that it is not clear to me what Kierkegaard understands by 'erotic love' – or as I prefer to call it 'sexual love'. Could it be that he identifies it with lust? I would say that sexual love is love which engages the lover's sexuality; it is a love directed to a person seen or affectively apprehended as a sexual partner. As such it can take different forms.

We have seen that Kierkegaard allows that a husband *can* love his wife as a neighbour; indeed he insists that Christianity enjoins the husband to do so. When he does so his love still remains a 'preferential' love. All right. But is its erotic or sexual character preserved? I have no doubt about what C.S. Lewis thinks. He thinks that it is preserved. I would myself say that it is preserved in a changed form in being integrated into a core of moral beliefs. In the process the love of which it is a part acquires a new dimension – spiritual in that it takes the form of a loyal friendship and a relatively selfless devotion. Where there is sexual reciprocity it enjoys it thankfully and where there is not it accepts this without complaint or bitterness. The earthly and the spiritual are *as such* each other's opposite. But they can live together in harmony. For where a person has gained maturity, the earthly can restrain itself in accordance with circumstances and the spiritual tones it down at its edges in its acceptance of it.

What about Kierkegaard? What does he think? Certainly I think that much of what he says is in agreement with such a view; but taken all together I find some ambiguity in what he says on this question which leaves me unsure.

In allowing that a husband *can* love his wife as a neighbour he says that Christianity should penetrate such a relationship, as it should *all* relationships, and in doing so transform the husband's love for his wife (p. 117). 'A person who in love belongs to a woman shall first and foremost absolutely belong to God, shall not first seek to please his wife, but shall strive first that his love may please God' (p. 118). In other words if, for instance, his wife wanted him to lie for her or to do something unkind or uncharitable, he should not do so. This is by no means in conflict with his love for her. If he were prepared to do absolutely *anything* to please his wife, this would not show that he loved his wife more; such a desire and willingness to please her at any cost would be servile. It would not be an expression of love, but of self-love. Indeed, if his wife did really love him she would not ask him to do anything that would compromise his integrity or to offend God. Thus my comments on Lady Macbeth's love.

Again Kierkegaard says that 'according to the secular point of view many different kinds of love are discernible', whereas 'Christianity ... recognizes only one kind of love, spiritual love' (pp. 144–5). I would agree, if this means that a love that has no moral core to it in the sense of being transformed with a commitment to goodness, and so one which has no spiritual dimension to its character, is not really love, or at any rate it is deeply flawed.

I think, however, that Kierkegaard is wrong to think – as he seems to – that all forms of love that have not come into contact with Christianity are forms of self-love and to be alien to any kind of spirituality. But God can be seen by a Christian to have entered into the soul of someone who has not come into contact with Christianity in the form of goodness and compassion and to have transformed his preferential loves. If Kierkegaard means to exclude all this where he speaks of 'self-love' and 'false love' then I have no quarrel with him on this point. All I wish to insist on is that the civilization or spiritualization of the soul and of its capacity for love is not confined to Christianity. What Kierkegaard means by 'secularity' would have to be taken in a very strict and extreme sense before I could agree with his verdict on our natural loves. But then this would be an unnatural sense of 'secular'.

Although, however, love of one's neighbour is not solely the possession of Christianity it is rare and often costly to come to.

Having been critical of Kierkegaard, in certain respects, I must add that I think he gives us a clear and profound insight into Christianity, shorn of all metaphysics, for which I admire him. In the following Chapter I shall examine some of this insight in what he has to say about 'works of love', that is about what Christian love can achieve in the human soul in the way it transforms it.

12

Kierkegaard on the Works of Love

12.1 Introduction

In the second part of his book Kierkegaard has more to say about the distinctive character of spiritual love and he talks about such love's work in 'forming the heart' and about its place in human life. 'Love [he says] is the deepest ground of the life of the spirit' (p. 205). Indeed I think he would agree that it is the source of goodness as he understands it. Those things that are part of goodness in a spiritual sense, such as patience, forgiveness, selfless service, generosity, mercifulness, humility, and courage too, the kind of courage that belongs to one's convictions, come from love; they are features of the distinctive character of spiritual love. One comes to such love by the purification of the soul, and that involves the purification of such love as one is capable of to begin with through self-renunciation.

What is in question is the psychological, affective and spiritual growth and development of the person in the course of his life and relationships. While the psychological and the spiritual are not one and the same thing they stand together. The spiritual growth of a person cannot take place without certain changes in his psychology. But while he has to take responsibility and labour to open his heart to love, and that means to a concerned appreciation of the existence of other people in their own right, such love and concern *in turn* have a way of working in his life, changing that life and 'forming his heart'. This is the work of love and its contribution is something he *receives*. We could thus speak of the labour in which he engages in the living of his life *and* of the fruits of what enters into his soul as a result. There is thus a division of labour between him and love. What he thus receives from love is what he learns from it.

12.2   Spiritual Love and its Character

Kierkegaard highlights some of the features that characterize spiritual love under six headings and in rather dramatic terms.

A. Under the first heading he says that 'love builds up', in other words it is spiritually constructive – a constructiveness that characterizes the person's relationships. Thus the difference between giving something or saying something to someone, giving him a present or encouragement or saying thank you to him with and without love. In the first case the giver will make contact with the person to whom his actions or words are directed and the recipient will feel that he is being considered as a person. In the second case the giver will be a giver only in name, his words or gestures will be devoid of significance, and they will leave the recipient either cold or wondering about the ulterior motives behind them.

Kierkegaard expresses what I take to be the same point in terms of the communication of knowledge with and without love. Here one can think of a school teacher who cares for his pupils, loves them and thinks of them, in contrast with one who possesses knowledge and competence but who is not interested in his pupils – his attitude with regard to the knowledge he communicates is 'take it or leave it'. Clearly the attitude of the first teacher towards what he teaches will be different. He will value it for what it is and this will communicate to his pupils. They will receive it as something valued and will therefore themselves feel valued. The pupils of the second teacher will not feel thus cared for and will not be encouraged to put themselves out to receive the knowledge their teacher makes available to them.

Knowledge can thus be 'edifying' or alienating according to whether it is given with or without love. Kierkegaard develops this further in the way he contrasts knowledge with love. One who has some specialist knowledge, especially someone whose knowledge and speciality have gained recognition and acclaim, may come to assume all others to be ignorant. His knowledge 'puffs him up'. In contrast spiritual love, having been gained through self-renunciation never does so. Kierkegaard says that loving means presupposing that others are loving, that the love of a person who is 'truly loving' presupposes that others have love (p. 211). This is puzzling on the face of it. For surely Kierkegaard does not think that everybody is loving or even capable of love. So what could he mean?

He connects what he calls 'true love' with 'the trustworthiness of one who loves'. Thus a person who has knowledge is related to something impersonal, objective. Purely as 'knower' his relation to what he knows is impersonal. By contrast in his love the lover stands in a personal relation to the person he loves. His relation excludes arrogance, looking down on the other. The lover, therefore, cannot treat the person he cares for as if he were incapable of love, appreciation and gratitude.

So he cannot treat the person he cares for in this way. But he can surely still recognize that the other is unloving and ungrateful, if this is the case, and ignore it. That is his love could be such that this fact makes no difference to it. This must be what Kierkegaard means. So what he claims is that spiritual love is a love that gives itself to the other *despite* his faults and deficiencies, *despite* his lack of love, *despite* his irresponsiveness to love. Why not put it thus plainly?

Even this last interpretation raises some questions. 'He loves despite the other's irresponsiveness to love, or even his lack of love.' In other words, this makes no difference to the love he gives. But does it make no difference? Does he not now love in sorrow – sorrow for just this, namely the other's hard-heartedness? Sorrow here is an expression of love; but for love to take this form it must apprehend the other's hard-heartedness. All right it is a love that is not put off by the other's hard-heartedness; but if it gives itself *despite* this it must be aware of it. So the point is that it is aware of it not in condescension but in sorrow. Kierkegaard of course does not wish to deny this. As we have seen, he stresses that while Christianity wants to turn the believer away from the external, its wants to do so without taking him out of the world (p. 354) and he often insists that Christianity is no fairy tale (p. 81). A love that does not recognize how often men are unloving would be a fairy tale love.

No, what Kierkegaard wishes to emphasize here is the patience that characterizes spiritual love and its indifference to whether or not it is returned. Its interest is to serve the other, to care for him; it wants nothing for itself. It is a selfless love and it is precisely because of this that it is constructive – 'builds up'.

B. Next and secondly Kierkegaard says that 'love believes all things and yet is never deceived'. Here is another dramatic statement; but what does it mean? Mistrust, he points out, believes nothing at all (p. 214). In other words, love is trust. Insofar as one mistrusts the other one's love is qualified. Trust is something one *gives* to the other. In French to trust is *'faire confiance'*. *'Faire'*, to make, indicates activity, a positive contribution on the part of the person who trusts another. In other words trusting here is not merely a matter of submitting to something independent – reasons, evidence. Thus trusting a person is very different from trusting that the structure one has erected will withstand the weather or trusting that one's calculations are correct. In the latter cases one trusts on the basis of evidence, of tests and checks. Trusting a person, however, is not like that; to trust here is to take a risk and only love is prepared to take a risk with the other. 'I trust him'. *'Je lui fais confiance'*: that is I *give* him my trust. But he may betray it.

Kierkegaard says that it is not 'from the standpoint of prudence that love is never deceived'. 'Experience will teach that one acts most prudently by not believing everything' (p. 214). But 'frivolity, inexperience, simplicity believe everything that is said; vanity, conceit, self-satisfaction believe everything flattering that is said; envy, spite, corruption believe everything evil that is said; mistrust believes nothing at all' (ibid.). These things are all of this world, human, whereas spiritual love and the kind of trust which forms part of it are 'other worldly', 'supernatural'. The lover who trusts the beloved is not naive, he trusts her in the knowledge that people are susceptible to temptation and change. But in his love he is prepared to be made a fool, to have his trust betrayed, to have his heart broken. That is a measure of his love, not of his naïvety, triviality or lack of experience.

He does not let these possibilities curtail his trust, qualify his love. If he did, then they would have cheated him out of unconditional love. That is if they stopped him from giving his heart and trust to those who called on his love he would have missed out on loving, serving, trusting another. The point is that from the perspective from which Kierkegaard is writing what he would thus have missed out on are good in themselves – part of what constitutes a life of the spirit. He would then have remained on or reverted to a level of existence which is poor by comparison, spiritually speaking, a level of existence which is a fertile soil for all sorts of evil.

Thus when Kierkegaard says that love believes all things he means that it is prepared to trust unconditionally, that is come what may. He makes it clear that *this* is 'the highest good and the greatest blessedness'. Why? One can answer only by bringing out what one sees in such love, service and trust, what it means to one. One does so from the perspective which such loves give one. Someone to whom this perspective is alien, someone steeped in worldliness, in the concerns for profit and prudence, will see nothing in it, expect foolishness.

The true lover, then, is not deceived so long as he keeps his heart open to true love so that this love maintains its hold on him. As Kierkegaard puts it, he 'abides in love and consequently in possession of the highest good' (p. 225). The deceiver on the other hand, the loved one who betrays his trust, deceives herself. She cheats herself 'out of the great blessedness'. This is at one with the Socratic claim that if you do evil, you hurt *yourself*, you damage your own soul. Thus, Kierkegaard says, 'to love in truth' (p. 225) that is unconditionally, 'without making any demand of reciprocity' (p. 226) is 'the highest good and greatest blessedness'. He continues in true Socratic fashion: 'next to this, to be loved in truth: the next highest good is to be loved by one who loves in truth' (p. 225). This is a gift from the gods; one cannot seek it. One must not look for it.

'Loving in truth.' 'Truth' here refers to what constitutes goodness in the spiritual world. So 'loving in truth' means loving in commitment to one's beliefs about what constitutes such goodness and therefore in loyalty to them. Kierkegaard contrasts 'loving in truth' with what he calls 'a lower conception of love; a love which has no notion of love in and for itself' (p. 223). What keeps such love going is the return which feeds it. Such a mentality, Kierkegaard suggests, is of the kind we find in the commercial world. When the feeding stops the love is withdrawn, it dies. Here where the beloved only pretends to love or cheats the lover the lover is deceived. As Kierkegaard put it: 'The lover was deceived; but the lover was not a true lover' (pp. 223–4).

In contrast, Kierkegaard writes:

Love believes everything – and yet is never to be deceived. Amazing! To believe nothing in order never to be deceived – this seems to make sense … But to believe everything and thereby, as it were, to throw oneself away, fair game for all deception and all deceivers, and yet precisely in this way to assure oneself infinitely against every deception: this is remarkable (p. 221).

By the criteria of what makes sense in the world of prudence and commerce, and more generally of 'worldliness', what Kierkegaard claims for spiritual love is, indeed, 'amazing' and what such love is capable of is 'remarkable'. What *such love* is capable of is indeed amazing! We should not cease to wonder at it. As for what Kierkegaard *says* about it, when understood properly, it makes good sense. To *understand* it properly, however, takes an imagination which takes a degree of detachment from the concerns which make for worldliness; it takes a capacity to appreciate that there may be other concerns beyond those of worldliness. But to *find* such love takes more than imagination. It takes faith, that is the capacity to open one's heart, to give oneself in commitment to something one finds significance in, a significance which calls one forth.

We have seen that when Kierkegaard says that 'love believes all things' he does not mean that love is naïve, that it is cut off or out of touch with what goes on in 'the real world'. Such knowledge 'does not defile a man'. 'The magistrate is not defiled because he knows more about the plots than the criminal' (p. 220). Indeed, it is necessary if the love one finds is not to be a form of sentimentality or a 'fairly tale' love. 'It is mistrust which defiles a man's knowledge, just as love purifies it' (p. 220). Mistrust defiles it by making such knowledge a source of cynicism. Love, on the other hand, is the source of hope, a hope which such knowledge cannot take away.

If one trusts nothing one can believe in nothing. And this 'is right on the border where believing evil begins'. For if one trusts nothing one cannot put oneself out for anything, one has nothing for the sake of which to put oneself out. If one believes in nothing, the self will be the only object of one's considerations when one acts or refrains from acting when tempted to so do. Consequently nothing will restrain one save considerations of self-interest and prudence. One will then be a prey to the call of evil, one will have no reason for wanting to resist it. As Kierkegaard puts it: 'one who believes nothing begins to believe evil' (p. 220). Thus spiritual love, trust, faith and goodness belong together and constitute a unified whole.

C. I now turn to the third heading under which Kierkegaard characterizes spiritual love: 'Love hopes all things and yet is never put to shame' (p. 232). In ordinary speech, Kierkegaard points out, 'hope' means 'longing-filled expectancy'. Hope in this sense is the relationship in which a person stands to possibilities that are open to him. Thus, he says, 'hope comes quite easily to the child and the youth, because the child and the youth are themselves still a possibility' (p. 234). 'But when a man has grown older, then his life mostly remains what it already has become, a dull repetition and re-writing of the same; no possibility rouses one to wakefulness and no possibility exhilarates the renewal of youth. Hope becomes something which nowhere has a home. ... Without the eternal he lives by the help of habit, prudence, conformity, experience, custom and usage' (p. 235).

Thus as in the case of 'deception' clearly Kierkegaard is not using the word 'hope' here in the ordinary sense that it has in the life which he contrasts with spirituality. In that ordinary sense to say that 'love hopes all things' would mean 'love is out of touch, extravagant, undisciplined'. Clearly this is very far from what Kierkegaard wishes to say. He points out that in the sense in which he speaks of hope here hope is the antithesis of despair. 'Hope,' he says, 'is related essentially to the possibility of the good and thereby to the eternal' (p. 235). Thus to have hope in one's heart means to believe in the good and so to be sustained by it. Thus, one can say, that hope is the outlook of someone who believes, i.e. does not doubt, that he is loved and, in that sense, that there is good in life. It is the unarticulated belief that one is not alone, that one is held in the way that in the past, as a baby, one was held by one's mother: that 'there are many beautiful arms about us and the things we know'.

> You the woman; I, the man; this, the world:
> And each is the work of all.
>
> There is the muffled step in the snow; the stranger;
> The crippled wren; the nun; the dancer; the Jesus-wing
> Over the walkers in the village; and there are
> Many beautiful arms about us and the things we know.

> (from a poem by Kenneth Patchen entitled
> 'The Character of Love seen as a Search for the Lost')

So 'love hopes all things' means that when one 'loves in truth' one is not discouraged, one does not give up, whatever happens. One does not give up, however, *not* 'because the eternal vouches for him' but because there is love in one's heart. It is that which carries the conviction that there is such a thing as goodness, however bad things may in fact be. Thus however badly one is treated one does not want to retaliate, one does not feel angry, one does not react in anger. One does not take it personally, one is ready to forgive.

One does not nurse a grudge, one is not embittered. One does not lose one's faith in goodness – not in what it will do for one, but one's regard for what constitutes goodness. More briefly, when one 'loves in truth' one is sustained; nothing makes one despair. But not because it gives one a rosy picture of the world: that would be a fairy tale love. No, the conviction in the reality of goodness which one finds in such love sustains one in the face of adversity. It gives one courage.

Here is one difference worth noting between Kierkegaard and Simone Weil. She contrasted the way Jesus faced death on the cross believing that he had been abandoned by his Father in Heaven and the Christian martyrs being thrown to the lions linked arm in arm and singing. Jesus remained loyal to his Father and did not stop loving him even when he believed he had been abandoned by Him. She calls this *'fidelité à vide'* – fidelity in the void. For Kierkegaard love, spiritual love, does not seek its return; but nevertheless gives one sustenance: 'hopes all things'. If I understand Kierkegaard rightly in this then where there is love in truth, self-renunciation's love, there may be mockery and persecution, such as suffered by Jesus, but there is no *void*. Yet for Simone Weil Jesus' 'fidelity in the void' towards his Father before his death on the cross is the pinnacle of Christianity. But, to be fair to Kierkegaard, the sustenance which I have identified with hope is *spiritual* and not psychological sustenance. So he may reply that Jesus may have felt abandoned but he did not give up on love. The void in question is the absence of any psychological sustenance. Yet his love enabled him not to give up even then. That is spiritual sustenance.

What does Kierkegaard mean when he says that love 'is never brought to shame'? Hope in the ordinary sense, expectation, is brought to shame when it is not fulfilled. One then thinks that one has been a fool and others may well treat one as such. But hope, as Kierkegaard speaks of it, is detached from what the world thinks of one and does not value what the world values. It scorns cleverness (p. 243). It is thus indifferent to being judged to be a fool. It cannot, therefore, be shamed by its lack of cleverness.

In any case the hope that Kierkegaard speaks of here is not a longing expectation. Hence it can neither be fulfilled nor remain unfulfilled. It is an affective attitude to life and its tribulations come what further may. While it is open to all that life can throw at it, it has its base 'outside life'. Hence however much it may be pained, hurt, shattered by what comes from life, it will not lose faith, it will not despair. For the good is 'outside the world' and so cannot be harmed by evil which belongs to this world (Plato).

The hope to which Kierkegaard refers, as I said, also has its base 'outside life' and the good to which it is 'essentially and eternally related' (p. 244) is 'outside the world'. It is a good which can only come into view and to which one can open one's heart when one turns away from the self and the world. These are the two sides of one and the same coin. As Kierkegaard puts it: 'Neither the eternal nor the Holy Scriptures have ever taught any man to strive to go far or farthest of all in the world; on the contrary, they warn against getting on too far in the world (p. 244). Linking this to what he said about hope, he says that 'hope for some kind of earthly future' is not hope at all. It is 'desiring, craving, expecting' (ibid.). As for someone who says 'I hope to God that vengeance would fall upon this man', Kierkegaard says that this is not hope. It is merely an expression of hate and as such belongs to 'this world'. There is nothing spiritual about it; it bears no relation to goodness (p. 245).

D. Kierkegaard expresses the fourth characteristic which he attributes to spiritual love by saying that 'love seeks not its own': 'it is essentially sacrifice' (p. 247). When one loves, genuinely loves and loves deeply, one forgets oneself and one's caring attention is centred on the other, the beloved. One would do anything for the other's good measured by one's love of goodness. Here comes Kierkegaard's 'triangular' relation. Where the sacrifice is not mediated by 'the third', but is a response to what the beloved wishes, or is imagined he wishes, the love one gives him or her becomes corrupt. Selflessness turns into subservience or domination and in each the self reappears. Hence Lady Macbeth's love examined in an earlier chapter.

'Love,' Kierkegaard puts in italics, 'seeks not its own; for in love there is no mine and there is no yours', and so 'no "mine" or "yours"', and 'no "one's own" either.' And so one cannot seek one's own, since there is no one's own to seek (p. 248). He contrasts it with a justice that concentrates exclusively on people's rights and so 'give to each his own'. Here Simone Weil speaks of a justice that puts the emphasis on one's obligations to others. It is not primarily concerned to restore their rights, as rooted in this world, but to see that they are not deprived of those needs which she describes as 'needs of the soul'. This is a justice – like Kierkegaard's hope – which belongs to a love not of this world, a love of self-renunciation.

In this love, Kierkegaard says, 'there is no distinction for the lovers between *mine* and *yours*'. 'Remarkable! [he goes on] There are a *you* and an *I* and yet no *mine* or *yours*! For without *you* and *I* there is no love, and with *mine* and *yours* there is no love.' He then points out a difficulty in understanding what he is saying: '*Mine* and *yours* are in fact formed out of *you* and *I* and consequently seem necessary wherever *you* and *I* are.' He adds: 'This holds true everywhere, except in love' (p. 248).

This is the question of love, its craving for union and the possibility of communion which I have discussed in earlier chapters. Love, human love, craves for union or fusion with the beloved in which either the other is appropriated or the lover sinks his identity as an individual into that of the other. Seeing the danger of this as a philosopher, Sartre, we have seen, supports an individualism which washes away love's spirituality. The lover has to maintain his individuality, be a separate individual; otherwise he would become a slave to the other, become the other's blind instrument. He needs to be himself if he is to have any judgement, if he is to be able to distinguish between good and evil.

But does this force one to an ethics of individualism? I don't believe so. Here we need to make several connected distinctions. To serve someone selflessly is not the same thing as being his slave. So first we need to distinguish between service and servility. In servility a person lowers himself for gain and thus debases himself. In such gain the self reappears. Self-renunciation is giving up that self – 'self' in that sense. But to be able to do so, to be able to serve the good and the other out of love one has to be oneself. That is one has to do so on one's own count, to think for oneself, to love for oneself. To think *for* oneself, not *of* oneself. These are by no means the same thing. The love and the thinking must come from oneself; it must not be an imitation. Where one obeys, where one serves, this must be what one wills oneself. Even where one says, 'your will is my command', this must be one's own will as rooted in one's love and convictions.

To be able to give or dedicate one's will to goodness or, if you wish, to God, one must own it. It must be one's own to give. Hence Kierkegaard's distinction between *I* and *mine* or, as I have put it elsewhere, between the self in 'He is himself', 'he has self-knowledge' and the self in 'he is selfish', 'all he thinks of is himself and his self-interest'. To be an individual is the same thing as to be oneself; but this is a requirement of most moralities: you have to *believe* in its values, give yourself to them. This in no way commits one to an ethics of self-realization, or to a philosophy of individualism – that is of putting the individual first.

Kierkegaard says that the distinction between *mine* and *yours* holds true everywhere, except in love – in spiritual love. While one is attached to the worldly – and all emotions, except those which derive from love do so – what is our own comes first, has to be protected, if not promoted. This is true, of course, of envy and jealousy, of possessiveness, of pride, of a low self-esteem which seeks compensation, of vindictiveness, that is of an offence or insult to the self which one cannot forget, of the thirst for revenge, of ambition, and of putting survival first where there is some threat to it, and of course of all expressions of hatred and malice – even in the case of a hate which overrides self-interest. There are also different forms of identification, some of which parade as love, in which the self is reinforced and looked after even where it seems to be subordinated to something greater – identification with one's tribe, one's family in the tribal sense, one's club, one's race, one's country in certain forms of jingoism. Here too certain distinctions have to be drawn – for instance between loyalty which is an expression of love on the one hand and a mindless tribalism in which the individual person loses his individuality and finds a false identity in which he finds protection and security. In it one also evades the burden of responsibility of having to think for oneself as well as the need for self-restraint on certain occasions.

The kind of love Kierkegaard is thinking of is the antithesis of all this. It is only in the ascent to love and spirituality that one turns away from all this. Hence the connection between love and goodness. This is at the centre of Kierkegaard's thought and that of Plato's as well.

Kierkegaard asks whether the distinction between mine and yours is dissolved in friendship and in erotic love (p. 249). C.S. Lewis's answer was that such loves are not enough in themselves; they have to be transmuted by a love of God. My question was: can they remain themselves, that is forms of erotic love and friendship, when they have been so transformed or transmuted? I took C.S. Lewis to be sympathetic to an affirmative answer. Kierkegaard, I said, is ambivalent in his sympathy to such an answer. Here he writes:

When mine has become yours and yours mine [he refers to the symbolic exchange of rings in a marriage ceremony and of friends mixing their blood and becoming blood-siblings], there are indeed a mine and a yours everywhere, except that the exchange which took place betokens and signifies that it is no longer the initial, spontaneous mine of self-love which stands contentiously against yours. Through the exchange the contentious mine and yours have become a communal mine and yours. Therefore it is a fellowship, a perfect fellowship in mine and yours. Since mine and yours exchanged become *ours*, in which category friendship and erotic love have their strength, they are strong at least in this. But ours is for fellowship exactly the same as mine is for the individual .... We discern, therefore, that friendship and erotic love, as such, are only augmented and refined self-love, although erotic love is undeniably life's most happy fortune and friendship the greatest temporal good! In friendship and erotic love the revolution of self-love is just not deep enough from the ground up; therefore the original self-love's contentious distinction between mine and yours still slumbers within as a possibility (p. 249).

My comment is that what Kierkegaard says here *may* indeed be the case. C.S. Lewis, we have seen, speaks of a shared egoism, and sees this as a *corruption* of friendship. Kierkegaard seems to think of it as *inherent* to friendship and erotic love. But, I ask, why must it be so? It would be so, no doubt, in a friendship between people who have no regard whatsoever for any spiritual values. But I doubt that in such a case what we have is genuine friendship, one that is anything more than companionship or camaraderie.

Imagine a husband and wife totally and genuinely loyal, faithful to each other in their love. If their love is not an *égoisme à deux* then they will think of others and will give of themselves to others. However not being saints their sympathies may be limited in that they may not be boundlessly giving to strangers. There may be situations in which they put their self-interest first. No doubt their love has not been totally purified from the self. Does 'the original self-love's contentious distinction between mine and yours' have to 'still slumber within' their love 'as a possibility'? Supposing the husband is willing to give his life for the wife; is this willingness bound to be false, not genuine? That is can it not be genuine self-sacrifice – not something he does for himself? Does it have to be something he does for 'us', for something which is a source of life for him in egoism?

Let me simplify: can I not be genuinely willing to sacrifice my life for someone I love preferentially – that is without being willing to sacrifice it for anyone else in the same circumstances? As I said, I may not be a saint, I may not have detached myself completely from this world. But my love for this other person – my wife, my friend, my mother, father, brother or son – may be perfectly genuine and deep 'spiritually speaking' for all that. If it cannot be so until I have become a saint, then I doubt that a saint is capable of erotic or parental, love or friendship. For these are preferential, they are indeed attachments. I ask again: can there not be a preferential love that is pure? That is can I not be totally giving towards another person while my givingness towards others, strangers, may be limited by reservations according to circumstances? If I love one person unconditionally does it follow, as Kierkegaard seems to think, that I so love *everyone*? And conversely, if I do so love everyone, that is if I genuinely love my neighbour, whoever he is, can I still love my wife or my parents preferentially?

If this means, can I still, other things being equal, put them before others, then I am inclined to say Yes. For I may still put others before myself. If it means, if I cannot always put others, my neighbour, before myself, can I put my parents or my wife before myself, then I find this question more difficult to answer. For it may seem that if I cannot always put my neighbour before myself, then there is something suspect, an impurity, in my putting my parents or wife before myself – i.e. that I am still putting 'my own' first. I would like to believe that this does not have to be the case, that it is not always so. At any rate people *normally* learn to love their neighbour, to put him before themselves, from the love they find and respond to in people they are intimately related to – such as their parents. That normally comes first. Hence even if in the case of someone such as I have in mind we could say, 'he has a long way to go', it need not be the case that what he has in this one case is impure or suspect. That is his love for his parents or his wife does not have to be a form of 'self-love', as Kierkegaard uses this expression.

Kierkegaard asks: 'how then is the distinction between mine and yours abrogated entirely?' (p. 250). He says that if you take away *yours* from the distinction 'mine and yours' then we have someone who has no respect for others and what they own. We have the thief, the robber, the seducer, the manipulator, the person who cons and preys on others. If, on the other hand, you take away *mine* then we have 'the sacrificing one who renounces himself in all things – we have true love' (ibid.). 'The category mine disappears completely only for self-renouncing love, and the distinction mine and yours ceases entirely' (pp. 250–1). One gives up *mine*, but one has to respect what others own. It is for the other to give up what he owns; it is *he* who has to will it.

If I understand him rightly Kierkegaard here says that a preferential love is inevitably a relation of polarity – if not of 'mine and yours' then 'ours'. By contrast, in love of one's neighbour the 'ours' yields to God. For such a love everything is God's; what you give to your neighbour you give to God. Kierkegaard quotes 'he who loses his soul shall win it' and adds that in friendship and erotic love the soul is not given up: 'only spiritual love has the courage to will to have no mine at all' (p. 251).

The true lover, Kierkegaard says, is totally unguarded against being fooled, deceived, ridiculed. In his self-renunciation he does not care about being duped or ridiculed; these things do not matter to him. None of these things can awaken the self in him – for instance being ridiculed does not humiliate him, make him feel lowered in himself. Genuine humility is immune from humiliation. As Kierkegaard puts it: 'he has eternally forgotten this distinction – between mine and yours' (p. 251).

Although such love is non-preferential, Kierkegaard points out, that is it gives itself to everyone without distinction, it is directed to each person as an individual, that is in what makes him distinct, in his uniqueness. He exclaims: 'What love! First of all, it makes no distinction. Second, which is like the first, it makes infinite distinctions in loving the differences. Wonderous love!' (p. 252). 'To make no distinctions' means to favour no individual. 'To make infinite distinctions in loving the differences' means not to forget or ignore anyone, to attend to him as an individual, not to treat him as an instance of a kind. There is an analogy to this in a mother's love for her several children. She must not favour any one of them, yet she must give each child attention – real attention, attention directed to each individual child.

At the end of this section Kierkegaard considers the question: 'Is, then, the life of the lover wasted, has he loved in vain, since there is absolutely nothing which witnesses to his work?' His answer is: 'is not seeking one's own the wasting of one's life?' (p. 260). From its own perspective this is so: those who seek their own – to take a blatant example: those who sell their stories to the papers – make a really poor and pitiable show. But from *their* perspective those who choose to remain anonymous and turn away from the opportunity of turning their 'assets' into profit are fools. 'In a certain sense his life [the true lover's] is completely squandered on existence, on the existence of others' (ibid.).

E. The fifth characteristic of spiritual love which Kierkegaard highlights, he expresses in the words 'love hides the multiplicity of sins' (p. 261). What he means is that 'the lover who forgets himself' does not dwell on the other's sins. In the attention he gives to the other he does not hold them against him, they do not diminish his love. He accepts the other as he is; the other's sins do not constitute a reason for him to qualify his love. On the contrary, they are a reason for sorrow and such sorrow is an expression of love.

'The lover,' Kierkegaard says, 'has no understanding of evil…he is and he remains a child in this respect' (p. 266). He contrasts him with the person one may describe as 'streetwise': 'What the world admires as shrewdness is really an understanding of evil.' 'Wisdom,' by contrast, 'is an understanding of the good'. An understanding of evil, he writes, 'involves an understanding *with* evil'. He means rubbing shoulders with evil, compromising with it, and hence contamination with it. The streetwise person knows the ways of those who carry out their business in the streets and he knows how to get on with them. He shares their perspective and has no objection to their ways. He belongs to the streets. The good man, the lover, finds them alien. Kierkegaard says 'like the child', in other words, pure. But he is not innocent like the child. He knows, but what he knows fills him with revulsion.

'Love *hides* the multiplicity of sins.' By contrast the streetwise person, in what makes him streetwise '*discovers* sin with the help of slander, backbiting, and the manufacture of lies', which is characteristic of the life of the street. 'Hides' does not mean buries its head in the sand. Conversely, 'discovers' does not mean 'comes to know', for as Plato's Socrates says, the evil person does not know evil, he does not know what he is doing – that he is doing evil. Similarly the streetwise person may be *initiated* to sin and become soiled; but he does not know what sin is and does not recognize that he is being soiled – or if he does initially when he resists it, when he no longer sees any reason to resist it he loses all recognition of having become soiled. He is no longer an outsider to the ways of the street.

As I said in my discussion of the *Gorgias* knowledge of good and knowledge of evil go together. To know evil you have to suffer it in one way or another, feel pain and revulsion at coming in contact with it. One comes in contact with it as its victim through suffering it, as a witness in compassion for loved ones who are its victim; also through being tempted to do evil and restraining oneself in horror, and where one succumbs to it, through the remorse one feels in retrospect. That is one comes to know it through pain, compassion, horror and remorse which are expressions of one's love of the good. It is through this love that one comes to know the good or goodness (see Dilman, 1979, Chapter 9, sec. ii).

'Love hides the multiplicity of sins.' Kierkegaard gives the example of Christ. He was ridiculed and scorned, but 'he discovered nothing; out of love he hid the multiplicity of sins' (p. 267). That is they did not touch him, they did not elicit the usual reactions in him. Instead he felt sorry for them, he forgave them – reactions or expressions of love. To forgive one must know what one forgives as offensive yet not be offended. It takes love and humility to do that. 'Ridicule and contempt really do no harm when the one scorned is not injured by *discovery*, that is by becoming embittered, for if he becomes embittered he discovers the multiplicity of sins' (p. 268).

Becoming embittered is a reaction that comes from the self, the ego. In one who is embittered, the embitterment is a participation in the sin. One is embittered because one is down and cannot do the same in return. This is a participation in the sin in that one would like to do the same if only one could. It is an expression of being soiled by the sin one 'discovers'. One is soiled because in being embittered the ego is alive and asserts itself in however a strangulated way. Embitterment thus is the very opposite of self-renunciation.

In the case of someone embittered by being cheated and deceived by the beloved the love that is embittered was a soiled love, one in which the self was alive even though invisible. Not being embittered is not insensitiveness however. The person cheated suffers but has no desire to get his own back on the other. As Simone Weil puts it, goodness converts evil into suffering, evil projects it back where it came from in revenge – in reality or in fantasy. As I said before, the good man knows the evil of which he is a victim in his suffering. He is not insulated from it – as Kierkegaard's child who finds himself in a den of thieves for a short time seems to be. For though he hears all their conversations and sees everything they are doing, and is able to report all this accurately when he comes out, it never enters his head that he was among thieves (p. 266). That is innocence. But goodness is not innocent of evil; if it were it would not be goodness. For it would be protected from suffering and will not have learnt self-restraint.

What Kierkegaard calls 'hiding' should not therefore include innocence. It certainly includes rising above and forgiving. It is the antithesis of rumour, gossip, passing on polluting knowledge, scandal mongering, what the French call *'mauvaise langue'*, that is the tongue of one who 'enviously and maliciously declares' instead of keeping silent (see pp. 269–71). Earlier we saw how in embitterment the sin is multiplied in participation. By contrast forgiveness, Kierkegaard points out, 'takes the forgiven sin away' (p. 273). However if I dwell on the forgiveness, make a big deal of it, so that my ego feeds on it, then 'no such miracle occurs' (p. 274). 'Every miracle (Kierkegaard says) is a miracle of faith' (ibid.). That is in the first case my forgiveness is gratuitous, in the second case it is untrusting: I push it down the other person's throat, trying to make him notice it, whereas in the former case I forgive him 'in good faith', I let him go. The way I let him go is an act of faith – faith in goodness *however things may go*.

In forgiving someone I let what he has done go, I do not hold it against him. I do not have to forget; I forgive. As Kierkegaard says: 'I put it behind my back' and in doing so 'I turn towards him', or rather 'in turning towards him I put his offence behind my back' (p. 275). That is I do not identify him with the offence, I do not let his offence become identical with who he is in my estimate of him. I see him past that offence and not through it. This is an expression of a love that has emptied itself of the self and an instance of the way, in Kierkegaard's language, such a love 'hides the multiplicity of sins'.

F. The sixth characteristic Kierkegaard attributes to spiritual love is its endurance: 'love abides' (p. 279). What Kierkegaard means is that a love that has purged itself of all traces of the self is *unconditional*; it imposes no conditions. It does not say, for instance, I shall love her provided she loves me, or provided she is true to me. Hence it does not change with any change in the beloved or her responses. It does not grow bitter or turn into hate if, for instance, the beloved stabs the lover in the back, nor does it fade away with the passage of time.

What we normally call a 'break between two lovers' Kierkegaard refers to as 'frivolous talk' (p. 282). For it makes it 'appear as if the love-relationship is a matter between two persons' (p. 282). But, as we have already seen, Kierkegaard says that there is a third concerned, namely God or love. 'When two persons relate themselves in love to each other, each one of them all by himself is related to *love* ... Before they reach the breaking-point, before one comes to break his love in relationship to the other, he must first fall away *from* LOVE. This is the important thing ... it has the seriousness of the eternal' (pp. 282–3). Kierkegaard goes on:

> When a relationship is only between two, one always has the upper hand in the relationship by being able to break it, for as soon as one has broken it, *the relationship* is broken. But when there are three, one person cannot do this. The third, as mentioned, is love itself, which the innocent sufferer can hold to in the break, and then the break has no power over him (p. 283).

The point made here is similar to the one made by Plato's Socrates in the *Gorgias* when he says that the good man cannot be harmed. Here one should add: he cannot be harmed *so long as he holds on to goodness*. For, spiritually speaking, that is the only true harm. Socrates should have said, goodness cannot be harmed. But the good man can be separated from goodness and so can be harmed, although he has by then stopped being good.

It is the same with Kierkegaard's claim that 'love abides'. He is saying something about spiritual love, namely that it is unconditional, that it is outside time in the sense that nothing that actually takes place can touch, change or diminish it. That is the kind of love it is. But this does *not* mean that one who has found such love cannot lose it. Kierkegaard does not always make this clear. Eternal love is unconditional, but whether or not it abides with the lover *depends on* whether or not the lover keeps his faith and holds to love: '*if* the lover does not fall away from *love*, he can prevent the break, he can perform this miracle, for *if* he perseveres the break can never really come to be' (p. 283). I have underlined the '*if*' to emphasize that the claim here is *conditional*. For love to endure 'the powers of the eternal are needed' – as Kierkegaard puts it. The lover can benefit from these powers through his faith. But the person who *has* faith *can* lose his faith. For holding to love, keeping one's faith are necessarily in time.

12.3 Love's Work in Forming the Heart

In the previous section I was concerned to elucidate, critically, what Kierkegaard often expresses in dramatic terms and in a paradoxical way and to indicate the conceptual problems behind his ways of expressing what he had to say. What was in question there are his perceptions of the characteristics of spiritual love – or to put it differently, what love *must be like* if it is to count as spiritual love. Those he dwelt on, in less dramatic terms, are (i) constructiveness, from a spiritual perspective, (ii) commitment in trust, (iii) spiritual sustenance, (iv) selflessness and generosity, (v) accepting forgiveness, and (vi) unconditional faithfulness.

It is through these characteristics that spiritual love works in forming the heart and in doing so commits the person to a relationship in which the other's welfare, spiritually understood, is paramount. Hence the characteristics of love I have discussed and its works in forming the heart are the two sides of the same coin. Thus, for instance, it is in the givingness of his love that a person is generous. So it is in the love that he finds that a person becomes generous. This is another way of saying that in love a person is generous and in hate mean. *His* task is to keep that love, *love's* work is to so change him that he becomes a generous person.

Kierkegaard concentrates on four aspects of this work: (i) 'the mercifulness of spiritual love', the compassion which turns a person away from the world and its values, primarily money and self-profit, or self-interest, (ii) the kind of reconciliation it brings and the attitude in the person towards it, (iii) 'the work of love in remembering one dead' and the kind of faithfulness it promotes in the heart and tests, (iv) 'the work of love in praising love', that is in service and dedication to it, in bearing witness to it.

A. In connection with 'mercifulness, a work of love' Kierkegaard speaks of a 'mercifulness which possesses nothing'. The person who is rich in the sense of possessing worldly goods runs the risk of attracting attention in what he gives and getting a boost to his ego – an instance of what Kierkegaard elsewhere called double-mindedness. He speaks of it here as 'the mercifulness of this worldly existence' (p. 294). Such a person does not give of himself. Kierkegaard contrasts what the world says with what Christ said: the world thinks that the rich man gives the most, whereas Christ said that 'the poor give the most' (p. 295). 'The world,' he says, 'has understanding only for money' – that is of what can be exchanged, of what one is paid with. Christ, on the other hand, has understanding 'only for mercifulness' – that which has no concern for repayment. He quotes what Christ said of the widow who gave only two pennies: 'She gave of her poverty' (ibid.).

Money, Kierkegaard says, 'is externally less than nothing'. That is we are morally deceived in attaching value to it, in measuring the worth of things in terms of money. He writes: 'Many think that the eternal is a construction of the imagination, money the reality.' But the truth is the reverse of this. From the perspective of the eternal it is money which is 'a construction of the imagination' (ibid.). 'Money is the world's god' (p. 296). Here Kierkegaard contrasts Socrates who would not accept money for his teaching with the worldly Sophists of his time who taught how to get on in the world in return for money.

Mercifulness lies in the spirit in which one gives rather than in what one gives. Therefore, says Kierkegaard, it can be seen more easily in the nothing which the poor give than in the everything which the rich give. The everything is 'spectacular', it 'affects the sensuous in one', 'it draws attention to itself' (p. 303). The spirit in which one gives: one doesn't want to be seen giving, one doesn't want to wound the pride – '*amour propre*' – of the needy. Thus Kierkegaard says that mercifulness is or lies in 'inwardness'. It is a work of love 'even if it has nothing to give and is able to do nothing' (p. 305). For instance there may be nothing that a doctor can do for his terminally ill patient; but in the patience with which he listens to his complaints of pain which, let us say, he is unable to relieve he shows real mercifulness. In this 'nothing' that he gives his patient he makes it easier for the patient to bear the pain. This is an instance of a work of love.

B. Kierkegaard next speaks of 'the victory of reconciliation in love which wins the vanquished'. He is thinking of the relation of the lover to the unloving beloved. The danger is that in time this will make him cold and indifferent. To remain sensitive to the call of love and so loving the unloving beloved is, he says, 'to triumph over evil with the good' (p. 308). This is an instance of love's work; it reconciles the lover to the unloving person. It takes goodness and nobility on the part of the lover to accept this situation while remaining loving and giving; and this is where 'the third' comes in. The lover battles 'not only so that the good may come to be in him, but he battles *reconcilingly* in order that the good might be victorious in the unloving one, or he battles *in order to win the vanquished*' – that is to win him to the side of love, of loving the good, but *not* in order that he may himself be loved in return. The love in him is first and foremost a love of the good, self-renunciation's love. Consequently, the relationship between lover and loved one is not 'an out-and-out relationship of combat' – as it often is, for instance, in the break-up of a marriage. There the partners become enemies, each thinking of himself now that the marriage has broken up and the love relationship has been soured. Whereas here the lover who is at the same time a true lover of the good is on the side of the other – the still loved one.

So far the loved one may remain untouched, alienated, not reconciled and unwilling to seek reconciliation. But the lover is reconciled: he doesn't think of himself, he wants nothing for himself, he has only one thing in mind, the good of the loved one. He does not hold anything against her. Forgiving may be difficult, but accepting the other's forgiveness may be even more difficult and calls for tact, delicacy and generosity on the part of the forgiver and humility and again generosity of spirit on the part of the forgiven. Here Kierkegaard speaks of winning the vanquished – vanquished in the sense that reconciliation for her means giving up the battle. In her coldness and indifference she was on the side of the self and everything the self values. For her to come round is the defeat of what she sided with. This is humbling and easily experienced as a humiliation and therefore resisted. Hence it is of paramount importance that the lover should never think of himself as the victor and genuinely believe that 'it is the good which has conquered' (p. 313).

> In order to remove the humiliation and mortification, the lover interpolates something higher between the unloving one and himself and thereby gets himself out of the way. When there is no third in the relationship between man and man, every such relationship becomes unsound, either too ardent or embittered. The third ... is the true, the good, or more accurately, the God-relationship; this third is a cooling factor in certain phases of a relationship and in others a soothing agent. In truth, the lover is too loving to take a posture over against the vanquished and himself be the victor who revels in the victory ... . With the help of the third, which the lover gets placed between them, both are humbled: for the lover humbles himself before the good, whose needy servant he is ... and the vanquished one humbles himself not before the lover but before the good. But when both are humbled in a relationship, there is no humiliation for either one of them alone (p. 313).

Both are humbled before the good; that is why Kierkegaard speaks here of the triumph over evil with the good. This is love's triumph which works in the hearts of the alienated parties, reconciling them by reintegrating each with the good – 'the third'. Reconciliation between the two parties here means the establishment or restoration of a relationship of mutual consideration and regard. This means different things in different relationships – that of a father and son who had become alienated, a wife and an estranged husband, a divorced couple, etc. It is not the restoration of the *status quo*. It does not mean requited sexual love. In the case of once close friends, it does not mean the return of the closeness, but the restoration of friendliness and good will. I said 'does not mean': I should say 'not necessarily'.

C. Kierkegaard speaks of 'the work of love in remembering one dead'. This is the work of love in forming the heart to remain faithful to the loved one 'in the void'. With the living we are in interaction – if we are not face to face, at least we can speak on the phone, write and receive letters, and if none of these is the case we can have news of them through a third party. Here there is always the risk of alienation and rupture, but at least the interaction sustains the relationship, keeps it alive, keeps it moving even when changing.

With someone dead, it is true that one can find out something new about him or her one did not know, and this may be something that hurts, but there is no interaction. One cannot remonstrate, ask, tell him or her off, hear what he or she has to say in response. This makes a radical difference. Kierkegaard says that 'if you could perchance watch someone shadow-boxing in earnest, or if you could get a dancer to dance alone in a dance he customarily dances with a partner, you would best be able to observe his movements, better than if he boxed with another actual person or if he danced with another actual person.' He adds: 'And if you understand the art of making yourself *nobody* in conversation, you get to know best what resides in the other person' (p. 319). This is, of course, what the psycho-analyst tries to emulate or approximate in a psycho-analytic therapy.

Kierkegaard continues: 'no one, absolutely no one, can make himself *nobody* as one dead can, for he is *nobody*' – i.e. he does not exist in reality but only in the heart of someone who continues to love him. So 'here the living becomes revealed' (ibid.). The loving person becomes revealed in his love: what kind of love did he have for the one dead when he was alive? Can he remain faithful to him in his acts now after he has gone? This is the litmus test, Kierkegaard argues, of the character of his love. For 'the dead make no repayment': 'one who is dead does not give joy to the remem-berer as the child gives joy to its mother' (p. 321). Furthermore 'one who is dead does not compel one at all. Yes, in the moment of sepa-ration, when one cannot get along without him who is dead, there is a shriek … [But] little by little, as the dead crumbles away, the memory crumbles away … little by little one becomes free of this – burdensome memory' (p. 324). Kierkegaard asks: 'Is this free love, is this love for one who is dead?'

In human love, he points out, 'there is usually something coer-cive, daily sight and habit if nothing else.' So there one cannot be absolutely sure 'to what extent it is love which freely holds its object fast and to what extent it is the object which in one way or another coercively lends a hand' (p. 325). One can see this clearly only when the loved one is dead and 'has become nobody.' The loving memory of one dead 'has to protect itself against time … it has to protect its freedom in remembering against that which would compel it to forget.' For there is much in life that beckons the one who gave a shriek when he died to forget him. The 'multiplicity of life's demands' beckon to him, the living beckon to him, but the one who is dead cannot beckon. 'Therefore no love is as free as the work of love which *remembers* one who is dead – for to remember him is something quite different from not being able to forget him at first' (ibid.). Thus remembering one who is dead, loved when he was alive, is a testimony of what love has wrought in the heart of the person who loved and continues to do so with a love undiminished. It is of course an expression of the depth and purity of his love.

A love that abides when the loved one is dead and long gone is 'most faithful, for there is nothing to aid the loving person in being faithful' (pp. 325–6), no 'holding together' such as is possible between two lovers who are alive. Where one of the lovers is dead 'the relationship is broken if the one loving does not hold on to him' (p. 326). Here Kierkegaard asks how real is faithfulness and how much of it constraint? The answer is we do not know until either the lover is tempted to turn away from the beloved or the constraint is lifted – as in the case of the loved one's death.

D. Last but not least Kierkegaard speaks of 'the work of love in praising love', that is in bearing witness to it and articulating what one has witnessed and learned: doing so out of love. Since it can only be done out of love this is itself a work of love.

Here Kierkegaard contrasts work with art. The idea is that the artist, the poet who felt called upon to praise love would 'wax lyrical', sing his praise of love, he would make a show of it and himself attract praise. Whereas work is hard, requires patience and humility. While Kierkegaard is correct in the point he wishes to make I do not think that what he thinks of the poet and the artist is applicable to the creators of great works of art, such as Bach, Shakespeare or Michaelangelo.

He has a further point in mind: 'art is related to the accident of talent; work is related to the universally human' (p. 330). All right, so *anybody* can work, anybody can bear witness to and praise love; what it takes is achieving inwardness: 'the work of praising love must be done inwardly in self-renunciation' (p. 331). It is something that requires inwardness which anybody can come to, and not talent which is rare. But this does not exclude the artist who has to work to produce a great work of art and which also calls for seriousness.

Let me quote Kierkegaard: 'Only in self-renunciation can a man effectually praise love. No poet can do it. The poet can sing of erotic love and friendship, and the ability to do this is a rare gift, but *the poet* cannot praise love' (p. 335). I can only repeat my dissent by citing the example of the religious music of Bach. I recognize the point about anonymity on which I quoted Kierkegaard at the beginning of the previous chapter. I also mentioned Father Sergius in Tolstoy's story who as he became famous was separated from God and who had to become a pilgrim and a beggar, that is give up everything, before he could find God. But does his mean that the acclaim which an artist finds must go to his head? A rich man cannot go to heaven because until he gives up his money he remains rich. Can he keep his money and think nothing of it? I doubt it. I doubt, however, whether this is entirely true of fame and of the acclaim a talented artist receives. It is possible for someone to genuinely shun fame while it is thrust on him by others. Could this not be a test of the genuineness of his humility?

Kierkegaard may well agree. But, he says, 'the work of praising love must *outwardly* be done in sacrificial disinterestedness': 'Sacrificial disinterestedness is required outwardly if love is in truth to be praised' (p. 336). I take it that this is because here one does not merely happen to be a witness, but bears witness – in which case one has to be seen doing so by others. Hence presumably one has to divest oneself of everything that shines in one to others. But does not Bach's religious music truly give praise to God in humility?

Kierkegaard points out that one who praises love is not concerned simply to win men's approval of love. This is the same as what Socrates says about oratory and sophistry in the *Gorgias* (see Dilman, 1979, Chapter 2). Thus love cannot be praised by flattery for instance. It can only be praised in love of truth (p. 336). Hence to praise love one has to be detached from the moment; that is one must bear witness to love and let the truth in what one says or shows speak for itself. One must be concerned with speaking the truth and not with persuading others. Recurring to the question of art and poetry, it is fair to say that Kierkegaard is probably afraid – as Plato was too – of the persuasive power of poetry and that is why he wants to avoid the poet's praise of love.

Poetry can make one believe. But even if what it makes one believe is the truth Kierkegaard would rather that truth should speak for itself. Only then would one believe the truth, believe in the truth, or believe 'in truth'. The relation in which one stands to the truth personally, as an individual, is all important here. Similarly, Kierkegaard points out, 'the love which loves the beautiful is not true love, self-renunciation's love' (p. 341). A bit earlier he speaks of 'what the world calls a lovable man'. He is charming, he makes one feel comfortable, he is friendly. It is easy to love him. Kierkegaard says that 'this love-worthiness of the lovable person ... is traitorousness towards the eternal' (p. 340). The easy love that he attracts from people is deceptive. In coming to love the likes of him one never comes to appreciate what 'true love' is; one is deflected from finding it. It passes one a false imitation of the real thing.

Kierkegaard contrasts the 'lovable man' with someone like Socrates:

> The lovable man knows about all the possible excuses and escapes and clever maxims for higgling and haggling and chiselling; and he is loving enough to let a little of his cleverness rub off on others, by whose help he organizes his own life advantageously, easily, and comfortably .... In [the] company [of the person it is difficult to love] the excuses and escapes do not look very good; all that one lives for takes on an unheroic cast. In his company one cannot simply take one's ease; even less does he

help one to adjust the pillow of ease by temporal or even by good-natured pious indulgence (ibid.).

Here I am bound to note that this second description reminds me of the psycho-analyst who in helping the analysand to self-knowledge makes him aware of his escapes and evasions and hopes to turn him away from a life in which self-deception runs deep. This leads to a time when the analysand comes to hate him for it and may well break off his analysis. Kierkegaard says 'Love to God means hatred of the world'. If I may continue the analogy with one more sentence: the will of an analysand to continue with his analysis means hatred of a life of self-deception – disgust with his own evasions.

To return to what Kierkegaard says about Socrates' qualification for praising beauty. He says that Socrates' physical qualification was part of this qualification. For if he were less ugly – if he had at least a beautiful nose – in praising beauty he would have been drawing attention to himself. 'But in the assurance of his being the homeliest, he believed that with good conscience he could say everything ... in praise of beauty without gaining the slightest advantage from it' (p. 341). There is a similar danger, Kierkegaard points out, in praising self-renunciation's love. Unless one genuinely feels one lacks it one cannot praise it. That is one can only praise such a love in total humility; one must believe that one lacks it, that one has a long way to go. Otherwise one cannot look up to it.

12.4   Kierkegaard, Plato and Simone Weil on Loving the Beautiful

We have seen why Kierkegaard says that 'the love which loves the beautiful is not true love, self-renunciation's love.' At the end of the chapter which I discussed in the last section Kierkegaard says of Socrates that he 'knew how to talk so beautifully about the love which loves the beautiful.' 'At times he spoke otherwise and spoke of *loving the ugly*. He did not deny that to love is to love the beautiful, but he nevertheless spoke, yes, it was a kind of jest, about loving the ugly.' He then asks: 'What is to be understood by *the beautiful*?' He speaks of it as 'the immediate and direct object of immediate love, the choice of inclination and passion.' He then repeats: 'the beloved and the friend are the spontaneous and direct objects of spontaneous love, the choice of passion and of inclination' (p. 342).

'And what is *the ugly*? It is *the neighbour*, whom one SHALL love.' He says that Socrates 'knew nothing of this; he did not know that one's neighbour exists and that one should love him; what he said about loving the ugly was only teasing' (pp. 342–3). He then repeats what he said many times earlier in the book: 'One's neighbour is the unlovable object, not something to offer to inclination and passion, which turn away from him and say, "What is that to love!" But for that very reason there is no advantage connected with speaking about having to love the unlovable object. And yet the true love is precisely love of one's neighbour, or it is not finding not the lovable object but finding the unlovable object to be lovable' (p. 343).

In the *Symposium* Plato put what he wanted to say about love and beauty in the mouth of Diotima and made Socrates the one who is instructed by her: 'initiated into the mysteries of love'. Diotima, or shall I say Plato, clearly recognizes what Kierkegaard says about the way beauty as the object of desire is beguiling and how love can be corrupted or soiled by such a desire. Yet he treats it as a ladder one can use to ascend towards a higher and purer love as one moves from beauty as an object of desire towards beauty as an object of contemplation. Kierkegaard rightly thinks of beauty – e.g., the beauty of a beautiful woman – as a barrier to spiritual love. Plato sees it as a ladder, a gateway to it. Simone Weil continually points out that there is no contradiction, that what is a barrier can at the same time be a gateway to God or the good for one who can learn to make the right use of it. Indeed what is a gateway to God has to be a barrier to Him. It has to offer resistance in the form of fear or temptation – in this case temptation.

Diotima describes love – the kind of love Kierkegaard is speaking about – as the child of Poverty and Contrivance. That is the lover approaches the beloved in full consciousness of his own incompleteness, much in the way Aristophanes describes it in the same dialogue. Yet he is not greedy; he is happy to make do with whatever the beloved is prepared to give him. He does not ask for more; indeed he does not ask. She describes love as 'not [itself] beautiful; but hard and weather-beaten and shoeless and homeless (Penguin Classics, 1952, p. 52). Secondly, love 'schemes to get for himself whatever is beautiful and good.' Thirdly, 'he is neither mortal nor immortal; but on one and the same day he will live and flourish (when things go well with him), and also meet his death; and then come to life again through the vigour that he inherits from his father' (ibid.). That is what worldly, 'human' love finds is evanescent. When it loses what it craves for and finds it dies: 'what he wins he always loses'. When it learns to surmount the loss in self-renunciation and contrivance it will come to life again transformed. In its poverty it will still crave for beauty but it will have learned to contemplate it from a distance. It will have learned not to try and possess or appropriate it.

The lover who has found such love, then, will 'no longer be the slave of a base and mean-spirited devotion to an individual example of beauty, whether the object of his love be a boy or a man or an activity, but, by gazing upon the vast ocean of beauty to which his attention is now turned, [will] bring forth in the abundance of his love of wisdom many beautiful and magnificent sentiments and ideas...' (p. 93). Plato expresses what he is saying here in terms of the particular and the universal towards which one moves by degrees of abstraction, and philosophers tend to think of what he is saying in terms of his 'theory of forms' which they take to be a 'theory of universals' such as is to be found in Locke. But this is a serious misunderstanding. What is in question is not 'abstraction' from particulars but *detachment* from the particular things that press on and tempt one in one's everyday life, and moving towards a spiritual perspective on them. This is not a perspective from which their particular individuality becomes a matter of indifference. Far from it: they lose none of their importance, but shine with a new and different light; they are seen as partaking in 'the beauty of the world'. As such they are loved for themselves as part of this beauty, as partaking of it and also contributing to it.

This is something which Simone Weil led me to understand – as she has led me to understand other aspects of Plato's thinking. In her book *Waiting on God*, the section called 'Love of the Order of the World', she writes:

> To empty ourselves of our false divinity, to deny ourselves, to give up being the centre of the world in imagination, to discern that all points in the world are equally centred and that the true centre is outside the world, this is to consent to the rule of mechanical necessity in matter and of free choice at the centre of each soul. Such consent is love. The face of this love which is turned towards thinking persons is the love of our neighbour; the face turned towards matter is love of the order of the world, or love

of the beauty of the world which is the same thing (Weil, 1959, p. 115).

What Kierkegaard rejects in the words 'the love which loves the beautiful is not true love' she simply qualifies:

A sense of beauty, although mutilated, distorted and soiled, remains rooted in the heart of man as a powerful incentive. It is present in all the preoccupations of secular life [including in those which absorb the sensual man – as she elaborates on the following pages]. If it were made true and pure it would sweep all secular life in a body to the feet of God, it would make the total incarnation of the faith possible (p. 118).

I take this as the key to understanding Diotima's initiation of Socrates to the mysteries of love in Plato's *Symposium*.

'All that is in the universe,' she says, 'is less than the universe' and if we call them 'beautiful', they are so only in an extended sense of the word. They only imitate what is strictly beautiful, namely the universe as a whole. Its beauty is 'universal' – i.e. of the universe. We normally call particular things beautiful without seeing them, to use Spinoza's word, *sub specie aeternitatis*. However, 'all these secondary kinds of beauty are of infinite value as openings to universal beauty. But, if we stop short at them, they are, on the contrary, veils; then they corrupt' (p. 120). They tempt us. She then adds that there are also aspects we see in things which make them 'seductive' to the person without discernment and so 'attract his love by fraud'. I take it she means that they are desired, found attractive, and simply on that account thought to be beautiful and described as so, instead of desired because they have beauty in them of however a 'mutilated, distorted and soiled' kind.

She then says: 'Beauty is the only finality here below.... We are drawn towards it without knowing what to ask of it' (p. 121). That is we are attracted to a beautiful woman, for instance, for no other reason than that she is beautiful. If we desire her it is not for the sake of anything other than that she is beautiful. Contact with something beautiful is pleasurable; but this pleasure is not something other than its beauty. If we crave for the continuation or renewal of such contact it is not in order to have or experience anything other than such contact. But there is more in this phrase she uses, namely 'without knowing what to ask of it'. She continues in what I find a very important passage:

> It [beauty] offers us its own existence. We do not desire anything else, we possess it, and yet we still desire something. We do not in the least know what it is. We want to get behind beauty, but it is only a surface. It is like a mirror that sends us back our own desire for goodness. It is a sphinx, an enigma, a mystery which is painfully tantalising. We should like to feed upon it but it is merely something to look at, it appears only from a certain distance. The great trouble in human life is that looking and eating are two different operations. Only beyond the sky, in the country inhabited by God, are they one and the same operation. While still children, we feel this trouble, when we look at a cake for a long time, and take it, almost regretting having to eat it, but unable to prevent ourselves. It may be that vice, depravity and crime are nearly always, or even perhaps always, in their essence, attempts to eat beauty, to eat what we should only look at. Eve began it. If she caused humanity to be lost by eating the fruit, the opposite attitude, looking at the fruit without eating it, should be what is required to save it (p. 121).

She adds: 'Only beauty is not the means to anything else. It alone is good in itself, but without our finding any particular good or advantage in it' (p. 122).

She then gives the example of St Francis who 'needed to be a vagabond and a beggar in order to feel it [the beauty of the universe or universal beauty]'. 'Poverty has a privilege. That is a dispensation of Providence without which the love of the beauty of the world might easily come into conflict with the love of our neighbour' (pp. 122–3). She has in mind the contrast between St Francis and the rich who surround themselves with luxury so as to feel they are living in a beautiful universe.

Having spoken about the way in which we are deceived by the kind of beauty we find in a beautiful woman, for instance, in the way we desire her and find her attractive, the beauty which Kierkegaard finds to be a barrier to self-renunciation's love, Simone Weil speaks of the way the mediocre in us, which constitutes the greater part of our soul, is afraid of pure beauty – the universal beauty the ascent to which is shown to be *one* of the ways to self-renunciation's love in the *Symposium*: 'This part of [our soul] is seized with panic every time that a little pure beauty or pure goodness appears; it hides behind the flesh, it uses it as a veil' (p. 129). This is another aspect of the way we are thrown back to substitutes of beauty and are held back from reaching where Diotima leads Socrates in her initiation of him to the mysteries of love.

I shall conclude this section by noting, briefly, that Simone Weil takes a diametrically opposed view of art and poetry to the one taken by Kierkegaard in her appreciation of *great art*. She devotes several pages to it here and what she writes about Homer's *Iliad* is itself a work of art. I shall simply quote two short paragraphs from the section in *Waiting on God* on which I have concentrated here:

> Art is an attempt to transport into a limited quantity of matter, modelled by man, an image of the infinite beauty of the entire universe. If the attempt succeeds, this portion of matter should not hide the universe, but on the contrary it should reveal its reality to all around.

Here I shall interject between the two paragraphs something that Tolstoy has said in one sentence: 'If you want to be universal paint your own village.' That is, you will only find it (i) in the particular and not the abstract, (ii) in your country 'here below' where your roots are and not in the sky. In the next paragraph Simone Weil continues:

> Works of art which are neither pure and true reflections of the beauty of the world nor openings onto this beauty, are not strictly speaking beautiful; their authors may be very talented but they lack real genius. That is true of a great many works of art which are among the most celebrated and the most highly praised. Every *true* artist has had real, direct and immediate contact with the beauty of the world, contact which is of the nature of a sacrament. God has inspired every first-rate work of art, though its subject may be utterly and entirely secular; He has not inspired any of the others. [She then agrees with Kierkegaard:] Indeed the lustre of beauty which distinguishes some of those others may quite well be a diabolical lustre (pp. 123–4).

12.5 Conclusion

I conclude with a few comments on Kierkegaard's conclusion to his work on love. Here he contrasts a worldly, natural conception of justice with an other-worldly, supernatural one. We find the former one in the Old Testament: it is 'the Jewish like-for-like: an eye for an eye, a tooth for a tooth'. The latter one we find in the Bible: it is the Christian one – 'the eternal's like-for-like' (p. 348). The former is justice without compassion, the latter is justice at one with love – a love of the good, self-renunciation's love. The former is concerned with redressing the balance or equilibrium which has been tipped against the victim of a crime. Kierkegaard describes this as an 'external' matter. The latter is concerned with the relation in which one stands personally with regard to goodness as a victim or witness of a crime. Here Kierkegaard speaks of 'inwardness'. 'Christianity,' he says, 'turns attention completely away from the external, turns it inwards, makes your every relationship to other human beings into a God-relationship' (ibid.).

As I explained in my book *Morality and the Inner Life* (1979), one's inner life is one's life, as an individual, in its relationship to the good. A person who is alienated from that relationship in being absorbed by worldly preoccupations, or one who lives a purely conventional life, has no inner life and so lacks inwardness. As I have already pointed out when Tolstoy's Father Sergius is taken over by the demands of the fame he acquires he loses his inner life, everything becomes external – it is, as he puts it, as if he had been turned inside out. But, as both Kierkegaard and Simone Weil point out, an inner life, a spiritual life, has to be lived and can only be lived 'in the world', 'here below'. Kierkegaard says: 'Christianly understood one has ultimately and essentially to do with God in everything, although one nevertheless must remain in the world and in the relationships of earthly life allotted to one' (p. 348).

Thus the worldly, the activist like-for-like, demands the righting of the balance tipped against the victim by the crime and injustice of which he has been the object. It says: 'see to it that in the long run you do unto others what others do unto you' (p. 354). 'But the Christian like-for-like is: as you do unto others, God does unto you in the very same mode' (ibid.). Kierkegaard adds: 'Christianly understood you have absolutely nothing to do with what others do to you; it does not concern you.' It is not your business; it is a matter between God and the criminal. Your business is in how you respond to accept God's will. What is important and of the greatest significance is how you fare in that relationship. As Socrates, who takes a similar line in the *Gorgias*, points out, this does not exclude earthly punishment so long as it is not the victim, the offended party who takes it into his own hands. It has to be administered by an institution who does not 'identify' with the victim and seeks revenge. Those who administer it must themselves be unsoiled by such a desire and have compassion for the criminal in his soul – the way Porfiry in Dostoyevsky's *Crime and Punishment* had for Raskolnikov. But Kierkegaard does not go into this. He is concerned to elaborate what distinguishes the Christian like-for-like from the Jewish one.

One example of the Christian like-for-like which he considers is 'forgive and you will also be forgiven'. This does not mean that necessarily others will forgive you and that things will go better for you. Whether or not they will is a purely contingent matter which should not be your primary concern. Your primary concern should be how you fare in God's eye and not how you fare among men. The forgiveness that you give you *necessarily* receive from God; what you receive from men is a contingent matter. In the *Gorgias* Socrates puts this clearly in answer to what Callicles says to him:

> You seem to me, Socrates, as confident that none of these things will happen to you as if you were living in another world and were not liable to be dragged into court, possibly by some scandal of the vilest character.

Socrates replies:

> I should be a fool, Callicles, if I didn't realize that in this state anything may happen to anybody. But this at least I am sure of, that, if I am brought to trial on a charge involving any of the penalties you mention, my prosecutor will be a villain, for no honest man would prosecute an innocent party (521).

What is important for Socrates is that in such a situation he should be innocent; not what other men think of him and consequently do to him. He has a clear conscience and he is represented in the *Phaedo* as facing his death with equanimity, not bearing any malice or ill will towards anybody, including his executioners.

Jesus' death was different. Like Socrates he was not concerned about what men were doing to him in nailing him on the cross to die. He forgave them. But his crucifixion with two thieves made him think that his Father had deserted him. This was the supreme test which Socrates was not put to. He came through it in that he remained faithful to his Father in Heaven in the absence of the kind of certainty Socrates had and of the sustenance Socrates received from it. Regarding 'God's abandonment of Christ at the supreme moment of the crucifixion' Simone Weil exclaims: 'what a gulf of love on both sides'. She takes the gulf to be an expression of God's love as mirrored in natural necessity. It is created by God's retirement from His creation out of love so as to force human love to become supernatural. Christ remained faithful to God in his love while believing that he had been abandoned by God: *'une fidelité à vide*, that is without the consoling belief that God was with him. For her that is an expression of the supreme grandeur of Christianity as a spiritual religion.

To return to the Christian like-for-like of which Kierkegaard speaks in his Conclusion. He gives many examples: 'God forgives you neither more nor less nor otherwise than *as* you forgive your trespassers.' 'To accuse another person before God is to accuse oneself.... If you wish to pretend to be completely outside the matter in hand and wish privately before God to complain of your enemies, God makes short work of it and opens a case against you – to complain against another is to complain against oneself.' 'It does not help that you intend that he shall judge someone else, for you yourself have made Him your judge, and He is, *like-for-like*, simultaneously your judge, that is, He judges you also. If, on the other hand, you do not engage in accusing someone before God or in making God into a judge, God is then a merciful God' (pp. 352–3).

Someone may ask: How does Kierkegaard or anyone else know God's ways, His like-for-like? Obviously what is in question is not something one finds out by experience. What we have are concept-forming statements, making connections which build up a concept of God – the Christian God. That is the God to which the believer gives his faith, in whom he puts his trust. To put his faith in such a God is for the believer to commit himself to a framework which such statements define and they give him a particular perspective on life. The vision they give him provides him with certain ways of taking particular situations and acting in them. He finds himself in that way of acting, in responding to the demands he sees particular situations making on him, in restraining himself in various situations which make sense to him, and in taking adversities as to be accepted, as 'the will of God', without questioning them. The framework of his faith and particular beliefs thus determines the significance of what he meets in life, they contribute to shaping the world in which he lives – 'the world of inwardness' as Kierkegaard calls it:

> This world of inwardness ... this is reality. In this world of inwardness the Christian like-for-like is at home. For, Christianly understood, to love human beings is to love God and to love God is to love human beings; what you do unto men God does unto you. If you are embittered towards men who do you wrong, you are really embittered towards God .... If, however, you gratefully take the wrongs from God's hand 'as a good and perfect gift', you do not become embittered towards men either. If you will not forgive ... you want to make God hard-hearted .... How, then, should He forgive you? If you cannot bear the offences of men against you, how should God be able to bear your sins against Him? (pp. 354–5).

Kierkegaard speaks of this as an 'echo' of what is in one's own heart. One who 'lives in urban confusion', one who has 'never been solitary' does not hear it. By being solitary Kierkegaard means being oneself, speaking and acting for oneself and shouldering responsibility for what one does, and it means being honest with oneself, not drowning oneself in the corporate 'we' – 'the crowd', 'the great beast'. It is only as such that one can find God. So Kierkegaard says: 'if you have never been solitary; you have also never discovered that God exists' (p. 355). That is, you may outwardly comply with the observances of Christianity, you may think you believe or take yourself to be a believer, but your beliefs are second-hand. *You*, in your solitariness as Kierkegaard would say, do not believe. You would not then hear what God 'repeats' to you: 'who believes in echo if night and day he lives in urban confusion!' (ibid.). For one who thus genuinely believes – and that means one who is himself and has found spirituality and the love internal to it – God holds a mirror to his heart. This is something Kierkegaard wishes to emphasize at the end of his book.

Bibliography

Anderson, John (1940) 'Freudianism and Society', *Australasian Journal of Psychology and Philosophy*, vol. XVIII, no. 1

Augustine (1973) *Confessions*, Harmondsworth: Penguin Classics

Balint, Michael (1952) 'Love and Hate', *Primary Love and Psycho-Analytic Technique*, London: The Hogarth Press

Dilman, İlham (1975) *Matter and Mind, Two Essays in Epistemology*, London: Macmillan

—— (1979) *Morality and the Inner Life. A Study in Plato's* Gorgias, London: Macmillan

—— (1980) *Studies in Language and Reason*, London: Macmillan

—— (1984) *Freud and the Mind*, Oxford: Blackwell

—— (1992) *Philosophy and the Philosophic Life, A Study in Plato's* Phaedo, London: Macmillan

—— (1993) *Existentialist Critiques of Cartesianism*, London: Macmillan

—— (1996) 'Psycho-Analysis as Ultimate Explanation of Religion' in *Can Religion be Explained Away?*, ed. D.Z. Phillips, New York: St Martin's Press

—— (1997) 'Psychoanalysis and Ethics: Some Reflections on the Self in its Relationship to Good and Evil', *Commonality and Particularity in Ethics* (ed. Lilli Alanen et al.), London: Macmillan

—— (non yet published) 'Dostoyevsky's Raskolnikov: Psychology and the Soul'

Dostoyevsky, Fyodor (1955) *The Idiot* (trans. David Magarshack), Harmondsworth: Penguin

—— (1956) *Crime and Punishment* (trans. David Magarshack), Harmondsworth: Penguin

—— (1957) *The Brothers Karamazov* (trans. Constant Garnett), London: Dent

Freud, Sigmund (1949a) *Three Essays on the Theory of Sexuality* (trans. James Strachey), London: The Alcuin Press

—— (1949b) *Group Psychology and the Analysis of the Ego* (trans. James Strachey), London: The Hogarth Press

—— (1949c) *Civilization and its Discontents* (trans. James Strachey), London: The Hogarth Press

Fromm, Erich (1950) *Man for Himself*, London: Routledge and Kegan Paul

—— (1979) *The Art of Loving*, London: Unwin Paperback

Guntrip, Harry (1964) *Healing the Sick Mind*, London: Unwin Books

Ibsen, Henrik (1971) 'The Master Builder', *The Master Builder and Other Plays*, Harmondsworth: Penguin

Jones, Ernest (1937) 'Love and Morality', *The International Journal of Psycho-Analysis*, January

Kierkegaard, Søren (1961) *Purity of Heart* (trans. Douglas Steere), London: Fontana

—— (1962) *Works of Love* (trans. Howard and Edna Hong), London: Collins

Klein, Melanie (1957) *Envy and Gratitude*, London: Tavistock

Lawrence, D.H. (1955) 'Love', 'Love was Once a Little Boy', 'A Propos of Lady Chatterley's Lover', *Sex, Literature and Censorship*, London: Heinemann

—— (1977) *Fantasia of the Unconscious and Psycho-Analysis and the Unconscious*, London: Penguin

Lewis, C.S. (1985) *The Four Loves*, London: Collins Fount Paperbacks

Malinowski, Bronislauw (1955) *Sex and Repression in Savage Society*, London: Meridian Books

Plato (1950) *Republic* (trans. A.D. Lindsay), London: Everyman's Library

—— (1952) *Symposium*, London: Penguin

—— (1973a) 'Phaedo' and 'Crito', *The Last Days of Socrates*, London: Penguin

—— (1973b) *Gorgias*, London: Penguin

—— (1973c) 'Phaedrus', *Phaedrus and Letters VII and VIII*, London: Penguin

Proust, Marcel (1952) *In Remembrance of Things Past* (trans. C.K. Scott-Moncrieff), Chatto and Windus

—— (1954) *A la Recherche du Temps Perdu*, vols i–iii, NRF, Paris: Bibliothèque de la Pléiade

Rhees, Rush (1965) 'Some Developments in Wittgenstein's View of Ethics', *Philosophical Review*, vol. 74, no. 1, January

—— (1969) 'Religion and Language', *Without Answers*, London: Routledge and Kegan Paul

Rilke, Rainer Maria (1952) *Duino Elegies* (trans. J.B. Leishman and Stephen Spender), London: The Hogarth Press

Sartre, Jean-Paul (1943) *L'Etre et le Néant*, Paris: Gallimard

—— (1947) 'Une Idée Fondamentale de la Phénomenologie de Husserl: L'Intentionalité', *Situations I*, Paris: Gallimard

—— (1948) *Esquisse d'une Théorie des Emotions*, Paris: Hermann

Scott-Maxwell, Florida (1957) *Women and Sometimes Men*, London: Routledge and Kegan Paul

Shakespeare, William (1947) *Macbeth*, *The Complete Plays of Shakespeare*, Oxford: Oxford University Press

Spinoza, Benedict (1960) *Ethics*, ed. James Gutmann, New York: Hafner

Suttie, Ian D. (1948) *The Origins of Love and Hate*, London: Kegan Paul, Trench, Trubner and Co

Tolstoy, Leo (1956) *Anna Karenina* (trans. Rosemary Edmunds), London: Penguin

—— (1960) 'Father Sergius', *The Kreutzer Sonata and Other Essays* (trans. Aylmer Maude), Oxford: Oxford University Press

Weil, Simone (1948) *La Pesanteur et la Grâce*, Paris: Librairie Plon

—— (1949) *L'Enracinement*, Paris: Gallimard

—— (1951) 'Lettre à une Elève' (1934), *La Condition Ouvrière*, Paris: Gallimard

—— (1953) *La Connaissance Surnaturelle*, Paris: Gallimard

—— (1959) *Waiting on God* (trans. Emma Craufurd), London: Fontana

—— (1960) *Attende de Dieu*, Paris: Gallimard

Winch, Peter (1972) 'Moral Integrity', *Ethics and Action*, London: Routledge

Wittgenstein, Ludwig (1963) *Philosophical Investigations*, Oxford: Blackwell

—— (1965) 'Lecture on Ethics', *Philosophical Review*, vol. 74, no. 1, January

Index

Abraham, 167
Albertine, 62, 64, 65, 67, 69–72, 81, 82, 93
Anderson, John, 86, 87, 121
Aristophanes, xx, 72, 119, 124, 125, 225
autonomy, xv, 6, 44, 45, 48, 50, 53–5, 58, 72, 119
authenticity, 5, 6, 122, 187

Bach, J.S., 222, 223
Balint, Michael, xii, 13, 14, 16, 20–2, 25, 121
beauty, 28, 81, 83, 84, 142, 151, 167, 224–9
Beethoven, 142

Cartesian dualism, 152
Cézanne, 27
Christ, Jesus, 134, 135, 158, 159, 162, 167, 168, 183–5, 206, 217, 231, 232
communion, xiii, xv–xvii, 58, 73, 80, 99, 102, 105, 107, 109, 111, 113, 120, 121, 208
concept-forming, 10
conceptual, xi, 73, 216
create, creativeness, xii, xvi, xvii, 85, 86, 89, 91, 96, 108, 109
courage, xii, 16, 20–2, 128, 199
culture, cultural, 48, 102, 113, 115, 117, 119, 134

David and Bathsheba, 151
destructive, xii, xviii, 23, 32, 37, 50, 53, 77, 83, 90, 96, 97
detachment, xx, 18, 20, 33, 64, 204, 226
Diotima, xii, xx, 138, 225, 227–9

Dostoyevsky, Fyodor, xvii, 50, 74, 95, 123, 124, 231
Don Juan, 27, 114

ego, egoism, ego-centricity, 1, 6, 17, 18, 21–3, 26, 74, 87, 88, 100, 103, 105, 114, 115, 127, 146, 147, 187, 190, 210
Eliot, T.S., 26
Erikson, Erik, 89
evil, 23, 207, 213, 218
existential, xi, xviii, xix, 119, 136

Fairbairn, Ronald, 141
faith, faithful, 20, 93, 128, 182, 192, 194, 215, 217, 221, 227, 232
Father Sergius, 33, 195, 230
forgive, forgiveness, xii, xviii, 19, 20, 22, 93, 161, 199, 205, 215, 219, 231, 232
Freud, Sigmund, xii, xvii, xviii, 14, 42, 43, 47, 60, 69, 72–8, 80, 81, 86–9, 94, 96, 97, 110, 117, 122, 125, 128, 132, 135–7
Fromm, Erich, xii, xiv, xv, xviii, xix, 117–22, 125–32, 134, 136, 137, 145

generosity, xviii, 10, 22, 38, 90–4, 127, 155, 156, 167
Gibran, Kahlil, x, xiii, xiv, xvi, xxi
goodness, xii, 16, 22, 39, 122, 123, 128, 166, 175, 188, 195, 199, 206, 207, 214, 216, 229
Good Samaritan, 184–5
grace, 139, 159, 166
gratitude, xix, 25, 38, 84, 93, 143, 201
Guntrip, Harry, 97

Hampshire, Stuart, 85
hate, hatred, 13, 16, 17, 19, 20, 21,
    67, 91, 92, 94, 95, 97, 100, 131, 136
Heidegger, Martin, 119
Homer, 229
humility, xii, 38, 81, 139, 140, 151,
    165, 166, 199, 212, 219, 224
Husserl, Edmund, 60

Ibsen, Henrik, 179
idealization, xix, 14, 25
ingratitude, 175
innocence, innocent, 143, 215, 216

Jones, Ernest, 179

Kantian, 190, 192
Kierkegaard, Søren, xii, xiv, xviii,
    xix, 39, 110, 116, 121, 122,
    171–86, 188–97, 199–204,
    206–25, 228–30, 232, 233
Klein, Melanie, 96, 128
Kundera, Milan, 27

Lawrence, D.H., xiv, xvi, 76, 77, 88,
    98–116, 191, 196
Lewis, C.L., xii, 116, 138–41,
    143–53, 155, 157, 158–61, 161n,
    163, 165–72, 174, 180, 189, 190,
    196, 209, 210
libido, libidinal, xvii, 86–8, 97
loyalty, xviii, 19, 22, 47, 58, 80, 90,
    93, 149, 182, 192
lust, 46, 47, 58, 81, 85, 151

Macbeth and Lady Macbeth, 32–7,
    39, 40, 178, 197, 207
Malinowski, Bronislaw, 87
Marcel (Proust's narrator), 62–7,
    69–72, 81, 82, 93
Marcel, Gabriel, xv, 120, 121
Maria, 28–30
Matisse, Henri, 2
mature, maturity, xii, xviii, xix, xxi,
    13, 14, 16, 17, 20, 21, 24, 26,
    30–3, 37–40, 100, 105,
    113, 118, 121, 125–7, 129, 133,
    134, 137, 170, 171, 188, 194–6

Maxwell-Scott, Florida, xx, 21, 35, 38
Meister Eckhart, 131
Michaelangelo, 222
Milais, Edna Vincent, 26
Morris, William, 138
Myshkin, xvii, 50, 74

narcissism, narcissistic, 14, 15, 87,
    94, 127, 129, 132
Nietzsche, Friedrich, 191

objective, 8, 9, 11, 12
Oedipus complex, 72, 96, 125
Othello, 39

paradox, paradoxical, xviii, xix, 4,
    53, 58, 94, 100, 105, 141, 146
Patchen, Kenneth, 205
patience, xii, xviii, 12, 22, 37, 93,
    106, 199, 201
Peer Gynt, 27
personal, 9, 11, 20, 26, 45, 50, 90,
    115, 188, 201
phantasy, xix, 15, 64, 65, 75, 78, 116,
    127
Phillips, D.Z., 26, 27, 33, 35, 140
Plato, xii, xvii–xx, 18, 42, 43, 45, 72,
    94n, 119, 138–40, 207
Proust, Marcel, xvi, 27, 60–4, 66–72,
    81, 82, 98, 149
prudence, 31, 39, 40, 202, 205
psycho-analysis, psycho-analytic,
    xi, 38, 39, 78, 117, 132, 141, 194,
    220, 224
'psychologism', 122, 130, 132

Raskolnikov, 95, 124
reciprocity, reciprocation, xiii, 1, 2,
    18, 24–6, 30, 37, 40, 43–6, 48,
    49–51, 53, 55, 57n, 193, 203
regress, 37, 76, 121
repetition, xii, 25, 71, 205
responsibility, 3–5, 24, 33, 47, 78, 80,
    96, 118, 119, 126, 129, 164, 178,
    233
Rhees, Rush, 83, 84, 101
Rilke, Rainer Maria, 173
Romeo and Juliet, 31, 122

Sartre, Jean-Paul, xv, 43, 44, 46, 53, 60, 63, 85, 119, 120, 208
self, self-, xii, xiii, xviii, xix, xx, 1, 6, 7, 12, 14, 15, 20, 22, 23, 25, 26, 32, 37–40, 46, 47, 56–8, 87–92, 96, 100–3, 109, 117, 123, 127, 129–32, 139, 140, 147, 149, 151, 153, 156, 158, 166, 167, 177, 178, 186, 187, 189, 190, 193, 195, 197, 199, 201, 202, 207–12, 214, 215, 217–19, 222–4, 226, 228
separateness, xvi, xviii, xix, 1–6, 8–13, 20, 44, 45, 66, 67, 69, 71, 98, 102, 104, 105, 107, 112, 119, 122, 124, 132, 146, 208
Shakespeare, 39, 222
Sims, David, 33, 35
Socrates, xii, 17, 18, 72, 143, 203, 213, 216, 218, 223–5, 229, 232
Solanas, 28
Sophist, 218
soul, xii, xiii, xviii, 10, 23, 29, 109, 147, 156, 162, 164, 166, 182, 194, 198, 199, 212
Spinoza, Benedict, 17, 18, 126, 137, 180
spiritual, xiii, xviii, 8, 30, 45, 109, 112, 115, 116, 133–5, 149, 151–3, 156, 164–6, 168, 169, 171, 173, 183, 196, 199, 200, 202, 204–6, 208–13, 217, 226, 233
St Augustine, 157, 170
St Nicholas, 157, 159
St Mawr, 103, 104
St Paul, 145
Stocks, J.L., 140
sublimation, xvii, 75

supernatural, xv, 91, 102, 138, 162, 163, 166, 168, 189, 202
Suttie, Ian D., 89
Svengali, 55
symbiotic, xv, 33, 72, 119

togetherness, 2, 4, 5, 30, 34, 48, 120, 148, 150
Tolstoy, Leo, xvi, 33, 64, 111, 153, 157, 195, 229, 230
transcend, transcendence, 19, 133, 135, 153, 156
transference, 69, 137
transmutation, 138, 147, 189, 196, 209
'triangular relation', 40, 158–9, 190, 193, 207, 219–20
troubadour, 26
trust, trustworthy, xii, xiii, 1, 11, 20, 22, 47, 53, 57, 68, 93, 95, 128, 164, 201, 202–4, 217

Vinteuil, 27
Vronsky and Anna, xvi, 63, 64, 108, 111, 153

Waismann, F, 11
Weil, Simone, xv, xvii, 31–3, 39, 41, 42, 45, 56, 91, 102, 109, 127, 134, 136–8, 141, 147, 160, 162, 164, 166, 168, 169, 172, 176, 179, 183, 184, 186–9, 206, 207, 224–6, 229, 230, 232
Wilde, Oscar, 61
Winch, Peter, 160, 179
Wittgenstein, 10, 11, 19, 84, 94n, 100, 183